TOTAL QUALITY MANAGEMENT

The Portable MBA Series

TOTAL QUALITY MANAGEMENT

STRATEGIES AND TECHNIQUES PROVEN AT TODAY'S MOST SUCCESSFUL COMPANIES

Second Edition

Stephen George and Arnold Weimerskirch

John Wiley & Sons, Inc.

New York • Chichester • Weinheim • Brisbane • Singapore • Toronto

Copyright © 1994, 1998 by Stephen George and Arnold Weimerskirch. All rights reserved.
Published by John Wiley & Sons, Inc.

Published simultaneously in Canada.

Library of Congress Cataloging-in-Publication Data:

George, Stephen, 1948–
    Total quality management : strategies and techniques proven at
today's most successful companies / Stephen George and Arnold
Weimerskirch. — 2nd ed.
      p.   cm.
    Includes bibliographical references and index.
    ISBN 0-471-19174-4(cloth : alk. paper)
    1. Total quality management—United States—Case studies.
I. Weimerskirch, Arnold, 1936–. II. Title.
HD62.15.G483 1998
658.5′82—dc21   97-38314

Printed in the United States of America

10 9 8 7 6 5 4 3 2 1

Preface to the Second Edition

In the first edition of this book, we described how 53 organizations were achieving impressive financial results by improving customer satisfaction and operational performance. This second edition features 51 high-performance companies, including 13 that were not in the first edition. These "models of excellence" (Alcoa's definition of benchmarks) represent a wide variety of industries, including aluminum, electronics, telecommunications, automobiles, hotels, office supplies, package delivery, ceramics, insurance, ice cream, photography, and baseball. They range in size from 30 employees to more than 300,000. They are at the leading edge of a sweeping transition from the old, inflexible management model to the new model we explore in this book.

BEST PRACTICES OF 51 SUCCESSFUL COMPANIES

One of the basic tenets of the new model is: Learning from successful companies. We have applied that same idea to this book. Our goal was to bring each element in the new model to life through the experiences of three or more models of excellence. Each chapter features at least one manufacturing company, one service company, and one small business ("small" usually meaning fewer than 1,000 employees). No company is featured in more than one chapter, primarily because we wanted to present as wide a variety of corporate cultures and experiences as possible.

We selected the companies through a benchmarking process similar to those described in Chapter 15. We identified the areas to benchmark and questions we wished to ask, talked to people and researched written material to come up with a list of candidates, conducted phone interviews to ascertain interest and qualifications, narrowed the list to our top choices, and interviewed our benchmarks. Initial lists of more than 175 companies were narrowed to an impressive group of 53 for the first edition and 51 for this edition, including 22 Baldrige Award winners, several others that have received Baldrige site visits, and companies that are leaders in their industries.

At the beginning of the revision process, we contacted all companies represented in the first edition to find out whether they still qualified as models of excellence. Some were removed because mergers and acquisitions had changed their structures and obscured a clear definition of their management practices. Others were replaced because changes in leadership or in the marketplace had taken their attention away from the area we wished to highlight.

We are excited about the best practices of the new companies we have included in this edition, including nine more Baldrige Award winners:

1. Dana Commercial Credit.

2. Armstrong Building Products Operations.

3. AT&T Consumer Markets Division.

4. Eastman Chemical.

5. GTE Directories.

6. Trident Precision Manufacturing.

7. ADAC Laboratories.

8. Wainwright Industries.

9. Ames Rubber Corporation.

They join an impressive list of companies we have all heard of—Motorola, Corning, Alcoa, Intel, FedEx, Xerox, Ritz-Carlton, Ben & Jerry's, Sprint, 3M, and Eastman Kodak—and some we may be less familiar with—Marlow Industries, Zytec, Lyondell Petrochemical, Solectron, BI Performance Services, Custom Research Inc., and Graniterock.

As with any such list, ours is neither perfect nor definitive. No company in this book can claim that all its processes run without problems or that it satisfies its customers all the time or achieves its corporate goals without fail. You may be able to think of others you believe would have been better examples. That is not the point. Each of our 51 benchmarks has something to teach us, depending on the nature of our business and the challenges and opportunities before us.

The point of this book is to teach by example. We invite you to explore the new management model not as a business theory but as a business reality. Consider how the lessons learned by our models of excellence could be applied to your organization, but be careful about copying any one particular piece. Quality has gotten a bad name because of all the companies that have tried to lift a single element, such as team building or benchmarking, and plug it into their old management models. The new model requires *systems thinking*, which means you must understand all the elements in your company—and how changes in one affect the others—to systematically improve it.

HOW THIS BOOK CAN HELP YOU MEASURE EVERY ELEMENT OF YOUR BUSINESS

Before we can talk about the key elements in a business, we need to agree on what those elements are. Chapter 1 introduces a model that is the most comprehensive and widely used in the world: *the Baldrige management model.*

In Chapter 2, we explore *how senior executives lead the transition from traditional management to the systems management inherent in the Baldrige criteria.* Senior executives are the gatekeepers for this cultural change; they are the only persons in the system who have the power to facilitate it or squash it. As quality pioneer J. M. Juran said, "To my knowledge, no company has attained world-class quality without upper management leadership."

Once the gates are open, a company's first task is to know its customers. Chapter 3 shows *how companies determine their customers' requirements* and then use that knowledge to drive their entire system. The customer connection at the top of our model closes the loop in your system, revealing the source of the requirements you need to meet and the results of your success in meeting them.

Chapter 4 examines *how companies internalize customer requirements.* Our benchmarks integrate strategic quality and business planning to create one strategic planning process for the entire system. People from throughout the company are involved in this process of translating customer requirements into short- and long-term plans that guide the activities of every division, department, team, and individual.

Although management of the system is the subject of this entire book, Chapter 5 looks specifically at *the roles of managers and supervisors in communicating customer and company requirements* throughout the organization and making sure those requirements are met. These roles require new skills: an ability to listen, persuade, coach, train, facilitate, and serve.

One reason for the change in roles is the new model's emphasis on employee involvement. Quality leaders have discovered that the planning process improves when more employees are included. They have realized that the people most qualified to manage and improve processes, including the processes that satisfy customer requirements, are the employees involved in them. Chapter 6 reveals *how companies are giving their employees the authority and responsibility for continuous improvement.* Chapter 7 describes *how companies provide employees with the knowledge and skills they need* to be effective in their expanded roles. Chapter 8 considers *the role that rewards and recognition play* in supporting employees' efforts to improve quality and satisfy customers.

Chapter 9 focuses on *employee satisfaction*, the result of the initiatives in Chapters 6 through 8 and of companies' pervasive belief in the value of their employees. Many believe employee satisfaction is a key indicator of customer performance. *People* are at the center of the new management model.

This pivotal position is especially important when building relationships with customers. In the new management model, companies work very hard at bringing customers into their organizations because this contact makes it easier to understand and meet the customers' requirements. Chapter 10 looks at *how our benchmarks stay close to their customers.*

Staying close to customers involves several different processes and subprocesses. The new management model is process-oriented; everything a company does is viewed in terms of the processes involved. Sorting through these processes is often one of the first tasks a company undertakes as it breaks out of the traditional management model. Chapter 11 examines *the processes used to translate external customer requirements into internal company requirements.* The design of products and services is a critical link between customers and a company.

Chapter 12 focuses on *how companies manage and improve all processes* in all areas. In the new management model, companies are organized around the core processes that meet customer requirements. Process management is about identifying and improving those core processes, then addressing all the other processes that feed into them. A number of those processes exist outside a company's control, with the suppliers of goods and services. Chapter 13 describes *how companies are continuously improving supplier quality.* (The final process element, assessments, is covered in Chapter 17.)

To manage processes, achieve company goals, and satisfy customers, a company must measure what it wants to manage, then analyze the information it collects and use that analysis as a basis for improvement. Chapter 14 shows *how people are using companywide measurement systems* to help them align and integrate their systems and to manage by fact. Chapter 15 looks at *how companies put their measures and performance into perspective* by benchmarking industry and world-class leaders. To encourage breakthrough thinking, our models of excellence excel at "borrowing shamelessly" from the best.

Successful companies do not look outside their walls solely to feed their internal processes; they also look outside to fulfill the public's expectations and to take the lead in publicly important issues. Chapter 16 explores *the relationship between companies and their communities,* and clarifies the connections between the new management model and a company's public responsibilities.

Chapter 17 describes *how companies check the health of their systems.* Companies that use the Baldrige criteria to define their management systems use the same criteria to identify their strengths and weaknesses in every area discussed in this book. The assessment process becomes an annual booster, rocketing companies to new levels of operational performance and customer satisfaction.

Chapter 18 presents *approaches your company can use to make the transition* to the new management model. As the companies in this book demonstrate, the transition does not follow any single path. Some companies use strategic planning to initiate the new order. Others begin by empowering, training, and involving their employees in continuous improvement. Still others turn to process management as the key to their cultural transformation. In this final chapter, we outline how these approaches can help your company shift to the new management model.

Chapters 2 through 17 end with a brief summary called "The Shift in Thinking." The emphasis is on *shift*, on the need for planned change. We're not talking about something you do *in addition to* what you are doing now, but about a way of understanding and organizing your activities—and those of your company—to be more efficient and effective. Such a holistic perspective allows you to stand back from the daily demands, study the system that serves your customers, and develop a course of action that improves performance, raises customer satisfaction, and increases profitability. That perspective is the greatest benefit of the Baldrige management model described in this book—a benefit our 51 models of excellence help to define.

Acknowledgments

We're all familiar with the customer's demand: *Higher quality at a lower cost in less time.* And with the company's addendum: *At a reasonable profit.* The demand is wearing us down; the pace is too fast, and the expectations are too great. We're being pulled in too many directions—barely able to react when we should be anticipating and planning. On the verge of disintegration, we seek models of integration, examples of companies that have a clue about how everything they do fits together to the customer's delight and the company's benefit.

This book presents a model of integration, defined by the criteria for the Malcolm Baldrige National Quality Award and exemplified in the stories of 51 leading U.S. companies. Taken as a whole, the book demonstrates how all of a company's processes and people can be focused on meeting customer requirements and improving operating performance. For you, the reader, it provides some context for the roles you assume and shows you how others are redefining those roles to add value to the process of achieving their companies' goals.

Arnie and I would like to thank all of the people quoted in this book for their cooperation. The men and women who agreed to be interviewed and who supplied us with valuable information helped bring the new management model to life.

I dedicate my part in this book to my wife, Ellen Carroll George, and my children, Dan, Katie, Allie, and Zachary.

STEPHEN GEORGE

Minneapolis, Minnesota
November 1997

xi

When the history books about the 20th century are written, I believe the chapter on industry must recognize three great revolutionary developments:

- Henry Ford's system of mass production.
- Japan's system of lean production.
- The Baldrige criteria for managing a lean enterprise.

The first revolution is universally recognized. The second has been widely adopted. In due course, the Baldrige criteria will be regarded as having the same stature as the first two. The full impact of the criteria is yet to be realized.

The Baldrige criteria are a road map by which a company can become world class. They represent a mental framework through which the management theories of leading experts can be integrated with tried and true management practices to yield a business excellence model.

By some, the Baldrige criteria are regarded as just another management technique, along with such management fads as reengineering, customer intimacy, or the horizontal organization. They are, in fact, much more than that. The criteria are evaluated and advanced each year by the consensus of leading experts. As a consequence, they represent the leading edge of validated management thought. They are not just another management fad. They are an enduring and complete management system.

It is to the mission of communicating this powerful message that Steve George and I have dedicated ourselves. In this book, we explain the Baldrige concepts; more importantly, we present role-model companies and how they apply the concepts in day-to-day management practice. It is our hope that we will bring to life the knowledge and insights necessary to lead your own organization to world-class performance.

I dedicate my part in this book to my wife, Anne. In our 37 years of marriage, she has been both my stability and my inspiration. We hope for many more years together.

ARNOLD M. WEIMERSKIRCH

Minneapolis, Minnesota
November 1997

Contents

1 THE NEW MANAGEMENT MODEL

Some scientists believe that Adam and Eve left paradise because of the tsetse fly. The insects carried "sleeping sickness," and because humans were easier to bite than the thicker-skinned animals around them, the tsetse fly drove the First Couple from Eden. One animal remained and eluded the fly's bites: the zebra. A tsetse fly could starve to death while flying past a herd of "invisible" zebras. The fly's eyes cannot accept the black-and-white pattern of the zebra's skin. To the tsetse, the zebra does not exist.

Today's business leaders and managers face a similar quandary. Responding to intense competition in a rapidly changing world, they have been forced to seek ways to become more competitive. Many devour the closest "meals" first: they lay people off, sell businesses, and demand more from those who remain. Eventually, these sources run dry. At this point, leaders and managers turn their full attention to their companies, and to the system they lead and manage. Many notice the "hoofprints" of inefficiencies, errors, dissatisfaction, high costs, slow responses, and defecting customers, but they cannot detect the sources of these problems. They cannot see the zebras.

When it comes to understanding the systems they lead and manage, most people see through tsetse eyes—and the zebras are frustrating the hell out of them. They *know* their companies could do significantly better if they could only focus everybody's attention on what is important; but what *is* important? Where do we look first? How do we make sense of this complex, confusing system we call our company? How do we attack something we cannot see?

Employees face similar frustrations with resignation, having been trampled by more than one invisible zebra. A problem that should have been solved reappears. A supplied component repeatedly fails. A time-consuming effort gets tossed aside when priorities suddenly change. For employees, the hoofprints up their backs remind them that the system has serious problems.

But then, the system has always had problems—and it always will. What has changed is that companies are finding it harder and harder to survive their problems. What has changed is *change*. When American companies could capture markets by the sheer volume of their production, when they could compete just by working hard, and when they could sustain growth with a stream of innovative products, they could afford to follow a business theory built on capital, driven by profits, and organized as a hierarchy. Change was slow and predictable, and the theory worked—for a while.

Global competition has made this old management model obsolete. One of America's leading management experts, Peter Drucker, described the transition in an article in the *Wall Street Journal*. Inspired by the major turnarounds under way at General Motors, IBM, Westinghouse, and American Express, he wrote:

> To start this turnaround thus requires a willingness to rethink and to reex-amine the company's business theory. It requires stopping saying "we know" and instead saying "let's ask." And there are two sets of questions that need to be asked. First: Who are the customers and who are the non-customers? What is value to them? What do they pay for? Second: What do the [successful companies] do that we do not do? What do they not do that we *know* is essential? What do they assume that we *know* to be wrong?

We will address both sets of questions in this book. Unlike the old model, the new management model is *customer driven*. The companies we will introduce make it their business to get and stay close to their customers.

THE NEW MANAGEMENT MODEL IS CUSTOMER DRIVEN

As Drucker suggests, the focus of the new model is not on how much we are making but on how well we are meeting our customers' requirements. The benchmark companies in this book—Motorola, Corning, FedEx, Xerox, Solectron, the Ritz-Carlton Hotels, and others—make understanding and satisfying customer requirements their top priority. They have

learned from experience that customer satisfaction determines financial
success.

The Institutes for Productivity Through Quality in the College of
Business at the University of Tennessee in Knoxville have more than 15
years' experience in executive education and field research with a majority of Fortune 500 companies. In an article in *Quality Progress*, associate
dean Michael Stahl described two themes that are of primary importance
to American competitiveness and that have surfaced from the Institutes'
experience:

> The first theme is that management should focus on creating and delivering
> the best net value to the customer, not maximizing stock price, return on
> investment, or shareholder equity—the typical measures of corporate per-
> formance. The second major theme is that managers must design and con-
> tinuously improve organizational alliances and consensus thinking that will
> cut horizontally across vertical organizational structures; integrate corpo-
> rate functions such as engineering, manufacturing, and finance; and foster
> teamwork.

Both themes fit the new management model. Both require a dramatic
shift in thinking. American businesses define themselves by financial measures. When *Fortune* Magazine announces its latest list of 500, it places
the successes and the failures into three categories: (1) biggest money
makers and losers, (2) biggest sales increases and decreases, and (3) best
and worst investments. Almost every article about company performance
in business newspapers and magazines uses a financial yardstick, whether
the article is about product innovation, quality improvement, customer
service, or any other of the myriad issues companies are addressing. This
system of financial measures has become the common language we use to
assess and compare performance, but it shows only one part of performance, and, as Stahl concludes, that part is not even the most important
one.

Our system of financial measurement is dragging us down, diverting
our attention from what we really need to work on to become more competitive. Our tsetse-fly eyes are incapable of finding the zebras that are
stomping all over the bottom line. Leaders who rely on these measures to
evaluate their companies' performance will never understand what will
eventually hit them.

By contrast, Stahl's themes—*customer orientation, consensus thinking, integration, and teamwork*—point to a solution. To take advantage of
this approach, leaders and managers must have a very good grasp of the
system in which they work. A company cannot take a haphazard approach
to knowing its customers, turning the organization on its side, integrating

functions, and working through teams. Those that have tried have failed. Studies by accountants and consultants at Ernst & Young have suggested that some companies have wasted millions of dollars on such quality initiatives as team building, benchmarking, and reengineering. You will read in this book about companies that have *saved* millions of dollars through similar initiatives. The primary difference is that the losers, without understanding their own systems first, adopted programs they had seen work for others. The winners become "systems thinkers" who integrate these initiatives into a broader process of continuous improvement.

FOCUSING ON SYSTEMS THINKING

Peter Senge defines systems thinking (the focus of his book, *The Fifth Discipline*) as "a discipline for seeing wholes. It is a framework for seeing interrelationships rather than things, for seeing patterns of change rather than static snapshots." The new management model is nothing more than a discipline for seeing your entire organization: the interrelationships among people and processes that determine success, and the patterns of change that demand vigilance. *In an increasingly competitive marketplace, you cannot hope to survive in a system that is out of control.* And it is out of control if you do not:

- Know exactly what your customers require.
- Have well-defined processes for translating those requirements into internal actions.
- Align all of your tasks and processes along common goals and objectives.
- Use key measures to manage by fact.
- Involve everyone in continuous improvement.
- Understand and improve all your critical processes.
- Satisfy your customers.

Most people are not used to thinking about their organizations in this way. We are dealing with complex structures here, from the operation of a company to the dynamics of a changing marketplace. People struggle to understand how it all fits together. They puzzle over where to begin. They lack the discipline for seeing wholes. "Systems thinking is the antidote to feeling overwhelmed and helpless," Senge writes. "It offers a language that begins by restructuring how we think."

USING THE BALDRIGE CRITERIA TO ASSESS QUALITY

The transition from the old management model to the new requires us to think differently. Chapters 2 through 17 end with summaries of the shift in thinking that our models of excellence have made in the areas common to every system. These areas have been identified by the criteria for the Malcolm Baldrige National Quality Award. *We believe the Baldrige criteria define the new management model because they provide the best guide to understanding, assessing, controlling, and improving an organization.*

No other model has gained such widespread global acceptance. As evidence, consider these facts:

- Since the Baldrige program was introduced in 1988, the National Institute of Standards and Technology (NIST) has distributed more than two million copies of the criteria. It estimates that people have made at least that many copies for their own use. NIST continues to improve the criteria every year.

- Companies also get the criteria from state award programs. Forty-two U.S. states now have quality award programs based on the Baldrige criteria.

- Many state programs have broadened the eligibility to include education, health care, and government agencies, all of which are able to apply the Baldrige criteria to their organizations. At the national level, NIST has piloted education and health care awards and has trained examiners to evaluate education/health care applications.

- Studies have shown that 70 percent of the companies that use the criteria use them as a source of information on how to achieve excellence.

- More than 20 countries, including Australia, Brazil, Sweden, Canada, India, and Japan, have implemented quality award programs based on the Baldrige criteria.

- The criteria for the European Quality Award, first presented in 1992, are patterned after the Baldrige criteria.

- More than $9 million in grants has been provided for research related to the Baldrige core values.

- Companies such as Honeywell, Intel, IBM, Carrier, Kodak, and AT&T have adopted the Baldrige criteria as their internal assessment tool and their criteria for their own corporate quality awards. Many other large companies are asking suppliers to assess their organizations by using the Baldrige criteria.

All these influences have helped expose thousands of companies to the Baldrige model. *The Baldrige Quality System: The Do-It-Yourself Way to Transform Your Business* (John Wiley & Sons, 1992) explains how the criteria evolved and how companies of all types and sizes are using them to improve. The book includes a statement by Joe Rocca, one of the leaders of IBM Rochester's 1990 Baldrige Award-winning application effort: "It's really a genius document, as far as I'm concerned, because it allows you to go back to the basics and see the common thread that exists in everything you do. Things get down to some very basic fundamentals that you know are at work. If you can put your finger on them, you look at life with a clearer vision of what it's about and why things are happening."

Rocca is describing a shift in thinking. *In our experience with companies that use the Baldrige criteria to improve, people who examine their organizations from a Baldrige perspective acquire a discipline for seeing wholes, for seeing interrelationships rather than things, for seeing patterns of change. They become systems thinkers.*

The Baldrige system was created to promote an understanding of the requirements for world-class performance. That the system also defines a new management model surprises no one who has been active in the implementation of total quality management (TQM). TQM has long been misunderstood as some kind of limited add-on program that may help improve quality but does not affect the rest of the organization. Our benchmarks and other quality leaders demonstrate that quality *is* the system.

Quality has been widely defined as "meeting or exceeding customer expectations," a criterion that also happens to be the focus of the new management model. *The best system for meeting or exceeding customer requirements is defined by the Baldrige criteria.* Speaking to the Canadian Life Insurance Association in 1992, Robert Shafto, president of the New England Mutual Life Insurance Company, said, "I've become more and more convinced that the Baldrige is a management guide for business success, and if you meet all the requirements, you will end up satisfying the customer—hence, grow the business." Shafto's conclusion is shared by a host of leaders who have made the Baldrige criteria their new management model. In the Baldrige model, they find a system that:

- Focuses on the customer.
- Aligns internal processes with customer satisfaction.

- Puts everybody in the company to work on shared goals.
- Facilitates a long-term approach to continuous improvement.
- Demands management by fact.
- Promotes prevention rather than reaction.
- Seeks ways to be faster and more flexible throughout the organization.
- Looks outside the company for opportunities to form partnerships with customers, suppliers, and other companies; to benchmark; and to fulfill the company's responsibilities as a corporate citizen.
- Values results.

For leaders who have been looking for a way to get their arms around their organizations—or to round up the zebras—this description of the new management model offers hope. The companies featured in this book are living proof of the benefits of systems thinking.

QUALITY IMPROVEMENT INCREASES PROFITABILITY

For leaders who are reluctant to turn their attention away from the bottom line, the final Baldrige characteristic offers a back door: The new model *values results*. The pursuit of quality excellence does not come at the expense of financial excellence. Rather, financial results are another way of measuring the effectiveness of the system. The difference is that the goal of the new model is not profits; it is customer satisfaction, with the understanding that profits will improve as quality improves. Figure 1.1 shows how delivering greater perceived value while continually refining processes improves profitability and delights shareholders.

Exhibit 1.1 reflects the experiences of quality leaders worldwide. Delighting customers, reducing waste, and increasing productivity are natural by-products of a systematic process of continuous improvement.

- Products and services that exceed customer requirements are of greater value to customers than competitors' products and services. Increasing numbers of customers are likely to purchase such quality, and that improves market share and grows revenues.
- Less waste and greater productivity result in lower costs, which, in turn, improve margins, asset utilization, and competitive position.
- Higher revenues and more favorable margins, asset utilization, and competitive position improve the bottom line, which delights shareholders.

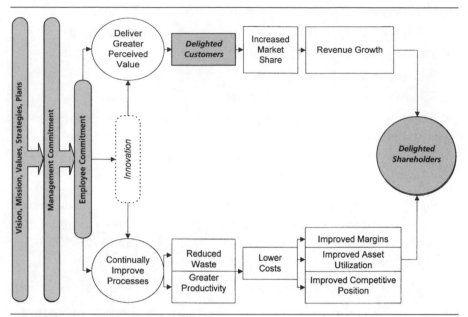

EXHIBIT 1.1.   Value creation model.

Exhibit 1.1 represents one way to look at the financial benefits of implementing the new management model. However, the connections between improving quality and improving profitability are not always this evident. We have all read about quality leaders that have stumbled financially. The business media are quick to hold these companies up as proof that the quality movement is a passing fad with limited value, which is like saying a baseball team finished the season in last place because it had a poor spring training. A company's financial success depends on many different factors, not the least of which is the company's leadership. *The new management model gives leaders the ability to control and improve their entire company, but it does not make the decisions for them.* Even the best management models are subject to the skill of the people who use them.

Skilled leaders are embracing the new management model because it makes them more effective. Financial performance depends on how well a company does in three areas, and the new model strengthens a company's position in all three:

1. *Strategy development.* It contributes to more efficient strategies and better business decisions, which improves the development of strategies and helps companies respond to a changing environment.

2. *Market performance.* It increases customer retention, market share, and revenues, which improves performance in the marketplace.

3. *Internal performance.* It improves asset utilization and productivity and lowers operating costs, which improves performance throughout the organization.

The new management model accomplishes all this by focusing the entire company on the customer, then identifying and improving the processes that lead to customer satisfaction. We will outline how companies are doing this, but before we present the elements in the system, it is important to "see the whole," to understand how the new management model works as a system before studying the parts in that system.

Exhibit 1.2 identifies the key elements in the new model and the ways in which they are interconnected. The model is driven by *customer requirements* and directed toward *customer satisfaction.* Leadership and information affect every part of the organization. *Leadership* commits everyone in the company to meeting customer requirements through continuous improvement; *information* is gathered from all critical points to evaluate and improve current operations and to help people make decisions based on facts. The *planning* process involves leaders, managers, employees, customers, and suppliers in charting a course that every department, team, and employee can translate into daily actions. People— leaders, managers, supervisors, and employees—are at the center of the new model, involved in planning, managing, and improving processes, and serving customers (see Exhibit 1.3). The new model is also a *process-oriented, horizontal organization aimed at fulfilling customer requirements (see Exhibit 1.4). And the measure of success, whether of

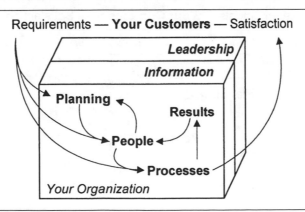

EXHIBIT 1.2. The new management model.

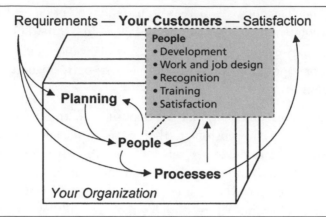

EXHIBIT 1.3.   How people contribute to the new management model.

processes, products, services, or performance, is the *results* that are then used to develop or modify plans, improve processes, and predict customer satisfaction.

The new model is directed toward results, which provide the link between customer requirements and the company's system. As the Baldrige criteria booklet points out, "The criteria are designed to help companies enhance their competitiveness through focus on dual, results-oriented goals: (1) delivery of ever-improving value to customers, resulting in marketplace success; and (2) improvement of overall company performance and capabilities." Successful companies use results to assess progress and to keep people focused on company goals. Because results are the measure of every element in a company's system, they are inherent in every chapter in this book.

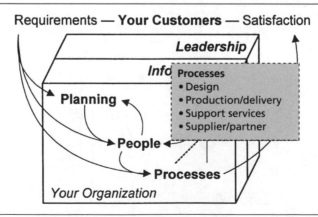

EXHIBIT 1.4.   Process management in the new model.

The following chapters introduce you to the different approaches companies are taking to achieve their goals, and to the ways those approaches are interconnected. It is a thorough examination of the system, but not of the elements in that system. Whole books have been written about the topics of each of the chapters in this book. Our purpose is to show how all of these elements fit together, how companies are using *systems thinking* to transform their organizations.

Systems thinking is a discipline for seeing wholes. As you explore the elements in your system, you will begin to acquire this discipline, and it will change how you view your organization. The shift in thinking is as dramatic as the transition from the old model to the new—a process of discovery that is exhilarating and enlightening.

And startling, when all those zebras begin to materialize.

2 LEADERSHIP

Corning

FedEx

Marlow Industries

Here is the one question every Baldrige Award winner hears too often: "How do I get my company's leaders involved in the quality improvement process?"

People ask this question because they know they must return to a company where quality improvement is not a priority; senior management has not made it one. They ask because they are tired of fixing pieces of the system, only to have apathy and resistance to change swallow up their efforts. They ask because they recognize that the company's leaders have the power to change the entire system by making quality improvement a cultural attribute.

Leadership holds the key to the door of continuous improvement. If the key stays in leadership's pocket, the organization has no chance of becoming a quality leader. None. Zero. The company may implement scattered improvements through the diligence of a quality champion. It may train everyone in the fundamentals of quality and urge their involvement. It may achieve ISO certification for the documentation of its processes. It may even win an award from a customer. But without clear and consistent leadership, the company will never be a quality leader. Its management system will never be sound and efficient, and its improvement efforts will eventually be replaced by an intriguing new management fad.

For a contrast, look at the Baldrige Award winners. They are driven by their senior executives' zeal for quality. Their leaders meet with employees frequently, to inspire and recognize their best efforts; they visit with customers regularly, to find out what they need and expect; they track quality improvements religiously, take and teach quality courses, demand excellence (100 percent customer satisfaction 100 percent of the time), and preach quality to every audience that will listen—and that includes civic groups, schools, government agencies, foreign companies, and trade associations, among others. They lead the quality improvement process because they are responsible for making the company more competitive and profitable, and the only way to do that consistently and for the long term is through continuous improvement of the entire system. That's not a one-speech, quick-fix kind of commitment; it is a relentless, all-consuming desire to make the company the best it can be.

So how do you make your leader a quality leader? You can't. You can no more make a CEO walk the quality path than you can make him or her convert to a new religion. In fact, the analogy to a religious conversion often surfaces in the way leaders talk about becoming quality believers. Many describe it as a "leap of faith." J. M. Juran likes to say that quality leaders have "the faith of the true believers," a faith they got by "witnessing the miracles."

Like those who experience a religious awakening, these leaders are eager to spread the gospel of quality. "When you get into quality, you become intolerant of the lack of quality in business, education, government, and other organizations," says James B. Houghton, former chairman of Corning Incorporated and the leader who initiated Corning's Total Quality strategy in 1983. "I made a lot of outside speeches because I think quality is in a spillover phase in our society."

Houghton did more than give speeches. Six months after he took the reins at Corning in 1983, he announced that the company would spend $5 million to set up a Quality Institute. "We were barely breaking even at the time," Houghton remembers, "and the cynics thought this was my new toy. Today there are very few cynics, for two reasons: we've never stopped promoting quality, and people now realize that quality means survival."

The survival issue is prominent in the minds of quality leaders. FedEx founder Fredrick W. Smith compares the awakening to quality to "a near-death experience. A lot of times it's brought on by trauma." Leaders often embrace total quality management because they see no alternative: improve or die. Whatever inspires them—the fear of failure, the promise of success, the achievements of other companies, the belief that there must be a better way to manage a company—triggers the leap of faith. Once they are on the quality path, the cultural changes they see all around them frequently breed a missionary zeal about the need for, and the benefits of, the quality improvement process.

In the course of becoming quality leaders, they seek to identify the words and actions that will bring everyone into the fold:

- What can we do as senior executives to personally lead the quality improvement process?
- What are our company's quality values?
- How can we communicate those values to our customers, employees, suppliers, and other groups?
- How can we improve as quality leaders?

In this chapter, we will see how the senior executives of three world-class companies—Corning, FedEx, and Marlow Industries—answer these questions. Although much of the chapter will focus on the highest-ranking officials of these three companies, their methods of leadership are shared by the senior executives who report to them. If you are a leader at your company, the perspectives of these senior executives will inspire you. If you wonder about the thought processes and actions of such leaders, their stories will enlighten you. If you wish to influence your leaders to embrace the quality improvement process, *good luck!* Our three benchmarks will give you some powerful ammunition, but you are probably facing a long campaign.

MODELS OF EXCELLENCE

Corning Incorporated was established in 1851 and today is a worldwide market leader in optical fiber and photonic components; television and computer display glass; advanced materials for the scientific, environmental, and consumer marketplaces with growing capabilities in polymers; and the physics and chemistry of surfaces. Headquartered in Corning, New York, the company has more than 20,000 employees worldwide. Corning Telecommunications Products Division won the Baldrige Award in 1995.

FedEx created the overnight air express business in 1973. Ten years later, it was the first U.S. company to top $1 billion in revenues in its first decade. The company is the world's largest express transportation company: more than 110,000 employees move more than two million items to over 200 countries each business day. In 1990, FedEx became the first service company to win the Baldrige Award.

Marlow Industries manufactures customized thermoelectric coolers—small, solid-state electronic devices that heat, cool, or stabilize the temperature of electronic equipment—for commercial and defense applications. Located in Dallas, Marlow employs 250 people and has total annual sales of $24 million. Marlow Industries won the Baldrige Award in 1991. CEO and president Ray Marlow founded the company in 1973 and initiated a systematic quality improvement process in 1987, even though Marlow's market share was more than 50 percent at the time. Its market share in its major markets is still greater than 70 percent.

LEADING THE TRANSITION

Step One: Commit to Quality

In leading the transition to systems management, the first step for any company president, chairman, or CEO is committing himself or herself, and the company, to the process. Jamie Houghton took this step in 1983, shortly after he became chairman. Fred Smith and his top executives founded a company on the idea of providing the highest quality of service, then participated in quality training in the first year of FedEx's existence. Ray Marlow initiated a systematic approach to quality improvement in 1987. All did it thoughtfully and deliberately, knowing that such a commitment would redefine their roles for as long as they remained leaders.

"When you start things as a leader," says Houghton, "you've got to make up your mind, then you've got to do it—even though you may not have one clue how effective it's going to be." In speeches, interviews, and articles, Houghton talks about leadership as a lonely art. Speaking to the Economic Club of Detroit, he said, "You're out front, the color guard, deliberately visible, encouraging and cheering on total quality, and you don't break stride for a second."

Step Two: Know Your Company's Systems and Values

Being "out front" can make you vulnerable to questions of substance about your new management system. The second step in leading the transition is to know your way around your system, because you will be looked to as the point person for continuous quality improvement.

Fred Smith, Ray Marlow, Jamie Houghton and his successor, Roger Ackerman, and their executive staffs created their companies' visions, missions, policies, and values. To do that, they looked at other companies' visions, studied their customers and their competition, assessed their own companies' strengths, and pinned down exactly what their companies stood for and aspired to achieve. Their values are presented later in this chapter. Each of the leaders has had to explain these values again and again, in myriad ways, to make sure the message sticks.

The explanations are often one-on-one. Fred Smith visits FedEx facilities and employees weekly; he invites their questions about any topic. Roger Ackerman, who took over as Corning's chairman in 1996, visits different Corning locations every year, on a rotating basis. After Ray Marlow introduced his company's quality policy, he went over it a phrase at a time at six straight monthly all-employee meetings. At recent monthly meetings, he has been reviewing the policy and talking about the company's quality pledge and quality tools. "You've got to keep it in front of people," he says.

At the end of one meeting, during which he had been stressing the understanding and use of Marlow's eight quality tools, an hourly employee asked for the microphone, then asked Marlow if he could name the tools. "I got 'em," he says proudly. In so doing, he showed his people that he could "walk the talk."

That is what quality leaders are asked to do every day. As the embodiment of their company's values, they are under constant surveillance to see whether they will "break stride." If they do, people become cynical about the value of the quality improvement process, and that cynicism poisons the process. We have all had leaders who say one thing and do another, and we are smart enough to know that what they do is what is really important. Leaders who talk about quality and actively participate in the quality improvement process leave no doubt about where their company's priorities lie.

Step Three: Participate in Your Company's Quality Processes

Active participation, the third step in leading the transition, can take many forms. At FedEx, Fred Smith has been directly involved in the development of every quality process and system the company has implemented. He founded the company on a belief that customers would value a time-definite express delivery service, then used on-time delivery as the company's primary measure of performance. In the late 1980s, he helped develop a more comprehensive, proactive, customer-oriented measure of customer satisfaction and service quality: the Service Quality Index (SQI).

The SQI measures 12 indicators that FedEx has determined are most important for customer satisfaction and service quality (see Table 2.1). As Smith said, "We believe that service quality must be mathematically measured." The company tracks these 12 indicators daily, individually and in total, across its entire system. Each indicator is weighted: the greater the weight, the greater the impact on customer satisfaction.

One of FedEx's service goals is to reduce the totals of the SQI every year. Service is one of the company's three overall corporate objectives: *People–Service–Profit. Every manager at FedEx, including Fred Smith and his senior executive staff, has annual objectives for each of these three corporate objectives.*

Smith sets his personal objectives with input from the board of directors, and the process cascades through the organization from there. Managers are evaluated on how well they achieve their objectives.

To develop and implement such broad measures and objectives, Smith and his staff had to understand the company's quality objectives, its customers' needs, and the potential effectiveness of SQI as a measure and motivator. Many other service companies are still trying to figure out what to measure. Smith led the development of a measure that tells all FedEx employees, every day, exactly how they are doing on customer satisfaction and service quality. Active participation in the quality improvement process doesn't get any better than that.

Roger Ackerman talks about a 14-year journey that turned a quest for quality into a powerful, driving force for the organization. "It has led to

TABLE 2.1. FedEx's Service Quality Indicators

Indicator	Weight
1. Damaged packages	10
2. Lost packages	10
3. Missed pickups	10
4. Complaints reopened	5
5. Overgoods (lost and found)	5
6. Wrong-day late deliveries	5
7. Abandoned calls	1
8. International	1
9. Invoice adjustments requested	1
10. Missing proofs of delivery	1
11. Right-day late deliveries	1
12. Traces	1

the creation of tools and strategies with operational, day-to-day applications," he says. "This, in turn, has focused us on customers and on achieving measurable results."

Good leaders know that a customer focus is critical. At FedEx, each officer is assigned responsibility for the major customers in a sales district. Smith and his staff talk to customers continuously at the executive level to make sure their needs are being met.

Quality leaders reinforce a customer focus by investing their own time in improving customer relationships. Marlow Industries has a standing rule: Every customer (which means anybody from a customer's company) who visits Marlow meets with either Ray Marlow or Chris Witzke, the chief operating officer. "We're not like Xerox," Marlow says. "We don't have something we sell to thousands of customers. Our products are customized for a select group, and we develop relationships with those customers. As we enter the commercial market and our customer base expands, that's much more difficult. You stay on the road a lot."

Leaders such as Marlow, Smith, and Houghton spend a great deal of their time discussing customer requirements and quality with employees, customers, suppliers, distributors, and other groups that affect and are affected by their companies. Later in the chapter, we will look at how they do this.

Step Four: Integrate Quality into the Company's Management Model

Once a leader is committed to management by quality, understands its basics, and physically participates in the transition, the fourth step is to institutionalize systems management as the company's business management model.

From the beginning, FedEx has been integrating quality into the way it runs its business. "Like many service companies, we're widely dispersed," says Anne Manning, marketing specialist, Business Logistics Services. "Half of our people—almost 45,000 employees—are front-line, customer-contact employees, and they're all expected to deliver the same standard of quality." FedEx senior executive leadership created the system that makes customer satisfaction and service delivery corporate strengths.

Marlow Industries hails integration as a breakthrough for the company. "We made the mistake of having two structures—business and quality—when we started to pursue quality," says Witzke. "We kept moving quality into the business area until we collapsed business and quality into one structure. Our agenda for quality is now the way we run our business." To reflect this broader scope, Marlow changed the name of its Total Quality Management Council to Total Quality Culture Council.

"As a Baldrige Award winner, we get a lot of requests about how to start this process," Witzke adds. "We recommend using the Baldrige criteria as a road map for your business from day one."

Ray Marlow agrees. "There's no doubt that the Baldrige criteria are the way to manage your business," he says. "The criteria continually change as we learn more about the depth and breadth of a quality system."

Notice Witzke said "for your business," not just for improving quality. To follow that advice, leaders must buy into the Baldrige criteria. They must demonstrate commitment, knowledge, and participation before integration can occur. And leaders must take all these steps all the time. "You have to be at least a zealot in your commitment to the quality improvement process to be effective," says Smith. "You've got to speak it and reinforce it at every opportunity."

EXPRESSING YOUR COMPANY'S VALUES

FedEx, Corning, Marlow Industries, and other quality leaders build their quality improvement processes on clear and precise quality values. These are not idealistic wish lists to be framed and hung in every conference room. The values of our three quality role models guide their quality efforts in tangible, measurable ways.

FedEx has three corporate goals: *People–Service–Profit.* As Smith summarizes, "When people are placed first, they will provide the highest possible service, and profits will follow." The three corporate goals are translated into measurable objectives throughout the corporation. Progress on the people goal is determined by the Leadership Index, a statistical measurement of subordinates' opinions of management's performance. Service is based on the Service Quality Indicators described earlier. The profit goal is a percentage of pretax margin determined by the previous year's financial results. Success in meeting the objectives for each area determines the annual bonuses for management and professionals. (The bonuses can account for up to 40 percent of their total compensation.)

FedEx has two primary corporate quality goals:

- 100 percent customer satisfaction after every interaction and transaction.
- 100 percent service performance on every package handled.

Many people doubt the ability to achieve 100 percent of anything. "We acknowledge that 100 percent is impossible," says Smith, "but that doesn't keep us from striving to achieve it. We have to be wary of being satisfied with 99 percent performance because the law of large numbers catches up with us. When you're handling millions of packages a day, a 1 percent failure rate is totally unacceptable. We believe the road toward 100 percent is worth the effort."

The business philosophy of Marlow Industries is expressed in its quality policy: *For every product or service we provide, we will meet or exceed the customers' expectations, without exception. Our standard of performance is: Do It Right Today, Better Tomorrow.*

Marlow's quality pledge is each employee's personal commitment to quality:

> *I pledge to make a constant, conscious effort to do my job right today, better tomorrow, recognizing that my individual contribution is critical to the success of Marlow Industries.*

The policy and pledge are further defined by Marlow's quality values:

- Senior executives must be the leaders.
- Employees have the authority to make decisions and take actions on their own.
- Honesty with customers, employees, and suppliers.
- Meeting the customers' requirements.
- Quality comes from prevention.
- Anticipate problems and take appropriate action before the problem happens.
- Do it right the first time.
- Continuous improvements toward customer satisfaction.

Nothing earthshaking here. Many companies espouse similar values. The difference is that Marlow Industries actually lives by them. The company's leaders will allow nothing less.

When Corning started its quality initiative in 1983, one of its first tasks was to identify the principles, actions, and strategies on which its system would be built. It introduced the foundations of its system in January 1984, and has been improving them ever since.

Corning's purpose is: "to deliver superior, long-range economic benefits to our customers, our shareholders, our employees, and the communities in which we operate. We accomplish this while living our values in an operating environment that enables corporate and personal growth to flourish."

"Corning's values are the unchanging moral and ethical compass of this organization," Ackerman writes, in a brochure that communicates the company's vision, "and they guide us every day." The seven values are:

1. Quality.
2. Integrity.
3. Performance.
4. Leadership.
5. Innovation.
6. Independence.
7. The Individual.

To help employees understand how to act on these values, Corning identified eight operating environment dimensions. The first five describe how to do business; the last three depict how to work together:

1. Customer focused.
2. Results oriented.
3. Forward looking.
4. Entrepreneurial.
5. Rigorous.
6. Open.
7. Engaging.
8. Enabling.

"We've worked hard to define an operating environment that is supportive of growth," says Ackerman. "It is built on the foundation of quality."

COMMUNICATING VALUES THROUGHOUT THE COMPANY

All three of our role models excel at communication. Ray Marlow and Chris Witzke use monthly all-employee meetings to reinforce the company's customer focus and values. During these meetings, Marlow hands out the Employee of the Month Award and Witzke presents the training awards. They frequently talk to employees in the manufacturing area, go to lunch with different employees, and act as mentors for employee effectiveness teams. They are involved in quality training: "If we're not teaching the class ourselves, we're there as students," says Witzke. In 1997, all employees had to have 50 hours of training, and all officers had to teach 10 additional hours.

Marlow's leaders talk about quality regularly with their customers and suppliers, and they have been strong quality advocates outside the company. Ray Marlow helped found the Texas Quality Consortium, a group of small companies that meets to discuss W. Edwards Deming's 14 principles of management. Marlow and his staff made 25 presentations on quality the year before the company won the Baldrige Award; they have made many more since then. In 1993, Ray Marlow helped to organize and incorporate Quality Texas as a not-for-profit state quality award presented by the Governor of Texas.

Unlike Ray Marlow, Fred Smith does not have the luxury of communicating his quality values to 250 people in one building. To provide what Smith calls "timely communication of the company's quality goals to our far-flung work force," FedEx invested $8 million in FXT, a television network that connects 1,200 downlink sites in the United States and Canada and six facilities in Europe. Each weekday morning, a five- to seven-minute morning news program is broadcast from FedEx's Memphis headquarters. The program includes features on company products and services, stock prices, package volume and service performance, forecasts of the day's volume, and frequent segments on company quality goals and initiatives.

"Open, two-way communication is absolutely essential to achieving our quality goals," says Smith. In the company's early days, Smith and his senior executive staff held regular meetings at a local hotel. Any employee could attend these "family briefings." When FedEx outgrew such meetings, the television network became the vehicle for continuing two-way communication. Smith appears on the network live every six months or so, to discuss the state of the company and to field questions from employees throughout the FedEx network.

Employees are not afraid to ask tough questions; open communication is part of the company's culture. During Smith's weekly forays to FedEx facilities, he asks for input and questions from the employees he meets. He and his staff also reinforce the company's customer focus and values by establishing and monitoring measures tied directly to each. On a quarterly basis, representatives of about a dozen employee teams come to

Memphis to share their "quality success stories." Smith frequently opens these meetings, then he and his staff remain to hear about the improvements being made—and to show by their presence that quality efforts at every level are important to FedEx.

Communication about quality extends to FedEx's customers and suppliers. "Fred Smith talks to customers continuously," says Tom Martin, managing director of public relations, "and he encourages his direct reports to do the same. Being assigned a sales district (which every senior executive is) certainly encourages communication with customers."

"I try to take a business trip to a different district every month," says Smith, "and to schedule one or two customer visits per trip."

The cumulative effect of this unrelenting communication about quality is the creation of a quality organization. Marlow describes it as "consistency of purpose," the leader's responsibility to nurture an environment where excellence is everyone's goal.

In an article in *Total Quality Management* magazine, Houghton described what leadership meant to him:

> In the end, quality is something that becomes deeply personal. It is a commitment to a way of life—to a way of interacting with others. Quality isn't just a little pool for wading. It is an ocean. If you don't take the plunge, if you don't totally immerse yourself, you can't hope to coax a whole organization to jump in. That's why quality starts at the top, with the leaders of an organization.

IMPROVING AS A LEADER

According to the new business management model, the key to improving as a leader is to establish key indicators of performance, track those indicators, and develop actions to improve. Ray Marlow monitors how many customer contacts he has, studies customer service measurements to determine how well he is leading in that area, and regularly reviews charts and graphs posted throughout his facility to see whether the company is improving.

Quality leaders tend to apply what they say about quality to what they do. "I'm always trying to find ways to engineer out rework," says Fred Smith, "and to be more effective in dealing with my external and internal customers. Not a quarter goes by that we don't formally evaluate that." Smith believes the ultimate measures of his effectiveness as a leader are

FedEx's measures of customer satisfaction and service quality. "The name of the game is driving the Customer Satisfaction Index up and the Service Quality Indicator score down."

In addition to working to improve their own leadership skills, the leaders at FedEx and Corning have helped develop a set of criteria or attributes that define leadership for their organizations.

In 1989, an internal FedEx task force implemented a Leadership Evaluation and Awareness Process (LEAP). An employee must complete this process before becoming a first-line manager. Since FedEx implemented the process, its manager turnover rate has dropped from 10.7 percent to 1.7 percent.

The LEAP identified three "transformational leadership behavioral dimensions" and six "leadership qualities" as the most important attributes a candidate for management must have in a people-first work environment. The dimensions are:

1. *Charismatic leadership.* Charisma derives from an ability to see what is really important and to transmit a sense of mission to others. It is found in people throughout business organizations and is one of the elements that separates an ordinary manager from a true leader.

2. *Individual consideration.* Managers who practice the individualized consideration concept of transformational leadership treat each subordinate as an individual and serve as coaches and teachers through delegation and learning opportunities.

3. *Intellectual stimulation.* Leaders perceived as using intellectual stimulation successfully are those who encourage others to look at problems in new ways, rethink ideas, and use problem-solving techniques.

The leadership requirements are:

1. *Courage.* A courageous leader stands up for unpopular ideas, does not avoid confrontations, gives negative feedback to subordinates and superiors when appropriate, has confidence in his or her own capability, desires to act independently, and does the right thing for the company or subordinates in spite of personal hardship or sacrifice.

2. *Dependability.* A dependable leader follows through, keeps commitments, meets deadlines, takes and accepts responsibility for actions, admits mistakes to superiors, works effectively with little or no contact with a supervisor, and keeps a supervisor informed on progress.

3. *Flexibility.* A flexible leader functions effectively in a changing environment, provides stability, remains objective when confronted

with many responsibilities at once, handles several problems simultaneously, focuses on critical items, and changes course when required.

4. *Integrity.* A leader with integrity adheres to a code of business ethics and moral values, behaves in a manner that is consistent with the corporate climate and professional responsibility, does not abuse management privilege, gains trust/respect, and serves as a role model in support of corporate policies, professional ethics, and corporate culture.

5. *Judgment.* A leader with judgment uses logical and intellectual discernment to reach sound evaluations of alternative actions, bases decisions on logical and factual information and consideration of human factors, knows his or her own authority and is careful not to exceed it, uses past experiences and information to gain perspective on present decisions, and makes objective evaluations.

6. *Respect for others.* A leader with respect for others honors rather than belittles the opinions or work of others, regardless of their status or position in the organization, and demonstrates a belief in each individual's value regardless of each individual's background.

These dimensions and qualities define leadership at FedEx. They prove that the senior executives at FedEx have thought carefully about what a leader is, using Fred Smith and other corporate leaders as their best examples. For any company, this is an awesome list of attributes that any leader can use to guide his or her improvement.

Corning's criteria for leadership at any level are: honesty, vision, caring, strength, and change. To be a leader within the Corning network, there are ten key traits a person must have and ten more traits he or she should have.

To be a leader, one *must:*

1. Believe in and live the corporate values.
2. Develop and communicate a rallying vision.
3. Be a strategic thinker.
4. Be a risk taker.
5. Have a proven track record.
6. Be a catalyst for change.
7. Earn the trust of the organization.
8. Be a listener and an enabler.

9. Develop good, strong subordinates for succession.
10. Be an optimist and have a sense of humor.

To be a leader, one *should:*

11. Have different work experiences.
12. Have an international orientation.
13. Be financially adept.
14. Understand and know how to deploy technology.
15. Be able to deal with ambiguity.
16. Be skilled at alliance management.
17. Have a balanced, healthy lifestyle.
18. Contribute to the local community, both personally and financially.
19. Be active in at least one business activity outside Corning.
20. Be active in at least one nonbusiness, nonlocal activity.

This list, drawn from more than 140 leadership characteristics identified during research, reflects Corning's culture and the values of its leadership. Like FedEx's dimensions and qualities, Corning's criteria remove leadership from the realm of the mysterious and make it tangible and measurable. And what can be measured can be improved.

The list also redefines leadership for the new business management model. "The way I see it, leadership does not begin with power, but rather with a compelling vision or goal of excellence," says Smith. "One becomes a leader when he or she is able to communicate that vision in such a way that others feel empowered to achieve success."

THE SHIFT IN THINKING

The new business management model requires a dramatic shift in thinking among senior executives who resist a systems view of their organizations. The model is not something you can fit into the way your company already operates, nor is it something you can do in addition to your normal operations. It is a different way of leading and managing, and it will change your view of your company—your "system"—and of your role in improving that system.

This new paradigm is the reason leaders talk about taking a "leap of faith" when they embrace its principles. Despite evidence that the new model works, you are confronted with the task of changing a culture—and many within the culture will hate the change. Like Smith, Ackerman, and Marlow, you will need to be a tireless advocate of daily, continuous improvement.

This means that you must first accept *your* responsibilities in the new management model. We discuss many of those responsibilities here and in other chapters; the following summary shows how you affect and are affected by the new model:

- You lead the quality improvement process. No one else in the organization can lead it as effectively.

- You are a quality zealot. The leaders introduced throughout this book do not lead the improvement effort by spending all their time on financial matters; they walk, talk, and think quality.

- You understand your customers' needs and expectations. Because quality is defined by the customers, you need to spend time with them and compare what you learn with what others in your company know about them and about your markets. Only then will you know whether your system is truly being driven by customers' needs and expectations.

- You empower everyone in the company to meet customers' needs and expectations. You get all employees involved in improving quality and customer satisfaction. You promote training so that they can achieve their objectives. You establish rewards and recognition that encourage employees to work together toward common goals. You create a culture in which every person is considered a valuable resource and employee satisfaction is seen as an indicator of customer satisfaction.

- You manage by studying facts. If you think of your business system as a car, you have within view all the gauges and indicators you need to assess the condition of the system and to decide what to do next.

- You promote process improvement. If you were to step back and observe any part of your company for any period of time, you would notice that work follows different processes. The better you manage those processes, the more productive people are and the higher their quality of work is. You can help your company focus on process improvement by studying the processes you are involved in.

- You use the strategic planning process to keep the company focused. Quality leaders establish clear missions, goals, and objectives for their organizations, then use the planning process to translate corporate objectives into team and individual actions.

- You demand rapid, continuous improvement. A business exists to meet customer requirements and to achieve superior operational performance. By setting ambitious goals for each purpose, you challenge people to change and improve, to channel their energy, knowledge, and determination toward a shared vision.

Leaders such as Ray Marlow, Jamie Houghton, Roger Ackerman, and Fred Smith run their companies according to this new paradigm. As the results of Marlow Industries, Corning, and FedEx demonstrate, such a systems approach to leadership results in profitable, successful organizations.

3 CUSTOMER FOCUS

Xerox

IBM Rochester

L.L. Bean

Staples

Louisville Redbirds

The new business management model is customer driven. *Stop!* You have read and heard this philosophy so much in the past few years that it rarely even registers anymore. After all, you deliver products and services to your customers, who buy what you sell and keep you in business. It is easy to assume that this means your company is customer driven. Such an assumption is wrong.

A company that is customer driven is fundamentally different from a company that is not. Consider IBM Rochester. "In the past, we measured and monitored customer satisfaction because we felt the measurement was important, but we were not quite sure why. Now, customer satisfaction is the focal point for running our business," says Steve Hoisington, senior manager of market-driven quality. "Virtually every business decision we make today is based on customer satisfaction or dissatisfaction. We look at every proposed action and ask, 'How will our customers perceive this?'

"Satisfaction used to be something that validated our performance," Hoisington adds. "Now it drives the way we do business."

In this chapter, we will explore how customers' requirements and satisfaction dictate a company's direction and actions. IBM Rochester is one of the benchmarks that will provide insight into how a system of customer satisfiers can be the foundation for continuous improvement.

Companies that build their systems on a foundation of customer satisfaction must be careful that the foundation is secure. This requires a thorough and accurate knowledge of customers' requirements. L.L. Bean, another of this chapter's models of excellence, found that its customer satisfaction data were not good indicators of its customers' actual buying behavior. Its surveys asked, "All things considered, how satisfied are you with the merchandise and service at L.L. Bean?" The company scored high because of its reputation for superior service, but the scores did not mean that people would buy from them again. L.L. Bean has changed how it segments its market and surveys its customers to get more predictive information.

We will look at how Xerox relies on "customer obsession" to sustain a competitive advantage. Xerox believes that such an obsession is critical, for four reasons:

1. *It improves financial returns.* This is how Xerox sees it: Putting the customer first leads to fully satisfied customers who exhibit superior customer loyalty, which improves market share, which improves financial returns. (For a more thorough discussion of this point, see Chapter 1.) Xerox launched a Customer First initiative that included training for all employees in 1997.

2. *It fulfills certain needs of Xerox's people.* Employees have a basic human need to receive positive feedback from those whom they serve. Giving them permission to do what's right for customers enables them to provide a quality of service that their customers will value. (For examples of how this looks, see Chapters 6 and 10.)

3. *It provides an integrating focus for empowerment.* Customer First is a unifying vision that guides everyone's efforts toward shared goals. (For more information about companies guided by a unified vision, see Chapters 2, 4, and 5.)

4. *It can be institutionalized to provide a sustainable competitive advantage.* When customers perceive that the entire organization is obsessed with satisfying their requirements, they become loyal, not because of the product's features and price, but because they know Xerox supports their business goals.

Staples, a deep-discount office supplier and another of our benchmarks, founded its industry. As competitors flocked to this new business opportunity, it quickly became apparent that anybody could build a new superstore around the same branded products. Staples decided early to differentiate itself by its customer focus.

The Louisville Redbirds have no trouble differentiating their entertainment product from others. Where else can you see Billy Bird vault over the centerfield fence, hear classic rock-and-roll tunes between innings, win 10 grand when a Redbird hits a grand slam, or get your kids in for $1.75 each? We will show how the Redbirds are driven to success by customer satisfaction.

We will use these five models of excellence to answer the following questions:

- Who are our customers?
- How do we determine their requirements?
- How do we use customer satisfaction to drive our business?

In the new business management model, total customer satisfaction is the goal of the entire system, and a pervasive customer focus is what gets you there. *The system is organized around customer satisfaction, which makes knowing what your customers expect and require the most important job your company has.*

MODELS OF EXCELLENCE

Xerox makes more than 250 types of document-processing equipment, including copiers and other duplicating equipment, electronic printers and typing equipment, networks, workstations, and software products. The U.S. Customer Operations Division featured in this chapter employs nearly 35,000 people and is the largest group within Xerox. Xerox Business Products and Systems won the Baldrige Award in 1989.

IBM Rochester develops and manufactures commercial computer server systems, nearly a half-million of which have been installed worldwide. The Rochester, Minnesota, facility employs 5,000 people who are responsible for worldwide product development and manufacturing. IBM Rochester won the Baldrige Award in 1990.

Staples, a deep-discount office supply retailer, operates more than 650 office superstores throughout the United States, Canada, England, and Germany. Merchandise includes general office supplies, computers and software, electronics, office furniture, and business services such as

photocopying, faxing, and business card printing. Staples's Contract and
Commercial Division operates a mail-order delivery business as well as
regional and national contract stationer operations. Based in Westbor-
ough, Massachusetts, Staples employs more than 26,000 associates. Staples founded the office superstore industry in 1986. In its first 11 years,
its sales soared to $4 billion.

L.L. Bean is the world's largest cataloger in the outdoor specialty field.
It employs nearly 9,000 people during peak times. Headquartered in
Freeport, Maine, the company distributes more than 100 million catalogs
worldwide each year. Sales in 1996 were $1 billion. Of the more than 16,000
items stocked for catalog sales, 94 percent carry the L.L. Bean label.

The Louisville Redbirds are the Triple-A (minor league) baseball club
of the St. Louis Cardinals. One of 28 Triple-A teams, the Redbirds play a
144-game schedule, plus postseason play-off games if they qualify. As the
first minor league franchise to attract a million fans in one year, the Redbirds established their leadership in providing entertaining events for
their customers. The focus on the events proved necessary because the
Redbirds organization has no control over the outcome for its primary
product: the Redbirds' team.

IDENTIFYING YOUR CUSTOMERS

Most companies assume they know who their customers are, and they
are probably right. But there are degrees of knowledge here, and the
greater the knowledge, the better your chances of satisfying customer
requirements.

The Louisville Redbirds maintain a database containing 90 percent
of their customers' names, addresses, and phone numbers. They use the
database for target marketing and frequent direct mailings. The primary
targets: children and their parents. "Kids, on the weekend, probably have
80 percent of the say in where the family goes," says Dale Owens, general
manager. "Parents want to do something with their children. Our goal is
to entertain and to provide a sense of community." Owens targeted children because of his own memories of going to Louisville Colonels games
when he was a child. The focus seems to be paying off: Attendance at
Redbirds games has grown steadily since Owens became general manager
in 1987.

Few people have the luxury of being able to relate so directly to their
customers. Employees who are making, selling, or servicing computers,

copiers, or office products have to work a little harder to put themselves in the customers' shoes. Some companies are making it easier by involving customers in such activities as strategic planning, product design and development, process management, and benchmarking. They are encouraging employees to participate in customer teams, interact with their peers at the customers' companies, and be aware of customer satisfaction measurements and results. They know what Owens has acted on: *The better you understand your customers, the more likely you are to satisfy their requirements.*

Staples pursues a variety of marketing strategies to attract and retain target customers. Its strategies include the use of broad-based media advertising such as radio, television, newspaper circulars, and print advertising, as well as catalogs and a sophisticated direct marketing system. In addition, the company markets to larger companies through a combination of direct mail catalogs, customized catalogs, and a field sales force. Through its store and catalog direct marketing system, Staples tracks the buying habits of many of its customers, measures the response rate to various catalog marketing and promotional efforts, and responds to changes in purchasing patterns and customer demands.

In 1995, Staples launched a loyalty program called Dividend$. The program rewards top store and catalog customers with rebates and a variety of other benefits. Staples introduced the program (1) to encourage its customers to buy more and continue to return to Staples, and (2) to create a database of its "best" customers, which will help the company understand them better.

To improve its marketing, L.L. Bean has changed the way it segments its customers. Historically, it grouped customers by the frequency, size, and timing of their purchases. Revolving-door buyers, big spenders, and recent customers attracted an overbalanced amount of the company's attention.

The segmentation was based on L.L. Bean's financial goals, which provided little guidance when it came to customer satisfaction. Now, the company has shifted to customer-defined segmentation. It has identified a half-dozen customer groups, based on what they generally purchase from L.L. Bean. For example, a customer who usually buys sporting goods will be placed in that segment. Perhaps more importantly, the company has aligned its customer satisfaction surveys and other monitoring systems to the new segments. This allows L.L. Bean to identify and track the specific requirements for each segment, and that information helps the company improve customer satisfaction.

Xerox segments customers according to their industry, environment, geography, and business need, then maps that information back to Xerox's core competencies. The process involves lengthy discussions with customer groups. Xerox listens to their requirements and checks to make sure it has heard them accurately. The process also involves market analysis, to understand the general field Xerox is competing in, the problems people have, and the ways in which Xerox can help solve them. The goal is to find the best synergy between where the customers have problems and where Xerox's competence lies. Xerox has positioned itself as The Document Company to help customers better manage their documents and information.

One of Xerox's core competencies is understanding document technology: how it is formed, developed, used, revised, thrown away, collaborated on, and so forth. Another core competency is work flow. These core competencies, combined with the customers' need to improve their work processes, revealed the "sweet spot": helping customers improve their information flow for work processes that are document intensive. "We're about helping people solve productivity problems or take advantage of marketplace opportunities, and our focus is on document-intensive work processes," says Sam Malone, director of quality services. "That gives us the shape of the market we are after."

Xerox's process for identifying its customers and market segments gives it great insight and flexibility. Rather than fall into the trap of assuming it knows who its customers are, it searches for needs that it is well suited to meet, then verifies the validity of those needs and the promise of the market as it talks and listens to its potential customers. Getting close to customers, talking and listening, checking, verifying, testing—the dialogue is endless, and priceless. There is no other way to know your customers.

DETERMINING CUSTOMER REQUIREMENTS

"It's not easy to collect, analyze, and act on customer satisfaction information on an ongoing basis. However, since the market and business change so fast, you could be out of business before you realize that customer satisfaction has gone in the ditch."

To stay out of the ditch, IBM Rochester's Steve Hoisington sails an ocean of data in search of anything that might tell him more about his customers. His group casts a wide net, regularly hauling in an abundant catch of information:

- IBM surveys its customers monthly and quarterly. The surveys ask how customers feel about all 44 attributes that are regarded as customer satisfiers (described in the next section).
- It does product-specific surveys, talking to customers of a particular product after anywhere from 90 days to a year after purchase.
- It calls all its U.S. customers within 90–120 days after installing its products. This customer contact is different from the product-specific surveys.
- It has a closed-loop process for responding to customer complaints, and the complaint information is fed into its customer management database.
- Its marketing teams conduct a win/loss analysis for every competitive bid.
- It forms councils and focus groups, bringing in present and potential customers to discuss their requirements. These meetings are held annually for worldwide customers and every three or four months for regional focus groups.
- It has a competitive analysis team that buys, uses, and studies competitors' products.
- It validates all its customer information with independent surveys and double-blind surveys conducted by its marketing organization.
- It aggregates customer satisfaction and dissatisfaction from a host of sources, and determines pervasive deficiencies and requirements.

When Hoisington was asked about sources of information, these are the items that came to mind, but they are not the complete list. IBM Rochester tosses many other meaty morsels into its customer satisfaction soup. That soup feeds its system, and IBM Rochester wants to make sure that nothing essential is missing.

Like IBM Rochester, Xerox collects customer information from a variety of sources, including:

- Telephone surveys, using a sample of customers who contacted Xerox during the previous month.
- Monthly customer surveys, to gauge level of satisfaction.
- Competitive benchmark surveys of the marketplace.
- Regular focus groups in which Xerox is not identified as the sponsor.
- Ongoing customer panels with which the company shares ideas and from which it gathers input.
- Roundtables with salespeople, to determine problems and solutions.

- Market research focused on potential product opportunities.

- Collaborative development with customers, in which Xerox installs prototypes at a few customer locations to see how the prototypes meet their needs.

- Competitive product analysis.

- Discussions with industry experts.

- Conjoint analysis, with customers, of specific product and service features.

- Problems and usage reported in real time by 30,000 copiers linked by phone lines to Xerox service offices.

- Collaboration with cosuppliers (such as computer hardware and software developers).

The information from these different listening posts is aggregated and used to evaluate and refine Xerox's market segments and facilitate continuous improvement. Both IBM Rochester and Xerox spend considerable time collecting, comparing, and correlating information. This is partly because of the changeable nature of the high-tech industries in which they compete, but the primary reason is that their management models are built on customer satisfaction. They have set up their businesses to move in the direction their customers point them. By aggregating and comparing information, they can feel confident that they have chosen the right path.

Staples uses its database of customer information to build evaluation techniques that help it identify sites for new superstores. It also uses analysis of the data to set up the new stores, anticipating the buying trends and types of services that will appeal to potential customers in the area. In addition to the database, Staples gets customer information through a variety of market research methods, including focus groups, outbound telemarketing, and customer comment cards placed in stores.

One of the great advantages of pulling everything into a database is that it offers the ability to manipulate the information, to use it as IBM Rochester, Xerox, and Staples do: grouping their customers into major markets, then extracting the precise customer requirements for each. However, the database is not a prerequisite for collecting, organizing, and using information to understand your customers. You may choose to have these functions performed by teams in the senior staff, marketing department, or customer service department. You may decide to identify key measures of customer satisfaction for each requirement, then post results on these measures so that every employee knows how things are going. The critical factor is not the database but the aggregation and use of all available customer information in a timely manner.

L.L. Bean can speak to the issue of timeliness. It used to do annual customer satisfaction surveys, but now conducts them monthly. "As a direct result of our involvement with the quality movement, customer focus has taken on a more significant role in our overall management," says Greg Sweeney, vice president of customer loyalty. "For example, we used to contact several thousand customers by phone or mail. That number has grown with our monthly customer satisfaction surveys and specific surveys in stores and packages and by phone."

The information fuels a new focus on customer-defined segmentation. "In the past, we had limited information about what we wanted to do— and we hoped the customers would go along with us," Sweeney says. "Now we have a better profile of our customers that allows us to develop better strategies to meet their needs."

Companies intent on staying close to their customers make it a point to factor information about dissatisfaction into the equation. L.L. Bean compiles all customer complaints and distributes that information within the company. The company uses a Product Suggestion Report to note all comments, suggestions, and complaints, broken down by area. The report allows L.L. Bean to aggregate customer feedback from a variety of sources and get it to the people who can identify the root causes of any problems.

The company also asks customers, through surveys and focus groups, to compare its performance to that of its competitors. "We monitor in absolute numbers how we're doing and how the competition is doing," says Sweeney, "then act on what we learn about our strengths and weaknesses."

Staples closely monitors indicators of customer dissatisfaction through a number of methods. Here is a sampling:

- Purchase patterns are reported monthly from response rates to catalog and merchandise offerings.
- Customer service measures are systematically reported. Problem orders and presidential complaints are tracked daily and reported weekly through the company's call center data collection. In addition, mystery shops are conducted and reported monthly.
- Comprehensive customer behavior analysis is performed and shared with top management quarterly. The analysis includes database patterns such as new customer additions, retention, and sales per average

account. It also covers merchandise sales patterns, customer feed-back, and operational performance.

Reviewing the different types of customer information our role models collect, it is easy to agree with the statement, by Steve Hoisington of IBM, that setting up such an information-gathering organization is hard work. Gone are the days when you can assume you know your customers' requirements. Xerox's Malone talks about the "science" of understanding customer requirements. "A lot of times they can't tell us what problems they have in specific terms, only vaguely, so we must listen carefully and use our knowledge of their work processes, any new technologies, and our core competencies to guide us."

Know your customers. Know your business. Know yourself. The degree of knowledge in all three of these areas will shape your success.

USING CUSTOMER SATISFACTION TO DRIVE YOUR BUSINESS

In 1991, the Louisville Redbirds' management spent $300,000 to rebuild the stadium's concession stands. They have spent $1 million on the state-owned stadium since 1987. The latest changes were hardly imperative—the old area was very good, with wide, clean halls and large, eye-catching signs—but the Redbirds are in the business of customer satisfaction. They made the ice cream stand bigger (so the kids could get back to the game faster), and they added closed-circuit television (so the parents would not miss the action). Parents and their children are the Redbirds' target customers, and the Redbirds' business is satisfying those customers. General manager Dale Owens and his staff circulate at every home game, talking to customers to find out what they like and dislike, then using that information to make each game fun, safe, and memorable.

The Redbirds developed mascot Billy Bird to appeal to their young customers. Before Owens came along, the mascot was a beady-eyed cardinal that scared small children—not the desired response. Owens hired one of the sports scene's most popular mascots, the San Diego Chicken, to redesign Billy Bird (which is why the mascot now looks like a red chicken), and the children adore him. Three- and four-year-olds, who are easily bored with baseball, love Billy Bird. When he "leaves" in the seventh inning, he races up a ramp in center field, leaps onto a trampoline, and flips over the fence, then goes to the concession area to sign autographs and talk to fans.

The Redbirds also target parents. They hired a great rock-and-roll organist to play music that couples would like. Off-duty policemen are paid to provide excellent security. A doctor is on duty at the stadium for every game. Attendants check the bathrooms three times a night to make sure they are clean and well stocked. This attention to details helps create a positive experience that brings customers back.

The Redbirds run a lot of contests to keep fans entertained during games. For example, if a Redbird player hits a grand-slam home run on a Friday night, some lucky ticket holder wins $10,000. The team also holds promotions for 50 to 60 of its 72 home games. (By comparison, the Minnesota Twins, a major league club, have only 20 promotions during their 81-game home schedule.) For example, the Redbirds have Quarter Night, when everything except admission costs a quarter, and Redbirds staff members tape quarters to 10,000 seats (which is as much work as it sounds). "I throw all of our promotions out every year, with a few exceptions," says Owens. "Typically, we determine next year's promotions, then match sponsors with them. There are thousands of companies you can approach about supporting these events."

The Redbirds' focus on satisfying its customers drives its business. According to Owens, the average minor league team runs in the traditional way—with a few promotions, basic concessions, and the game itself as the sole entertainment—can make money drawing 250,000 people. In 1992, the Redbirds drew nearly 650,000 fans. "We run it as a community asset," Owens says. "We want to pass it on to the next generation of Louisville youth. And it also happens to be a way to make money."

Few companies have the luxury of focusing on customer satisfaction to the point where making money is almost an afterthought. Efforts to satisfy customers obviously cannot be allowed to wipe out a company's financial resources, but improving customer satisfaction can still be the company's driving force. The Louisville Redbirds are making money. They could also make money while doing far less for their customers, but they have chosen their course because they want *satisfied* customers. As a result, the Redbirds have a shared vision of what they wish to be: a company with a much sounder customer base, a strong competitive position in their marketplace, and a clear understanding of their customers' requirements. And they're making 650,000 customers happy in the process.

Owens and his staff get feedback from these customers at least 72 times a year, when the Redbirds play at home. They learn from them what works, what does not, and what they would like to see added or changed. Owens uses that knowledge to improve. He understands that customers' requirements constantly change (usually becoming more demanding), which is one reason the Redbirds offer a fresh slate of promotions each season and continually update their facilities.

Larger companies recognize the same dynamics at work in their customer base. "We believe that managing to satisfy customer requirements is a little like the hierarchy of needs," says Xerox's Malone. "We look at the basics people expect to have, understanding that the line keeps going up." He gives an example. People expect Xerox to be easy to do business with. In 1990, the company began offering a customer satisfaction guarantee that basically said, "If you're not happy with a Xerox product, we'll replace it at your request with no hassle, period." Malone says, "At the time, the guarantee was an industry first and a differentiator, but now others are following and it's become an expected service."

As noted earlier, Xerox aggregates into a database all the customer information it gathers. The database is then used to generate customer satisfaction levels and trends. This information is updated weekly and reviewed during regular management meetings. Always one of the first topics on the agenda, customer satisfaction data are used to identify gaps and to develop action plans that will address them. The levels and trends are also communicated to employees. Control charts for overall customer satisfaction and the supporting internal process measures are prominently displayed on walls and in work areas throughout the organization—including the boardroom, where the top management of U.S. Operations meets. The trends are easy to track in the charts:

- Xerox's overall customer satisfaction has improved more than 43 percent since 1985.

- In the category of low-volume copiers, Xerox improved 33 percent, compared to a 16 percent improvement for its competitors.

- For the past several years, Xerox has been recapturing market share from Japanese competitors.

- In the category of both mid- and high-volume copiers, Xerox remains the leader.

Outside research companies confirm these trends and levels. At the same time, adverse indicators, such as sales returns and accommodation adjustments, have declined.

IBM Rochester tracks customer satisfaction in six general categories, using what it calls the customer view model (Exhibit 3.1). Like Xerox, IBM Rochester recognizes that the items that satisfy customers are constantly changing. "Image" only recently made the list when IBM Rochester's information showed that its customers were factoring a company's image into

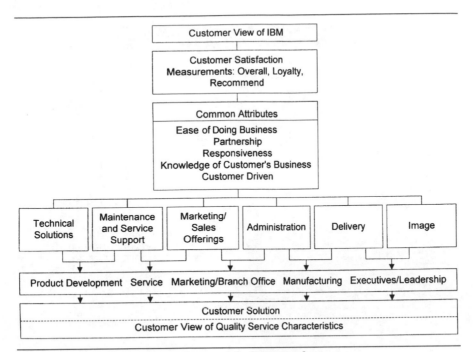

EXHIBIT 3.1.   The customer view model of IBM Rochester.

their buying decisions. Other items, such as ease of doing business, have become attributes a company is expected to have. "An element may be a satisfier today, but when everyone is doing it, it is no longer a satisfier; it is expected," says Hoisington.

IBM Rochester's goal is to be the undisputed leader in all six satisfiers: technical solutions, maintenance and service support, marketing/sales offerings, administration, delivery, and image. Under these general headings are 44 more specific satisfiers. Monthly customer surveys ask for input on all 44, except for those not valid for a particular customer. The executive team reviews the results monthly. If an area shows a potential problem, the executive in charge of the general satisfier establishes an action team to address it. Exhibit 3.2 shows how IBM Rochester uses customer satisfaction information to drive its business.

Hardware quality is a key quality indicator under the "technical solutions" satisfier identified in Exhibit 3.1, and the measurement of hardware quality is the first step in the closed-loop process shown in Exhibit 3.2. The six steps in the improvement process are:

Step 1.   Measure and benchmark the key quality indicator.
Step 2.   Trend the results.

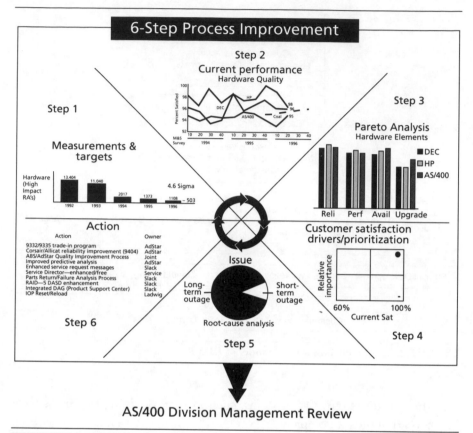

EXHIBIT 3.2.   IBM Rochester's process for measuring customer satisfaction.

Step 3.   Prioritize the key elements that affect the indicator (Pareto analysis).

Step 4.   Use a leverage matrix to determine which elements to work on.

Step 5.   For each element chosen, perform a root-cause analysis to identify the drivers of dissatisfaction or the satisfaction inhibitors. Choose the key drivers that will be addressed.

Step 6.   Identify actions to reduce the driver defects. Assign owners to each action. Track the impact of the actions.

The process continues with measurement of the key quality indicator to gauge the effects of the improvement actions—the return to Step 1 that closes the loop.

By institutionalizing customer satisfaction, IBM Rochester steers an entire organization along a course charted by its customers. It according to one agenda: *customer satisfaction.* It analyzes and improves its processes in order to improve performance in its six primary satisfiers. It is not in the business of making computers or servicing computers or selling solutions; *it is in the business of satisfying customers better than anyone else.* That is what it means to use customer satisfaction to drive a business.

THE SHIFT IN THINKING

In the new management model, business begins with *customer focus* and ends with *customer satisfaction,* which are two sides of the same coin. The customer requirements that you focus your business on are the same requirements you use to measure satisfaction. Changes in customer satisfaction or requirements trigger changes in how you do business, and those changes affect customer satisfaction. The new management model is a closed-loop system driven by customer satisfaction.

The remainder of the book demonstrates how the desire to satisfy customers translates into action. Companies that are accustomed to defining their activities by other criteria (such as departmental goals, financial

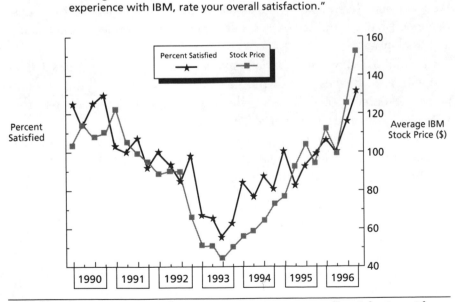

EXHIBIT 3.3.   Comparison of customers' responses on overall satisfaction with IBM Rochester (solid pattern) and average price of IBM stock (shaded pattern).

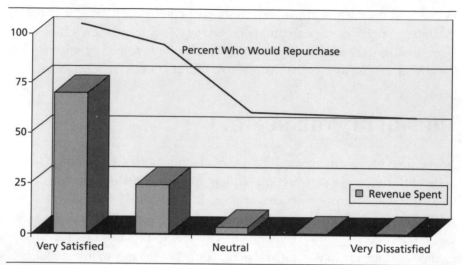

EXHIBIT 3.4.   Revenues correlated with customer loyalty at IBM Rochester.

targets, or quality measures) find that the shift in thinking to a total customer focus requires *deep-rooted cultural change*.

"We are learning about the way customer satisfaction affects our entire system, including measuring, planning, processes, and results," says IBM's Hoisington. "Winning the Baldrige Award in 1990 was a catalyst for expanding our use of customer satisfaction information even further. We have since been able to determine a direct correlation between customer satisfaction and business results, including revenue, market share, and stock price."

Exhibit 3.3 shows the correlation between customers' overall satisfaction with IBM Rochester and IBM's average stock price. Exhibit 3.4 compares the percent of customers who said they would repurchase from IBM Rochester and the actual revenue spent.

As these graphs and our models of excellence show, companies that get close to their customers, and develop strong customer loyalty, can anticipate strong financial performance. The proof is in the numbers.

4 STRATEGIC PLANNING

Zytec

Cadillac

Dana Commercial Credit

The function of strategic planning in the new management model is to align all the efforts of the organization to customer satisfaction, quality, and operational performance goals. Deployed to its fullest, a world-class planning process would make it possible for all employees to match their tasks to specific company objectives. At Zytec, Cadillac, and Dana Commercial Credit, the planning process is definitely world-class. All three companies use their strategic planning processes not only to align quality improvement activities within their organizations but to drive the whole improvement process.

Zytec calls its process (which is patterned after the Japanese *hoshin kanri) management by planning*. Cadillac states that its business plan is its quality plan. Dana Commercial Credit's annual strategic planning process integrates customer, operational, people, supplier, and quality plans into seven business and financial plans, one for each decentralized product group.

All three companies blend business and quality planning into a single strategic plan. We will introduce the planning processes of these companies separately, to show how they work. We will then examine the manner in which they address the following issues:

- Who is involved in the planning process?
- What data and information, including customer requirements and company capabilities, feed the planning process?
- How does the planning process address continuous improvement?
- How is the plan deployed throughout the company?
- How is the planning process improved?

MODELS OF EXCELLENCE

Zytec is a leading designer and manufacturer of custom electronic power conversion equipment for original equipment manufacturers in the communications, networking, computer, and other electronic equipment markets. In addition, the company provides logistics and repair from its California operation, and repair of power supplies in its Redwood Falls, Minnesota, site. Zytec employs 2,300 people at facilities located in Eden Prairie and Redwood Falls, Minnesota; Broomfield, Colorado; Lincoln, California; Richardson, Texas; Vienna and Kindber, Austria; and Tatabanya, Hungary. At the company's first strategic planning meeting, in the summer of 1984, its senior executives committed to follow the concepts of W. Edwards Deming as the basis for its drive for quality improvement. In 1991, Zytec won the Baldrige Award and the first Minnesota Quality Award.

Cadillac Motor Car Company is a division of General Motors North American Automotive Operations. A Baldrige Award winner in 1990, Cadillac earned quality recognition as early as 1908, when it was the first American company to win the prestigious Dewar Trophy. Cadillac's quality leadership declined in the early 1980s, but a reorganization in 1987 spurred a transformation built on three strategies: (1) a cultural change, (2) a constant focus on the customer, and (3) a disciplined approach to planning.

Dana Commercial Credit (DCC) is a leading provider of business lease financing services in the capital markets, dealer products market, diversified capital market, international operations, asset management, technology management, and energy management. Headquartered in Toledo, Ohio, DCC is an indirect, wholly owned subsidiary of Dana Corporation. DCC has approximately 550 employees. The company won the Baldrige Award in 1996.

ZYTEC: MANAGEMENT BY PLANNING

Zytec's original long-range strategic planning process boiled down to three steps:

1. Data are gathered.
2. Cross-functional teams set goals.
3. Departmental management-by-planning (MBP) teams implement the goals by developing detailed action plans.

Zytec got most of its data from customer feedback (primarily on a factory-to-factory basis), formal and informal market research, and benchmarking. The data had to be: consistent from year to year; within the control of the area doing the collecting; and able to be presented using statistical methods. Examples of the types of data collected include:

- Customer on-time delivery.
- Customer reliability (mean time between failures).
- Production cycle time.
- Employee quality training.
- Supplier dock-to-stock percentage.

The planning cycle began when senior management identified the company's strategic issues. Each issue was assigned to strategic planning groups in marketing, technology, manufacturing, materials, the product renewal center, and corporate administration. Each strategic planning group consisted of eight to ten employees from throughout the company. Over a three-month period, the groups researched their issues by using the data that had been collected and interviewing internal experts, customers, and suppliers. The groups then prepared reports that identified what had been examined and laid out a five-year plan.

The reports were discussed at two off-site, one-day planning meetings attended by all managers, all exempt employees, representatives of the rest of the workforce, customers, and suppliers. In 1992, nearly a third of Zytec's employees participated in these meetings. Following the meetings, a consensus document was written that identified Zytec's long-range (five-year) goals. The people who attended the meetings shared the results with and requested reactions from employees, major customers, and any key suppliers who did not attend.

When agreement was reached on the company's vision, Zytec had its long-range strategic plan (LRSP). Attention then turned to short-term planning. *At this point, the company's strategic planning process translated its vision into action plans.* Senior management used the LRSP to set broad corporate objectives for the company to address. Zytec's corporate objectives are to improve:

- Quality.
- Cycle time.
- Customer service.
- Cost structure.

With these objectives and the LRSP as their guide, MBP teams in every operating department developed their departmental objectives for the year and created detailed action plans with measurable and specific monthly goals. The MBP teams completed a standardized matrix to show how they were translating corporate objectives into team objectives and measurements. They used a standardized action plan to identify activity steps, resources required, measures, and time of completion. The standardization of these techniques, combined with a common set of problem-solving tools all employees had been trained to use, kept everyone in the company on the same path toward shared goals.

To prevent conflicts between departments, senior executives played "catch-ball" with the MBP teams. "Catch-ball" involved meeting with the teams to exchange information and negotiate specific objectives and actions that fit with those of the other teams and with the LRSP. The senior staff had to sign off on the teams' objectives, plans, and measurements. Zytec then established detailed department budgets, staffing plans, and capital plans to support the objectives.

After the plan was implemented, departments reviewed their measurements and action plans with senior management monthly. These meetings reinforced interest in and support for the departments' efforts to improve quality while giving management an opportunity to help departments that were not performing according to plan.

After completing the LRSP process, Zytec asked participants how each major step in the process could be improved. Senior management evaluated the suggestions and initiated appropriate changes for the next planning cycle. The feedback generated continuous improvement: the number of employees participating in the process was increased, customers and suppliers were brought into the process, and training was expanded to give employees more tools for meeting their objectives.

CADILLAC: BUSINESS PLANNING PROCESS

In its Baldrige Award-winning application, Cadillac Motor Car Company wrote, "At Cadillac, the Business Plan is the Quality Plan." The business planning process in place when Cadillac won the Award spurs quality improvement at Cadillac because:

1. It drives an *annual review* of the division's mission and strategic objectives, to make sure they are aligned with the business environment and the mission of General Motors.
2. It guides the development and implementation of *key processes* such as simultaneous engineering and the labor–management quality network.
3. It builds *discipline* into the ongoing process of creating and achieving short- and long-term quality improvement goals.

Exhibit 4.1 illustrates Cadillac's planning process. The planning process began every June, when the executive staff reviewed current objectives to make sure they were aligned with corporate objectives. The staff then gathered relevant data from throughout the organization to assess Cadillac's strengths and weaknesses. The data included benchmarking of competitive products and processes used by world-class companies. Key suppliers and dealers also contributed to the planning process.

On the basis of this situational analysis, the executive staff proposed business objectives for the next year. In 1992, Cadillac had 29 business objectives in six major areas: leadership, people, quality, customer satisfaction, cost, and speed to market. The proposed objectives were reviewed across the division, and the feedback generated by this review was used to develop the final business objectives. The executive staff shared the objectives with top union and management leaders of the company and its various divisions at the business planning kickoff meeting.

Next, the functional staff, plant quality councils, and human resource management developed goals and action plans that supported the business objectives. "Just about everybody in Cadillac got involved in this process," says William Lesner, former superintendent of manufacturing.

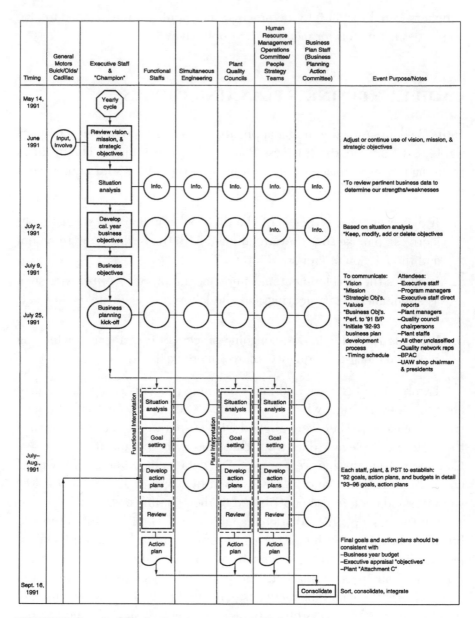

EXHIBIT 4.1.   Cadillac's planning process model.

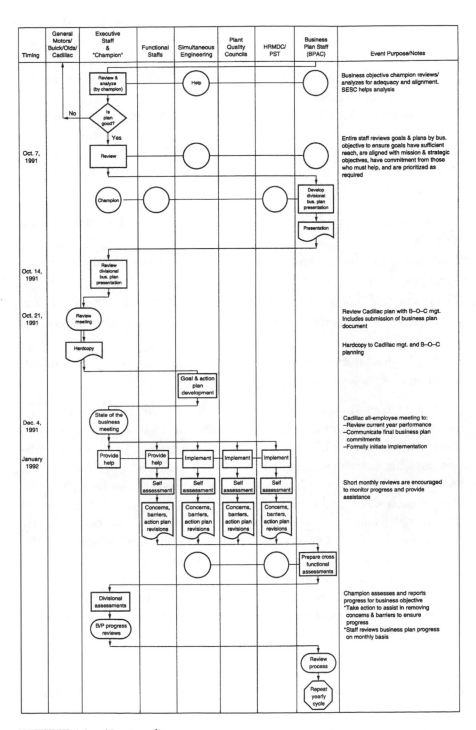

EXHIBIT 4.1. *(Continued)*

"Plants and departments came up with their own plans to meet the division's plans." The executive staff reviewed all plans, for alignment and adequacy. In December, the entire business plan was presented to all Cadillac employees at the annual state-of-the-business meeting. Implementation began in January.

For example, Cadillac identified three business objectives for quality in its 1991 plan. The first, labeled Q1, was: "Cadillac will continuously improve the quality of our processes, products, and services." The Detroit-Hamtramck assembly center developed five goals to achieve this objective (all labeled Q1 also):

1. Continually improve first-time quality through the Quality Planning process.
2. Achieve greater awareness and responsiveness to internal customer expectations.
3. Continually implement the approved Quality Network action strategies.
4. Expand implementation of the Pull System throughout general assembly.
5. Establish a Level Schedule Index (LSI) to measure variation in scheduling of vehicles to assembly.

The Detroit-Hamtramck plant simplified its 1992 plan to focus on fewer key goals and measures. Every day, management distributed a single-page handout. On one side of the page were Cadillac's vision, mission, and business objectives and the plant's vision and problem-solving process; on the other side were six critical measures. The first five minutes of each day's quality audit meeting were spent reviewing three of the critical measures: two measures for daily audits and one for daily production. Weekly team meetings included reviews of progress on the business plan. Monthly division management meetings focused on performance relative to the business plan.

By using a variety of communication tools to keep its key goals and measures in front of people, Cadillac focused everyone's efforts on activities that contributed to achieving its business objectives.

DANA COMMERCIAL CREDIT: STRATEGIC PLANNING

At most companies, strategic planning is the domain of senior leaders. Dana Commercial Credit (DCC) prefers a "bottom-up" approach. "If you look at our eight-stage planning process, the ideas come from the product groups closest to our markets," says Kevin Moyer, president of DCC's Capital Group and champion of the planning process for DCC. "What our planning process does is provide a disciplined framework that forces people to think about what they ought to be doing and to get the processes in place to do it."

The disciplined framework is an eight-phase process, as shown in Exhibit 4.2. Phase 1 affirms the business philosophy that guides the strategic plan. DCC's vision is "to be the preferred, knowledge-based, service-oriented leasing company in our selected markets, both domestically and internationally." DCC's mission is "to be first in customer satisfaction, by being first in knowledge and first in quality."

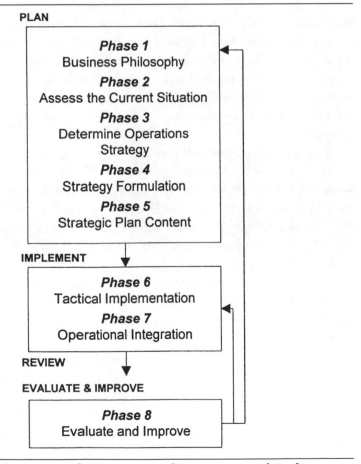

EXHIBIT 4.2.   The strategic planning process of Dana Commercial Credit.

During Phase 2, Product Group Operating Committees consider the "trendynamics" of the leasing industry that are outside the control of the organization. Trendynamics is DCC's term for changes in key areas—customers, competitive, financial, market, technology, social, economic, tax laws, accounting regulations, and legal issues—that affect the company. "If I were to boil down what's key to the planning process, that's an area we spend a lot of time on, thinking about what's out there, because we're not the biggest in the market," says Moyer. "This company has always been a niche, opportunistic player in the market. Being able to spot trends and provide high-value products to our customers is our competitive advantage."

With trendynamics in hand, each Product Group then performs a SWOT analysis—a review of its *Strengths* and *Weaknesses* with respect to *Opportunities* and *Threats*—for each of its targeted market segments.

During Phase 3, the Product Group Operating Committees conduct a SWOT analysis of issues within DCC's control, including leadership style and culture, technology gap analysis, business process capabilities, and supplier capabilities. Key business drivers are developed at the product group level. According to Moyer, "Our key business drivers are set up around knowledge, quality, profit, and customer satisfaction. Each product group will have measurements that relate to these key business drivers."

The next two phases pull together the findings of the product groups into a strategic plan for the organization. "This is an ongoing process," Moyer says. "We are constantly gathering data. On a semiannual basis, product groups get together with senior management to present strategies. We don't make people sit around and write strategic plans every year. We focus on the key things you need to get done and whether your strategy has changed."

During Phase 6, each Product Group Operating Committee develops a supporting tactical implementation plan. All involved product groups and division staff review the plans as part of Phase 7, to make sure they are aligned.

The final phase involves evaluating and improving the process. "The biggest thing people struggle with is how to get started," observes Moyer. "Somebody at the top has to say 'We're going to do this.' When we were in the early stages, we educated ourselves in the best way to do planning. We got a process in place and we worked it. It didn't happen overnight. Leadership and education really drive the improvement."

WHOM TO INVOLVE IN STRATEGIC PLANNING

At Zytec and Cadillac, senior management initiates the planning process; at DCC, product groups take charge of the first phases in the planning process. Leaders are responsible for identifying strategies that reflect their company's long-range vision, which typically reaches five years into the future. They develop those strategies with input from people throughout the company, and often get feedback from key customers and suppliers.

Once the corporate strategies and objectives have been determined, the planning process involves more employees. Departments, teams, and work units must translate the corporate vision into specific goals, action plans, and measures. The more employees involved in the process, both in developing and carrying out the strategic plan, the greater the understanding and deployment.

The completed plan may be circulated among major customers and suppliers for their input. The advantage of involving external people in the process is one of *alignment:* The plan will reflect what customers need and expect, and what suppliers are able to provide and support.

Once the plan has been implemented, managers and employees report progress on action plans and objectives. The employees participate in the reporting process as members of teams that work on related issues or as representatives of their departments.

WHAT DATA AND INFORMATION TO USE

As with any decision a company must make, the better the data and information available to understand the situation and evaluate options, the better the decision. For a decision on where to focus the company's resources, the sources of data might include the following:

- Customer service, sales, and marketing functions usually report on customer satisfaction and current and future needs.
- The human resources department describes the talent and skills that are available to achieve the company's vision, and how those talents and skills can be enhanced through involvement, training, reward, and recognition.
- The quality and finance departments outline the company's condition and the resources available for the coming year.

- Other departments provide relevant data on environmental issues, government regulations, process capabilities, supplier capabilities, and similar areas.

- Ongoing teams formed to address major issues or problems summarize their progress and their needs and expectations for the year ahead.

Typically, the data provided include performance on key measures over the past year, results of competitive comparisons and benchmarking studies, survey results, and perceptions and ideas about current and future capabilities.

Senior executives and others involved in developing the plan use all these data to establish corporate goals, objectives, strategies, action plans, and key indicators. Data collected on the key indicators during the year are used to evaluate progress on the plan.

ADDRESSING CONTINUOUS IMPROVEMENT

The best strategic plans include specific measures for achieving every objective, a means for gathering and publishing data on these measures, and a process for timely review by management. It is critical to identify, collect, and use the right data; otherwise, continuous improvement on the company's most important areas cannot be made.

At Zytec, Cadillac, and Dana Commercial Credit, the strategic plans focus the organizations' resources on a few key processes. The indicators for these processes include current levels and targets for the end of the next year. Progress on the indicators is communicated regularly and frequently:

- Cadillac's Detroit-Hamtramck plant distributes a page of graphs showing daily performance on six critical measures, discusses three of those measures at daily quality audit meetings, and reviews progress on the business plan at weekly team and plant meetings and at monthly division management meetings.

- Zytec's senior management reviews all key indicators and action plans monthly. Departments track performance on their key measures and report progress at the monthly meetings.

- Dana Commercial Credit has semiannual senior management meetings to study the trends, share ideas, and listen to the product groups' strategies. Every product group has a scorecard linked to the company's key business drivers.

A business truism states: "What gets paid attention to, gets done." Many companies find that just posting trend charts in a department immediately improves performance because people naturally want to see that their efforts are making a positive impact. By assigning responsibility for keeping trends moving in the right direction, a company institutionalizes continuous improvement in those areas it considers most important.

Deploying the Plan

The most effective strategic plan would be so well implemented that every task performed by every employee would support one or more corporate objectives. The connections would be traceable, and the employees would understand the connections.

As our quality role models show, world-class planning processes are only half over when the plan is complete. In the second half, plans must be turned into action. This involves identifying the steps necessary to achieve the objectives at the corporate, division, department, work unit, team, and individual levels. It is not a particularly mysterious or difficult process, but it does require a deployment process for each level to translate corporate goals and objectives into action items, and an evaluation process wherein management can monitor performance and assist those units that are having trouble.

At Zytec, the plan is deployed by MBP teams using a standard matrix and action plan to show the translation of corporate objectives into team objectives, measurements, and actions. Cadillac translates corporate and division objectives into plant objectives, then uses a few visible, broad measures to focus everyone's attention on what is critical. DCC devotes two phases of its planning process to implementation. One of DCC's "secrets to successful strategic planning" is: "Strategic thinking by the entire Dana Commercial Credit organization is essential to move everyone in the same direction."

Improving the Planning Process

All three models for this chapter can point to improvements in their planning processes because they solicit input from those involved, through either feedback sessions or surveys. Zytec asks for feedback after each major step in its planning process; DCC has an improvement cycle built into its planning process.

THE SHIFT IN THINKING

Early in their quality improvement process, many companies attempt to do quality planning separately from business planning. *This doesn't work.* Baldrige Award-winner Marlow Industries (profiled in Chapter 2) is quick to point out the mistake it made by trying to have two structures, one for quality and the other for the rest of their business. "We kept moving quality into the business area," says Chris Witzke, chief operating officer. "Now, we can't make any distinction. We make quality part of our business by integrating it into our business plan."

Leading companies affirm Cadillac's claim that the business plan is the quality plan. Treating the two as separate entities suggests to employees that quality exists outside the rest of the business, that they can work on quality over here and everything else over there. Senior executives create an environment for continuous improvement by demonstrating that quality is inherent in *everything* that *every* employee does.

Leading companies also show that the planning process can benefit from a wide variety of inputs. They involve more employees in the process, which typically involves additional training and is another method of increasing employee involvement. Some invite customers and suppliers to participate, which improves both customer satisfaction and supplier quality. They pull in a host of data and information to make sure they understand their customers' needs and their companies' capabilities. These inputs produce a plan that accurately reflects the real world, by having goals and objectives that everyone in the company can support. Efforts to improve processes can then center on those that are identified as most important to the company.

Finally, leading companies have proven that the strategic planning process can be used to coordinate and fuel rapid quality improvement. Employees work on what is important to the company.

The alignment of activities through the strategic planning process makes it possible for a company of any size to focus all its resources on the strategies and objectives that are critical to its success.

5 MANAGEMENT

Ritz-Carlton Hotel Company

Motorola

Engelhard-Huntsville

Since 1988, when Motorola won the first Baldrige Award, its people have given thousands of speeches about how Motorola became and remains a successful company, the "big company that acts like a small company," as some have called it. The standard presentation includes a slide that states:

We have been successful because of our management process.

There is no vacillation here, no all-encompassing list of reasons Motorola succeeds. It is the management process. Put simply, Motorola's process is:

1. Have a set of metrics.
2. Determine results.
3. Pick a problem.
4. Address the problem.
5. Analyze the solution.
6. Move on.

The process is far from earthshaking. "This is no magic solution," says Paul Noakes, former vice president and director of external quality programs for Motorola—the man responsible for a good portion of those speeches. "The basic tools are there for everyone to use. The rest is a management process."

How you manage your company—your system, your quality improvement process—determines your success. That statement sounds so obvious it is almost trite, but somewhere between thinking it and actually believing it lies a wall of disclaimers:

- Management is the key *except* when competition is unfair.
- Management is the key *except* when employees don't do their jobs.
- Management is the key *except* when the market goes bad.

Motorola accepts no exceptions. "If we don't make a goal," says Noakes, "we've learned it's because management isn't involved enough in the process."

This chapter focuses on managing the quality improvement process. It looks at how three successful organizations convert their customers' and company's requirements into goals and standards for their managers, supervisors, and other employees. The processes they have developed respond to three critical management questions:

1. How do we translate our customer focus and quality values into requirements for our managers, supervisors, and other employees?
2. How do we communicate these requirements throughout the organization?
3. How do we make sure the requirements are being met?

In answering these questions, we have tried to pin down the changing roles of managers and supervisors. The new business management model has not been kind to old-style bosses, who would have answered our questions with one simple, blunt command: "Do it." To create flatter and more flexible organizations, managers and supervisors have had to learn how to listen to their subordinates, encourage their feedback, persuade rather than demand, support their initiatives, coach, train, facilitate, and serve. This is not the job many managers envisioned. As if these expectations were not enough, the specter of "self-directed work teams" threatens to eliminate supervisory jobs altogether.

All this seems to suggest a contradiction: If the key to success is the management process, what exactly should management be doing? Answers to that question appear in this chapter and in every other chapter in this book. Managers need to understand the *system* in which they work and for which they are responsible. They need to tune that system to customer requirements and get every person and process they are responsible for humming the same tune.

MODELS OF EXCELLENCE

The Ritz-Carlton Hotel Company is a management company based in Atlanta that develops and operates luxury hotels for W. B. Johnson Properties. The company operates 23 business and resort hotels around the world. It also has 9 international sales offices and 2 subsidiary products: restaurants and banquets. It employs 11,500 people. The Ritz-Carlton Hotel Company targets primarily industry executives, meeting and corporate travel planners, and prestigious travelers. In 1991, the company received 121 quality-related awards and industry-best rankings by major hotel-rating organizations. In 1992, Ritz-Carlton won the Baldrige Award.

Motorola is one of the world's leading providers of electronic equipment, systems, components, and services for worldwide markets. Its products include two-way radios, pagers, cellular telephones, semiconductors, and automotive and industrial electronics. Motorola employs more than 138,000 people in facilities around the world. In 1988, Motorola won the first Malcolm Baldrige National Quality Award.

Engelhard-Huntsville is a major manufacturer of catalytic parts for controlling air emissions from automobiles, forklifts, and stationary pollution sources. It also produces silver chemicals. Engelhard invented catalytic converters in the early 1970s and built a plant in Huntsville, Alabama, to manufacture them. By the early 1980s, productivity and quality were so bad that the plant was close to being shut down. Today, the Huntsville plant's 380 employees proudly point to their dramatic productivity gains, incredible safety record, and low turnover rate as indicators of their success. Among the many quality awards and citations the plant has received, two of the most notable are the Ford Total Quality Excellence Award (only 8 of Ford's 3,300 suppliers have won this award) and the United States Senate Award for Productivity, which it won in 1991.

MAKING THE SYSTEM HUM

Leadership sets a company's vision and values. Customers indicate what to focus on. Strategic planning converts vision, values, and customer requirements into company goals. And the system stands ready to pursue those goals. But first the *goals* must be translated into *requirements* that rivet the attention of all employees on the specific improvements they can and must make. Without these shared requirements, clearly communicated and reviewed for progress, the system is out of sync, clanking and wheezing instead of humming along with continuous improvement.

The primary methods our role models use to make their systems hum are:

- Set challenging goals.
- Develop action plans to pursue those goals.
- Train people to achieve the goals.

Ritz-Carlton: Striving for "Gold Standards"

The Ritz-Carlton Hotel Company translates customer requirements into employee requirements through its Gold Standards and its strategic planning process. The Gold Standards include a credo, a motto, three steps of service, and 20 "Ritz-Carlton basics." The credo states:

> The Ritz-Carlton Hotel is a place where the genuine care and comfort of our guests is our highest mission. We pledge to provide the finest personal service and facilities for our guests who will always enjoy a warm, relaxed yet refined ambiance. The Ritz-Carlton experience enlivens the senses, instills well-being, and fulfills even the unexpressed wishes and needs of our guests.

The company's motto is: "We are ladies and gentlemen serving ladies and gentlemen," and its three steps of service are:

1. A warm and sincere greeting. Use the guest's name, if and when possible.
2. Anticipation of and compliance with guests' needs.
3. Fond farewell. Give them a warm good-bye and use their names, if and when possible.

The 20 "basics" include understanding and following the credo, motto, and three steps, and other requirements.

Employees are expected to adhere to these Gold Standards, which describe processes for solving problems guests may have, as well as detailed grooming, housekeeping, safety, and efficiency standards. "We've taken the things our customers want most and come up with the simplest ways to provide them," says Patrick Mene, vice president of quality. "And then we continuously emphasize them. We define our employees' behavior." The Ritz-Carlton's data show that its employees' understanding of the Gold Standards is directly correlated with guest satisfaction.

Ritz-Carlton employees are charged with mastering the basics first, then improving. The requirements for improving are set through the strategic planning process. Teams that include corporate leaders, managers, and employees set objectives and devise action plans, which the corporate steering committee reviews. Quality goals draw extensively on customers' requirements, which are determined by travel industry research and the company's customer reaction data, focus groups, and surveys.

Employees also determine and respond to customer requirements at the individual level because, as Mene points out, "This is a highly personal, individual service." Ritz-Carlton's 11,500 employees are trained to read customers' reactions and to detect their likes and dislikes. "You're fully deploying customer reaction detection," says Mene. Customer likes are documented on a simple piece of paper and entered in a computerized guest-history profile that provides information on the preferences of 240,000 repeat Ritz-Carlton guests. "When the customer returns, we know his or her personal preferences, which are distributed to the employees providing the service," Mene says. "What's unique is that employees correct and use customer reaction data to deliver premium service at the individual level. Our business management system is almost driven by the individual employees, running the business at the lowest levels."

If an employee detects a dislike, he or she is empowered to break away from the routine and take immediate positive action, to "move heaven and earth" to satisfy the customer. Any employee can spend up to $2,000 on the spot to make a customer happy. Or, the employee can call on any other employee to assist. The Ritz-Carlton refers to this as "lateral service." Such a system depends on trained, empowered, and involved employees, which is why the Ritz-Carlton is careful to hire perceptive people, define their behavior, and train them to serve. With more than a million customer contacts on a busy day, the Ritz-Carlton understands that its customer and quality requirements must be driven by each individual employee.

Motorola: Setting "Stretch" Goals

Motorola is a very goal-oriented company. In 1987, it announced aggressive corporate quality goals:

- 10 times improvement by 1989.
- 100 times improvement by 1991.

- Six-Sigma performance by 1992 (Six Sigma roughly equates to 3.4 defects per million opportunities).

Such ambitious goals clearly define the level of improvement that Motorola expects from every business unit, division, department, work team, and individual in the company. "I believe the fundamental reason total quality management fails is because no level of expectations has been set," says Noakes. "You need *results* or people will get disillusioned—and that includes management."

Motorola has produced results. From 1987 to 1996, its cumulative savings from quality improvement was $11 billion. Over the same period, sales increased 4.75 times and sales per employee tripled, while the number of employees increased just 46 percent. This translates into an average increase in employee productivity of 12.3 percent per year.

To achieve these goals, Motorola changed its system. Keki Bhote, senior corporate consultant on quality and productivity for Motorola, listed the changes in an article in *National Productivity Review:*

- Reducing the number of managerial and supervisory layers, and increasing the spans of control.
- Organizing to a more manageable size to build teamwork and give employees a greater sense of control.
- Integrating related functions to break down artificial departmental walls and overcome the "vertical silo" syndrome.
- Changing the organization's traditional role of policing to that of coaching.
- Enhancing every standard, expectation, process, and system in a few businesses that have now become the models for others to follow.
- Making quality the first order of attention on meeting agendas, reviews, plans, compensation, and rewards.

Notice that every change affected the way in which managers and supervisors managed the process. The fundamental change in Motorola's system was to redefine management's roles and responsibilities. Only then could the management process achieve the company's "stretch" goals.

Motorola's current "stretch" goal is 10 times improvement in quality every 2 years, which works out to a 68 percent *annual* improvement in whatever is being measured. Managers and supervisors are expected to reduce the amount of defects in the products and services for which they are responsible by 68 percent this year. Then they must do it again next year and the year after that. They are also expected to reduce cycle times by 10 times in 5 years—approximately 40 percent improvement per year. Through clearly defined goals, Motorola focuses the efforts of its managers, supervisors, and other employees on *five initiatives* that capture the company's customer focus and quality values:

1. Six-Sigma quality.
2. Total cycle time reduction.
3. Product, manufacturing, and environmental leadership.
4. Profit improvement.
5. Empowerment for all in a participative, cooperative, and creative workplace.

Engelhard-Huntsville: Aiming for "Exceptional Quality"

Both the Ritz-Carlton and Motorola use formal processes to translate customer requirements and quality values into requirements for managers, supervisors, and other employees. The scope of these companies' operations demands goals, action plans, and performance reviews, to make sure their requirements are being deployed and met. At Engelhard's Huntsville operation, customer requirements and quality values are converted into employee requirements through its Quality Operating System, which includes measures and requirements for three areas, identified as customer focus, internal focus, and prevention focus. However, the size of the Huntsville plant makes it easier for managers and supervisors to communicate, review performance on, and help meet these requirements. Leadership deploys its customer and quality requirements by giving clear direction about what is expected, serving as examples of what customer service and quality improvement mean, and promoting training.

Engelhard's version of total quality management is called *Exceptional Quality.* The entire plant has been trained in Exceptional Quality, which formalized what Huntsville had been doing since the mid-1980s. Among the twelve principles that support the commitment to Exceptional Quality are pledges to be flexible and adaptable, work together, train and empower each other, encourage innovation, and promote long-term relationships with customers, suppliers, and fellow employees. The twelfth principle is a pledge to "provide management support and accountability for the quality commitment and principles through direction, example, and appropriate resource commitment."

The Huntsville operation knows from experience that management is key to success. When Joseph Steinreich became general manager of the plant in 1981, it had 590 employees. In 1982, they filed 82 grievances and lost 22 workdays because of accidents. Turnover was at 150 percent per year. Eighteen percent of product was being wasted because of poor quality. Not surprisingly, the plant was losing money. Engelhard gave Steinreich six months to turn things around or the plant would be closed.

Steinreich began by ditching the plant's confrontational management style. He instituted a supervisors' training program to foster a more people-oriented management culture. Managers and supervisors changed or were replaced. "We focused on skill building, on how to get along and solve problems," says Carl English, human resources manager.

Fifteen years later, employees recognize the dramatic changes that have occurred. Asked to list the changes during training sessions, employees came up with more than 500, of which 498 were positive. Many items on the list described how the new management style had contributed to the operation's success, such as "Management is concerned about everything," "People will listen to you," "A good job is recognized," and "We're partners with each other and with our customers and suppliers."

In 1994, Steinreich retired and was replaced by Ken Rogers, who had been the manufacturing manager at Huntsville from 1986 to 1991. Rogers led an effort to redesign the organization around employee teams, which are now totally responsible for order fulfillment, including receiving customer orders, planning, scheduling, production, maintenance, quality control, shipping, and billing.

The Huntsville plant expanded in 1996 to serve a growing worldwide market share. Such growth is only one measure of Engelhard-Huntsville's success. Other achievements are:

- Turnover has been reduced from 150 percent to less than 3 percent annually.
- Scrap has been cut by more than 50 percent since 1994.
- In over 13 years, not one workday has been lost because of an accident.
- The plant provides 70 percent of the automotive catalysts for the Japanese market.
- Huntsville has earned top quality awards from Ford, BMW, and Honda.

Engelhard-Huntsville has achieved these successes by setting specific requirements through its Quality Operating System and by empowering its managers, supervisors, and other employees to meet these requirements. As described in the next section, it also uses training to translate customer requirements and quality values into requirements for its employees, then relies on frequent communication, through meetings and personal contact, to clarify and reinforce these requirements.

COMMUNICATING REQUIREMENTS THROUGHOUT THE COMPANY

When asked how to manage quality, the first thing Joe Steinreich says is, "Set an example." As the man responsible for initiating the turnaround at Engelhard's Huntsville operation, Steinreich knows how important it is for managers and supervisors to exemplify the attitudes and behaviors they wish to encourage.

For example, Steinreich met with his staff weekly. Every month, at one of those meetings, he asked five "monthly EQ (Exceptional Quality) questions" he carried with him on a laminated card the size of a credit card:

1. What are you personally doing to improve EQ?
2. What are your plans for improving the work climate in your area?
3. What are your plans for empowering your people?
4. What have you identified that needs to be fixed and how can I help you fix it?
5. What successes have you had with EQ in your area?

"I went around the table and asked each person to respond," says Steinreich, "after I answered them first." In this way, Steinreich communicated what was important to him as a leader and to his operation. The managers took the five questions to their direct reports, cascading the requirements throughout the organization.

Steinreich also communicated directly, frequently, with employees. Every quarter, he met with all employees to discuss the state of the business, which included customer requirements and quality issues. In addition to these meetings, Steinreich and one of his human resources department managers conducted 16 to 18 roundtable discussions each year. "We selected a group of hourly people to participate, and they always asked their coworkers what they wanted or needed to know," says Steinreich. "We met for lunch or dinner. I talked briefly about the state of the company, then we went around the table for discussion and questions. If we couldn't answer a question, we wrote it up and posted the answer."

Employees make a habit of checking bulletin boards. "We do a lot of communicating," says Carl English, human resources manager. "A well-run company communicates well. We have about 40 new postings every month on customers coming to the plant, recognition, promotion, policy statements, company stock prices, and general information." Every new posting has a blue "NEW" sticker on it to catch employees' attention.

Another form of communication helps managers and supervisors understand what employees go through to meet their requirements. The program is called "Working with the Folks." Once a month, managers and supervisors work with people in the plant for two to four hours. "You get a new appreciation for the lack of control workers must face," says English. The work takes place in noisy, dusty areas, in jobs that consist of lifting fragile ceramic substrates off conveyors and placing them on another conveyor or in a box. "Working with the Folks" helps managers and supervisors see their requirements in a different light.

Engelhard-Huntsville emphasizes working together to satisfy customers and achieve goals. In a training course called "Working," employees are taught how to contribute ideas and get along with their supervisors, peers, and subordinates. One or two people from all areas of the plant, including supervisors, attend sixteen two-hour sessions. The class takes ten months to a year to complete. "We begin by talking about customers and suppliers, so that people start seeing the connection," says trainer Stan Creekmore. "This leads to being a team player, to building trust and sharing values."

All three companies profiled in this chapter emphasize *constant communication of shared values and expectations.* At the Ritz-Carlton, service standards are continuously emphasized during all work activities, beginning on day one. "On the first day of work for every employee, our president and chief executive officer personally and aggressively communicates our vision, values, and methods," says Mene. "You are expected to internalize those values and vision and to use our methods quite naturally." Service standards are reinforced during training and daily "line-ups" (brief meetings between managers and employees). The constant communication about requirements is effective. In a 1991 survey, 96 percent of all employees identified guest services as a top hotel and personal priority—and 3,000 of those employees had been with the company less than three years.

Like Engelhard-Huntsville and the Ritz-Carlton, Motorola communicates its requirements through extensive training (Motorola spent $170 million on education in 1996) and shared goals (Six-Sigma quality and its other initiatives). Motorola also believes that management accountability is critical. "We want to involve people in the improvement process," says Noakes, "but we must change ourselves first."

One way Motorola encourages change and communicates customer and quality requirements is through rewards and recognition. Since the early 1980s, Motorola has tied 25 percent or more of its managers' bonuses to improvements in quality, customer satisfaction, and cycle time. The goal of 68 percent improvement per year clearly communicates management's requirements.

In 1987, Motorola began paying a bonus twice a year for performance on one measure: return on net assets. If a business unit does not make its goal, no one in the unit receives the bonus. If the company does not meet its goal, no one in the company gets the bonus.

In 1990, Motorola began a worldwide competition among teams, an idea it picked up from the Japanese. As long as a team is working on something that relates to one of Motorola's five initiatives, it can enter the competition. More than 5,000 teams competed in 1996.

Through rewards and recognition, frequent meetings, personal contact, and training, successful companies tell managers, supervisors, and other employees exactly what is expected of them. World-class performers make sure every message reflects the same central themes and key requirements. The Ritz-Carlton has its Gold Standards, Motorola has its five initiatives, and Engelhard-Huntsville has its Quality Operating System. By communicating the same basic requirements over and over, in a variety of venues and situations, leaders help their people internalize those requirements and act on them naturally. And their systems hum as many voices become one.

REVIEWING AND BOOSTING PERFORMANCE

Our role models compare performance with requirements frequently, in many ways, to make sure the requirements are being met and to identify and help those who need assistance. In the new management model, the purpose of the review is not to fix blame, or scare people into action, or punish. Quite the opposite. Managers and employees mutually discuss the working relationship, ever mindful of the need to enable and empower everyone in the organization to achieve the stated goals.

That does not mean our benchmarks do not evaluate individual performance. We discuss this subject in more detail in Chapter 8, but to close the loop here, consider what the Ritz-Carlton does. Individual performance is judged by the employee's ability to master the company's Gold Standards. Performance is measured and evaluated constantly, and assessed through opinion surveys. "We evaluate people's performance because we're coaching them every day," says Mene. "We're constantly evaluating the process."

Service companies have long resisted the idea of measuring their performance. When FedEx became the first service company to win the Baldrige Award, an honor it received in no small part because of its measurement system (see Chapter 2), other service folks were quick to claim that FedEx was really no different from a manufacturer: It handled commodities—in this case, packages. Not at all like an insurance company. Not one bit like an ad agency. Nothing like a bank. Nope, they said, we cannot measure what we do.

"People who haven't measured," says Mene, "haven't tried. They're making excuses." The Ritz-Carlton gets information from training sessions, observations of performance, employee evaluations, customer evaluations, and assessments by independent groups. Mene emphasizes that the measurement of performance does not have to be statistics controlled; it can be behavior controlled. "The difference between us and high-tech firms is that, when they do analysis, they have more data and more strident analysis. But even without hard data, you can still meet and talk through data analysis and prevention. Nobody said you had to have Deming in your plant to look at a control chart. The only difference I find from manufacturing to service is how detailed you're going to be. Managing people isn't always detail data, it's judgment."

Process data stay at the hotels, where they are used to evaluate and improve performance. The only results that get to the corporate level are data on key products, customer satisfaction, customer complaints, market share, turnover, profits, safety, and employee satisfaction. "If a hotel is worse than the norm, there's some special reason unique to that hotel," says Mene. "Usually, they can find it themselves and get it in control. If they can't, we try to help." Based on results, the Ritz-Carlton Hotels are doing an exceptional job of translating customer requirements and quality values into requirements for all employees, then communicating those requirements. Ninety-seven percent of the Ritz-Carlton's customers report having a "memorable experience" while staying at one of the hotels.

Engelhard's Huntsville operation relies on fewer data to review performance, but then, with only 380 employees and one plant, its managers are getting constant feedback on performance. Senior management reviews performance during its weekly meetings. Performance is also studied as part of the Quality Operating System and in employee opinion surveys.

At Motorola, each month, business units submit charts on their quality and cycle time performance to the corporate quality division, which selects specific charts to discuss during the corporate performance reviews, held eight times a year. During these four-hour meetings, quality is the first item on the agenda, and issues of quality and cycle time typically take up half the meeting. (When Robert Galvin was chairman, he would leave the meetings at this point, before the group discussed financial issues. The message: If quality and cycle time are improving, the bottom line will improve with them.)

The heads of all major operations are accountable for their performance. The goal is 68 percent improvement. If they are meeting the goal, there is no discussion. If the trend is on target, there is little discussion. If the trend is flat, the group identifies the causes and develops an action plan to address those that are most important. The action plan lists who is going to make what happen, and when.

Divisions hold quality review meetings at least monthly, but it is common to see weekly and daily quality review meetings—and even hourly meetings in the factories. Motorola conducts quality system reviews of its major business units and suppliers every two years. Seven-person teams spend a week auditing the unit's system. Ninety days after the audit, the team presents its finding. The general manager must then respond with plans for improvement.

Motorola also uses the Baldrige criteria as an internal system assessment. (Chapter 17 explains how companies are using Baldrige assessments to improve internally.) In 1991–1992, every business unit wrote and submitted a full Baldrige application, identifying how it would address areas for improvement. Motorola is now working on uniting its quality system reviews and Baldrige assessments into a single tool. (For more about data collection and analysis, see Chapter 14.)

THE SHIFT IN THINKING

At the beginning of this chapter, we referred to a slide in Motorola's standard quality presentation that says, "We have been successful because of our management process." It is a statement any role model in this book could make, a summary of the single overriding factor that contributes to continuous improvement and long-term success.

It is also the subject of this book. In the new business management model, the management process is a *systematic approach* to meeting and exceeding customers' expectations. The approach includes every element in the system. The shift in thinking is dramatic. Companies are driving out of the narrow tunnel of daily departmental supervision and discovering a panorama stretching from suppliers on one edge of the horizon to customers on the other. The ever-changing landscape is populated with planning, extensive measuring and analysis, process improvement, and employee involvement, as far as the eye can see. In this new horizontal organization, managers manage processes, not results. They become process owners in charge of the processes that lead to customer satisfaction.

To manage quality is to manage the process is to manage the system. As Motorola's standard presentation summarizes on its final slide:

> *Quality is not an assignable task. It must be rooted and institutionalized in every process. It is everyone's responsibility.*

Management's job is to do the rooting and institutionalizing, to manage the system. As self-directed work teams have shown, people can pretty much manage themselves. It's the system that causes the problems—and that is management's responsibility.

6 EMPLOYEE INVOLVEMENT

Lyondell Petrochemical

AT&T Consumer Markets Division

ADAC Laboratories

In the previous chapter, we looked at managing the system to make it hum. The sweet music that results does not come from factory lines or computers or stock market tickers, but from the people who make the system work. Employee empowerment, responsibility, and innovation produce long-term success.

However, before managers grab this concept off the shelf and install it as the latest symbol of their company's dedication to quality, a word of warning. If management is not prepared to give employees control over their activities, freedom to make important decisions, and responsibility for their actions—forever—this idea belongs back on the shelf. Employee involvement is a long-term commitment, a new way of doing business, a fundamental change in culture. Employees who have been trained, empowered, and recognized for their achievements see their jobs and their companies from a different perspective. They no longer punch a clock, do what they are told, and count the minutes until the weekend rolls around. They "own" the company, in the sense that they feel personally responsible for its performance. As Shirley Helms, a lab technician at Lyondell Petrochemical (one of the role models described in this chapter) says, "If

I see something that needs to be done, I do it or find someone who can. That's empowerment to me."

Managers who try to take back some of that power end up with bitter, frustrated, and disillusioned employees. Performance will suffer, and future attempts to involve employees will be met with cynicism.

Employee involvement works, but only as a way of running a business. It is not something to dabble in. It does not work as a short-term solution or an intriguing experiment. It is truly a Pandora's box, tempting to open but powerful enough to change your world forever.

The main difference is that instead of releasing all the ills that could plague humanity, unlocking this box produces a torrent of positive energy; enthusiasm, ideas, and improvements. In this chapter, we describe how three quality leaders benefit from employee involvement. All three have been at it for several years, with notable successes: two have won Baldrige Awards and the other has had a Baldrige site visit. We will explore how they address these key questions:

- How do we get people involved in the quality improvement process?
- How do we keep them involved?
- How can we use teams to improve?

Employee involvement, like managing quality, touches every other part of the business management model, as described throughout this book:

- Employees nurture relationships with customers (see Chapters 3 and 10).
- Employees translate customer expectations into products and services (see Chapter 11).
- Employees manage and improve a company's processes (see Chapter 12).
- Employees work with suppliers (see Chapter 13).
- Employees determine and use measurements to improve (see Chapter 14).
- Employees compare their processes to others (see Chapter 15).
- Employees contribute to their communities (see Chapter 16).

Employees are empowered to do all this by management (as discussed in Chapters 2 and 5). At some companies (for example, our role models in Chapter 4), they are empowered through the strategic planning process to contribute individually and in teams to corporate objectives. In this chapter, we will briefly discuss how AT&T Consumer Markets Division uses a shared vision, which it communicates through "Common Bond" and "Ask Yourself," to align employees' activities with the division's values and goals.

Companies also empower people through training, rewards, and recognition. We mention these briefly here, then devote more time to training in Chapter 7 and rewards and recognition in Chapter 8.

In this chapter, we focus on how to initiate and sustain employee involvement. One of the fastest growing methods is through teams, with many companies moving toward self-directed work teams. We will look at how our role models use teams to get the most out of their human resources.

In the process, the models have permanently changed their corporate cultures. "We haven't had a supervisor on our shift for seven years," says Helms. "I don't think it's ever going backwards." After ten years, it is hard to imagine how it could—or why Lyondell would want it to.

MODELS OF EXCELLENCE

Lyondell Petrochemical Company produces a wide variety of petrochemicals, including olefins (ethylene, propylene, butadiene, butylenes, and specialty products), methanol, polyethylene and polypropylene, and, through an affiliate, refined petroleum products (gasoline, heating oil, jet fuel, aromatics, and lubricants). It has more than 1,500 employees at four manufacturing sites in Texas. Its headquarters is in Houston.

AT&T Consumer Markets Division (CMD) provides long-distance communications services to primarily residential customers, numbering more than 80 million. The largest unit of AT&T, CMD has 75 million daily transactions with customers, more than 90 percent of whom rate the overall quality of CMD's services as good or excellent. CMD's headquarters is in Basking Ridge, New Jersey. The division employs approximately 44,000 employees. CMD won the Baldrige Award in 1994 as AT&T Consumer Communications Services.

ADAC Laboratories designs, manufactures, markets, and supports products for nuclear-medicine imaging, radiation-therapy planning, and managing health care information. ADAC has installed about 5,000 systems at more than 2,500 hospitals, clinics, and other sites around the

world. Most of ADAC's 700 employees are based at its corporate headquarters and production facility in Milpitas, California, or at offices in
Houston. ADAC won the Baldrige Award in 1996.

INITIATING AND SUSTAINING EMPLOYEE INVOLVEMENT AT LYONDELL

In the early 1980s, Atlantic Richfield executive Bob Gower was on a team
that suggested lumping together the company's petrochemical and refining operations, which were losing money, and forming a new company. Atlantic Richfield called the company Lyondell Petrochemical and asked
Gower to run it. Choosing to regard as a challenge an organization that
had lost a total of $200 million each year for the past three years, Gower
accepted.

Serious red ink was not Gower's only problem. The new company had
no assets that set it apart from the competition. It had no unique technologies, nor did it enjoy any special advantages in the marketplace. The
only way it could differentiate itself, the only way to return to profitability, was to improve productivity. But, as Gower notes, "Morale was low
and costs were way too high."

To make matters worse, Lyondell had to build a new management
team. "I was told that I could have anybody I could talk into joining me."
No doubt Atlantic Richfield's leaders felt pretty safe with such a generous
offer, but they did not count on Gower's persuasive powers. He not only
pulled together a management team, "but the people who came were risk
takers who believed, as I did, that people are the key to a successful turnaround."

And Lyondell has succeeded. In 1989, *Fortune* ranked Lyondell first
in sales per employee among all industrial companies in the United States.
It earned the same honor again in 1990 and 1991. It received Baldrige site
visits in 1991 and 1992. And in 1993, it was identified as one of the 100
best companies to work for in the United States. The key to Lyondell's
success has been employee involvement.

Employee involvement begins with a change in management's attitude. Lyondell's leaders turned to employee involvement as the key to
continuous improvement because they knew Lyondell would have continued to lose money without it, and because they believed that most people
want to do their jobs well, are proud of their work, have valuable ideas to
share, and want responsibility.

The Process of Empowerment

Empowerment at Lyondell begins with:

- A willingness by managers and supervisors to give others responsibility.
- Training supervisors and employees in how to delegate and accept responsibility.
- Communication and feedback to tell people how they are doing.
- Rewards and recognition.

Giving Employees Responsibility

Here's how they do it. Lyondell helps its managers and supervisors turn over responsibility through a two-day training course called "Managing the Lyondell Way." The course identifies ten key management behaviors that Lyondell values:

1. Low-cost production.
2. Quality.
3. Entrepreneurship and innovation.
4. Action orientation.
5. [Recognition that] people are the difference.
6. Responsibility and accountability in all jobs.
7. Teamwork.
8. Communication.
9. Safety of people.
10. Social responsibility and ethics.

The course covers what to communicate for each behavior, what actions to take, and how to follow up and monitor progress. Many of the actions encourage employee involvement. For example, one of the *quality* actions "involves employees in achieving and improving quality performance." For *entrepreneurship and innovation,* managers are told to "encourage others to use sound, creative thought and action that can lead to innovations." For *people are the difference,* managers must "assure that people understand their responsibility to make the greatest, most positive difference they can."

The behaviors and actions overlap, forming a cultural web that defines continuous improvement for Lyondell. "One of the greatest strengths of 'Managing the Lyondell Way' is integration. It works as a whole," says David Lindsay, manager of purchasing and quality.

Training Employees to Accept Responsibility

This second part of empowerment at Lyondell is often overlooked in a company's eagerness to empower. Managers soon discover that most people lack the skills or experience they need to take responsibility, make decisions, and act confidently.

People need to be trained in their new roles, given opportunities to succeed, supported, and encouraged. The transition will be faster for some than others; a few will never make it. "It's scary for some people," one employee notes. "When you become empowered, you get additional responsibility, and some people don't want that."

Communicating and Giving Feedback

Lyondell provides feedback, the third part of empowerment, frequently and in a variety of ways. Teams are given feedback at every meeting. Each team has a management sponsor who provides support and advice. Managers and supervisors are trained in giving feedback during the "Managing the Lyondell Way" course. Teams make presentations on their progress, and management offers on-the-spot feedback. All these opportunities and more are encouraged as integral to continuous improvement.

Giving Rewards and Recognition

Lyondell ties its rewards and recognition, the fourth part of empowerment, to the behaviors identified in "Managing the Lyondell Way." In place of annual performance reviews, employees participate in more frequent dialogue sessions with their supervisors. The sessions focus on linking employee activities to the company's results. Employee contributions to Lyondell's quality and performance objectives are honored in a host of recognition programs.

EMPOWERMENT AT AT&T CONSUMER MARKETS DIVISION

With operations and field personnel scattered across the country, AT&T Consumer Markets Division (CMD) needed a way to encourage individual initiative and self-directed responsibility without compromising the integrity of its communication network. CMD accomplished this delicate task through six interconnected approaches:

1. Common Bond.
2. Ask Questions.
3. Process Management Teams.
4. Quality Improvement Teams.
5. Corrective and Preventive Action System (CPAS).
6. Communication.

Common Bond is AT&T's statement of values, created in 1992. The company relied heavily on internal focus groups and external expertise to develop a fundamental slate of values that could drive behaviors. AT&T's Common Bond is:

We commit to these values to guide our decisions and behavior:
- Respect for individuals.
- Dedication to helping customers.
- Highest standards of integrity.
- Innovation.
- Teamwork.

To internalize these values, AT&T conducted employee focus groups to talk about what the values meant to them and how the values could guide their decisions and behavior. Leadership teams were asked to talk to their people about what the values meant to them. The Common Bond was published and widely distributed throughout the organization. But the real test was: Does it make a difference in how people act? Will they use it in their daily work?

"The values have really become embedded in the organizations—but it wasn't that way in the beginning," says Larry Theleman, quality director. "Now it's not unusual at meetings to hear someone say, 'In the spirit of Common Bond, I think we need to consider another viewpoint.' It's become our common language."

While Common Bond became CMD's common language, the "Ask Questions" program provided more specific guidance. An organization cannot empower employees to take initiative without guidelines about acceptable and unacceptable actions. In CMD's case, technicians could easily create problems in the network just by working on things. To help prevent this from happening, CMD created a program for employees to ask themselves questions in eight areas. The questions include:

- Why am I doing this?
- Have I notified everybody directly affected by this work?
- Can I prevent or control service interruptions?

- Is this the right time for the work?
- Have I been trained or am I qualified to do this work?

"There was a point in our history when, if a craft person was asked to do something and he declined because he didn't have the training, that response wouldn't have flown," says Theleman. "With the launching of Ask Questions, that attitude has changed. People are empowered to stop the line and not do the work if they answer any of the Ask Questions 'No.'"

As with the Common Bond values, CMD has internalized the Ask Questions program in a variety of ways, but the most effective has been its real-life application. For example, CMD had to upgrade processors in its switching machines while they continued to operate. As Theleman notes, "People compared this to having brain surgery while running a marathon." The changeover process was extremely complex; it took two years just to plan it. When the time finally arrived to change processors at the Oklahoma City site, one of the people on the team had to bow out at the last minute for personal reasons. When the team then went through the Ask Questions before starting the changeover, they found they couldn't give a definitive "Yes" to all the questions. They didn't change the processors as scheduled, then held their breath as they awaited the repercussions.

They didn't have to wait long. The head of the organization pulled together a conference call with his managers and the team members. He told them he was not happy about stopping the schedule—but he wanted to recognize the team for doing the right thing. "I don't think there was a technician in AT&T who hasn't heard about that," says Theleman.

By remaining true to Common Bond and Ask Questions, CMD has created a culture in which employees understand how they are expected to behave without being told exactly what to do in every situation. The shared vision provided by Common Bond and the guidelines inherent in Ask Questions allow CMD to give employees the freedom and responsibility to do their jobs to the best of their ability.

Employees do this by managing their processes. "We have defined six fundamental processes at the top of the organization, which we then break down into roughly 50 subprocesses. Some of those subprocesses are further subdivided," says Theleman. "We have around 125 Process Management Teams (PMTs) in place to continuously examine our key processes, identify metrics, make sure the metrics are aligned with customer expectations, and do continuous improvement."

PMTs are ongoing and continuous. Membership rotates, drawing on people who are involved in the work of the process. When a PMT identifies an area for improvement, it launches a Quality Improvement Team that typically includes members of the PMT plus others in the organization. The Quality Improvement Team addresses the area to improve, which may take a couple of meetings or several months, after which the team is disbanded.

Employees who identify opportunities for improvement are encouraged to use the Corrective and Preventive Action System (CPAS) to elevate the issue. Local issues are handled locally, but if the issue affects the network, it typically goes to a PMT through the CPAS. "We want participative empowerment," says Theleman, "a direct avenue for getting information to a larger group of employees that will make fundamental decisions about how to do this across the nation."

As organizations get flatter by empowering frontline people to take more responsibility, their needs for communication change. The process of moving information must also be analyzed and improved, if that information is to reach the right people when they need it. CMD communicates through focus groups, training, newsletters, work instructions, and other formal methods. Involvement in PMTs and Quality Improvement Teams also helps communicate the vision and policies of the organization. CMD has an internal video broadcast network to keep technicians up-to-date, and is currently equipping technicians with laptop computers for the same purpose.

All of these means of communication supplement the informal methods—lunch chats and casual conversations and phone contact—that help define a culture. Based on CMD's high customer satisfaction, the strength of its management system, and the shared vision of its employees, CMD's culture reflects a Common Bond.

ADAC'S TEAMWORK APPROACH

At ADAC, most workers participate on highly empowered function and/or process teams, and all manufacturing employees are members of self-directed work teams. Throughout the course of a year, every ADAC employee is on at least one team.

Self-directed work teams are, typically, groups of 4 to 25 people, drawn from within a function or department, who work with a high degree of autonomy to produce a complete component or to perform a particular service. The concept of self-directed work teams was introduced in the mid-1920s and more thoroughly developed in the late 1950s. The Japanese have been leaders in institutionalizing the concept, having learned about it from IBM. In 1984, Toyota had 5,800 self-directed work teams.

The members of self-directed work teams are typically cross-trained to perform most or all of the jobs in the team's area. They monitor quality, schedule work, control costs, plan, hire, interact with customers and vendors, and handle discipline. Most members need extensive training and encouragement to handle such a wide range of activities. "We have a two-day course on our Total Quality Management approach and problem-solving methodology," says Doug Keare, vice president of quality at ADAC.

ADAC's function teams focus on a specific function, such as accounts payable; the process teams encompass many functions. Any manager at any level can form a process team. The only stipulation is that the team must address a strategic need or imperative. "At the beginning of our quality journey, we used to identify things for teams to work on," says Keare. "Some were successful, but others weren't because they weren't working on leveraged activities. Now teams are formed to address a strategic need, not formed first before identifying their strategic connection."

Individual initiative is not limited to team participation. "At some companies there's a lot of asking for permission. Here it's the opposite. The expectation from management is that employees can and should make improvements without permission. We value not getting in the employee's way," says Keare.

As with AT&T Consumer Markets Division, ADAC makes sure employees know which direction their actions should take. Methods of communication include:

- The company's planning meetings, which feature discussions of all areas of the business, are open to all employees. Employees come to meetings that interest them. The meetings take place over four days, every quarter.

- Weekly customer quality meetings, also open to all employees, include a review of large amounts of data on how things are going at ADAC's sites. "Most employees don't come every week," says Keare, "but they'll come every other week or so."

- An operational data and performance meeting, where the focus is internal, is also open to employees and enjoys the same levels of participation.

- Quarterly all-employee meetings focus on the state of the company, including current financial information.

The effectiveness of ADAC's efforts to empower its employees are measurable. From 1990 to 1995, company revenues nearly tripled. Defect rates fell by 40 percent. Customer retention rates have risen from 70 percent in 1990 to 93 percent in 1995.

THE SHIFT IN THINKING

One of the hottest topics in business these days is *change.* Companies need to change. People need to change. Gone are the days when today's job is the same as yesterday's, when months pass with no discernible difference in people, processes, or output.

According to a study of workers' attitudes and behavior, headed by psychologist G. Clotaire Rapaille, Americans are threatened by change when it is imposed, but feel positive about it when they can control it. Carl Dildy, a maintenance mechanic at Lyondell, agrees: "The marketplace is constantly changing, and people need to change. Being involved in teams helps people accept this change."

Across America, companies are looking for the best approach to: the demands for higher quality, the pressure of increasing global competition, the necessity to be more efficient and productive, and the effects of rapid change. To compete, companies must produce a high-quality product or service at the lowest possible cost in the shortest possible time, and be prepared to change any part of that equation at a moment's notice. Successful companies believe the only way to compete is through employee involvement. They have learned that the employees who perform the tasks that produce a product or service:

- Are in the best position to ensure and improve its quality.
- Are best able to lower costs by eliminating waste throughout the process.
- Are in the best position to speed up their processes by reducing cycle times.
- Are the ideal agents of change when they are in touch with their processes, trained through education and experience, and empowered to act decisively.

Companies are choosing to empower people because it makes good business sense. In the process, they are blurring the lines between manager and employee as they create a "boundaryless" company. Employees on self-directed work teams perform all the tasks formerly done by managers. They plan, schedule, buy, hire, control, and improve. They work closely with customers and suppliers. In every respect, they are responsible for how well their company meets its customers' requirements. The culture of a company that understands this will be significantly different from the culture of a company that still treats its employees like commodities.

The other dramatic difference is in how employees see themselves. In Chapter 10, we mention MetLife's training program, called *Achieving Personal Quality*. To help serve customers better, employees are taught the fundamentals of personal quality, including treating others as you would like to be treated, taking responsibility, learning, and sharing. These are universal values: we teach them to our children, and we try to live by them every day. Employee involvement is another way of teaching these values.

"The biggest thing Lyondell has done for me has been to give me confidence and ownership. It even helps me work with my three teenagers as a single parent," says one Lyondell employee. A coworker adds, "You can go home and feel good about your day, and that spreads to your family."

In the process of empowering people, companies are also blurring the lines between work and home, giving people the tools they need to succeed in all facets of their lives. That, too, makes good business sense.

7 TRAINING

Eastman Chemical Company

Northern Trust

Globe Metallurgical

The Plumley division of Dana Corporation manufactures rubber hoses and ducts for the automobile industry. In the early 1980s, Buick stopped using Plumley because its defect rate was too high. To address the problem, Plumley bought and installed high-tech equipment to improve the production of its rubber products.

It didn't solve the problem. Employees had trouble using the new equipment, and even when they got it running, mistakes were common. Training was the obvious solution. When the Big Three automakers told Plumley that they expected it to use statistical process control (SPC) to improve the quality of its products, the training path seemed clear: Plumley began training its workers in SPC.

That didn't solve the problem either. Larry Moore, who was then director of education, remembers chairman Mike Plumley bumping into an employee who had had 30 hours of SPC training. As they talked, Plumley realized that the employee didn't know that a quarter-inch equaled 0.25 inch. A closer look at just how much the employees knew revealed that many lacked basic math and reading skills. Although new equipment and SPC training were the obvious solutions to a high defect rate, both assumed a level of knowledge that did not exist. Before Plumley could improve quality, it had to train employees in the basic skills they would need to run the equipment and implement SPC.

Baldrige Award-winner Motorola took nearly a decade, from 1980 to 1990, to develop a training program that did what Motorola wanted it to do. Initial executive training did little to improve quality. Motorola then developed a five-part curriculum that included courses in SPC, problem solving, and goal setting. Every employee received about 20 hours of training, but this failed because the employees were not motivated to apply what they were learning, and their managers were not receiving the same training.

From 1985 to 1987, Motorola's top 200 executives had 17 days of training in manufacturing, global competition, and cycle time. The training was then cascaded down through the company. However, when Motorola converted a facility from radio technology to cellular technology, it discovered *the wall:* elementary reading and math. Only 40 percent of the facility's employees passed a simple math test, and 60 percent of those who failed could not read the questions. Motorola surveyed its 25,000 manufacturing and support employees in the United States and found that half could not do seventh-grade math and English.

When one of Northern Trust's business units wanted to learn how to attract and retain skilled, flexible employees, the company conducted a workplace study to establish benchmark performance levels and training needs. The study revealed that some of the most important skills were reading, grammar and writing, math, and problem solving.

Learning from Plumley, Motorola, and Northern Trust, a company would be wise not to assume any level of knowledge when it assesses the need for training. Training for continuous improvement involves everything from remedial reading and math to design of experiments and concurrent engineering. Without such training—and lots of it—continuous improvement is not possible.

Leading companies across the country have shown that training is one of the pillars of improvements in quality and performance. Motorola spent $120 million on education in 1992. Corning expects all employees to spend 5 percent of their work time on training—about 92 hours per employee per year. Solectron's employees averaged 110 training hours in 1993—all during normal working hours. Custom Research Inc.'s employees averaged more than 130 hours of training per person in 1995.

These top performers treat their workers as assets to be developed, not commodities to be used. They invest in their people because they must; their expectations of their employees are too high, and their demands too great, to send them forward unarmed. Consider just a few of the things high-performance companies are asking their employees to do:

- Contribute to work unit, department, and cross-functional teams.
- Solve process problems in all parts of the company.
- Communicate with customers and suppliers, both internal and external.
- Measure and analyze indicators of performance and improvement.
- Manage processes to improve quality and reduce cycle time.
- Learn a wide range of skills to improve flexibility.
- Take the initiative in identifying and addressing improvements.
- Assume responsibility for quality and productivity.

These tasks require a host of advanced skills in such areas as teamwork, problem solving, communication, process management, and leadership. Employees cannot do any of these if they check their brains at the door—and if employees cannot improve quality, the improvement will not get done. Companies that want to improve quality fire up a quality training program early in the process. To develop an effective training process, every company must wrestle with these questions:

- What kind of training do we need?
- Whom should we train?
- How will we deliver the training?
- How will we know whether the training is effective?
- How can we improve the training process?

In this chapter, we look at how three quality leaders are answering these questions. In the process, we will examine how they use training to achieve their performance goals.

MODELS OF EXCELLENCE

Eastman Chemical Company is a leading international chemical company that produces more than 400 chemicals, fibers, and plastics. Eastman does not sell consumer products, but supplies billions of pounds of products for countless uses by consumers. Founded in 1920 in Kingsport, Tennessee, as a unit of Eastman Kodak, Eastman Chemical Company was spun off in 1994 and is now an independent, publicly held company. Eastman employs 17,500 people in more than 30 countries. The company won the Baldrige Award in 1993.

Northern Trust Corporation opened for business in Chicago more than a hundred years ago. Today, it employs more than 7,000 people in 61 locations in seven states, Canada, Great Britain, Hong Kong, and Singapore. Although Northern Trust has long been a leader in the trust side of the banking business, it determined in 1990 that a systematic quality improvement process would improve its position. It developed a process it calls Commitment to Absolute Quality, with the goal of consistently exceeding clients'/partners' expectations while striving to become their ideal provider.

Globe Metallurgical is a major producer of silicon metal and ferrosilicon products. Its 475 employees report to four plants, including its headquarters in Beverly, Ohio. In 1988, Globe was the first small business to win the Baldrige Award. Since then, it has earned the first-ever Shingo Prize for Manufacturing Excellence, Ford's highest award for Total Quality Excellence, and the U.S. Senate Productivity Award for Alabama. Globe is a flat organization run by self-directed work teams; of the 175 people working in the Ohio plant, only 14 are managers. Training is driven by customer and/or team needs, and it focuses on skills that can be put to use immediately.

DETERMINING TRAINING NEEDS

The rush to improve quality frequently leads to poor decisions about what kind of training to provide. These are some of the most common mistakes:

- A customer tells you it expects a new skill from your company, so you begin training employees in that skill without knowing whether they are ready to learn it.
- You discover a competitor is implementing a certain quality technique, or you read about how such a technique turned a business around; you quickly organize your own training, before finding out whether the technique is a good idea for your company.
- You install new equipment, prepare to make a new product or offer a new service, or redesign a process, and you only consider training as an afterthought.
- You begin general training in broad quality concepts without knowing how each employee will apply those concepts in his or her daily work to improve quality.

The mistakes suggest a more effective way of determining your company's training needs, a process anchored in the business management model. The process begins with data and information that will tell you what skills employees now have and what skills they will need to have to achieve your short- and long-range plans, satisfy customers, improve quality and operational performance, and grow personally and professionally. At the three benchmark companies profiled in this chapter, the human resources departments gather their data and information from a variety of sources, perform an analysis, and determine training needs.

The nature of the assessment depends primarily on the size of the company: The smaller the company, the less formal the assessment. "There's no room to hide in this company," says Norm Jennings, Globe's quality director. "Everybody knows what everybody else is doing to contribute, which makes our training needs very obvious. Teams identify what skills their people need. Individual employees suggest training. Looking at what we as a company will need for the future reveals training needs. And our customers' changing expectations inspire new training."

Because of Globe's size and structure, it is able to practice more just-in-time training than a larger company could accomplish. The danger in this less formal approach is that training can end up being short-term and reactive, a response to problems rather than a means to anticipate and prevent them. Globe avoids this by collecting, correlating, and acting on information from a variety of sources—teams, individuals, corporate goals, and customers—and by responding quickly to a training need when it is identified.

"One of our customers, General Motors, told us it wanted its suppliers to be more sensitive to reductions in lead times, cycle times, and costs," Jennings says. "We determined that the best way to continue to improve in those areas was through synchronous management [i.e., performing a series of tasks in parallel, also called concurrent engineering], and we're now doing training in that area."

Globe has also been introducing more formal training programs in such areas as the nature of teams and teamwork, safety, and job skills. "We acquired two new plants, one here in the United States and one in Germany, and the melding of the three cultures has presented some obstacles and opportunities," says Jennings. "Our U.S. acquisition was in a formal training mode, and we've adapted some of their ideas."

Eastman Chemical is also in the process of changing its approach to training. In the summer of 1997, it opened Eastman University, an idea more than a place. Its goal is to create learning systems that provide common solutions to Eastman employees worldwide.

"In our culture, training priorities and support are determined by functional areas," says Edd Baldock, manager of Eastman University. "They run their own programs in terms of employee development. They analyze jobs to determine what the needs are. Eastman University is a strategic initiative aimed at developing employees as a whole."

Eastman University flows from a history of employee development, beginning with the company's roots in Eastman Kodak Company. A formal development and coaching process brings employees and their supervisors together to discuss learning opportunities and plan future training and development. "We started out thinking these meetings would be annual, but more of them occur semiannually and some are even going to quarterly development and coaching meetings," says Baldock. "The learning cycles have gotten so fast that you can't just plan development on an annual basis."

Another goal of Eastman University is to implement systems that accelerate the cycle time of learning. The company wants to match people and knowledge faster than in the past, a task that requires a more centralized approach.

Northern Trust strives for a balance between corporate-level training and training determined by its business units. The company identifies training needs by:

1. Determining what *skills* its employees will need to achieve the company's strategic quality initiative. Its 24-hour training curriculum, "Training for Absolute Quality," includes skill building in the four key goals Northern has identified for achieving absolute quality:

    • Unrivaled client satisfaction.
    • Continuous improvement of all processes.
    • Inspired leadership.
    • Active involvement of all Northern people.

2. Conducting periodic needs assessments to identify *topics* to be addressed. As a result of recent assessments and other data, Northern is now focusing on bringing training to employees who need it when they need it, similar to Globe's philosophy.

3. Using an ongoing *needs identification* process, which includes employees' evaluations of courses they complete, and suggestions by Northern's business units and managers for new training.

4. *Benchmarking other companies* within the industry, to find out what they are doing and where their training programs are going.

The skills taught as part of the "Training for Absolute Quality" course target the areas Northern has identified as essential to achieving its goals.

The course is filled with individual and team exercises that help employees understand and act on each of the principles listed under Northern Trust's four quality goals. The list is as follows:

Unrivaled Client Satisfaction

- Client needs drive improvement decisions.
- All areas need an ongoing process for establishing client and partner requirements.
- Prevention of defects is essential to meet or exceed client and partner requirements.

Continuous Improvement of All Processes

- Everything is a process—and every process can be improved.
- Process measurements provide the facts that will guide decisions.
- To solve problems, look beyond symptoms so you can find and remove root causes.

Inspired Leadership

- Absolute quality management is achieved through attention to both process *and* results.
- We will deliver absolute quality to our clients and partners through cooperation and teamwork between areas.
- Managers can lead improvement by creating a climate of support and respect for all Northern people.

Active Involvement of All Northern People

- Everyone has a vital role in delivering unrivaled client satisfaction through absolute quality in everything we do.
- We exceed client expectations when all Northern people apply a systematic and disciplined approach to process improvement.
- Skills improvement and knowledge of the Bank are fundamental tools for Northern people.

The course on unrivaled client satisfaction is the only course mandated for all employees. Northern is a very decentralized organization; each business unit is responsible for customizing training to its unique needs.

As with Plumley and Motorola, that training ranges from basic to advanced skills. A workplace survey of more than 200 employees revealed that fundamental reading, writing, and math skills were critical to success. At the other end of the spectrum, an analysis of Northern's goals and principles pointed out the need for courses on the Baldrige criteria, benchmarking, advanced SPC, service delivery, and team skills. Northern is addressing the full spectrum through a comprehensive training program that reflects where employees are and where they will need to be.

WHOM TO TRAIN IN WHAT

All employees require some quality (and related) training. For example:

- Every Northern Trust employee is trained in client satisfaction.
- Every Globe employee has had team problem-solving and safety training.

To varying degrees, these and other quality leaders train all their employees in quality awareness, problem solving, reducing waste, process simplification, teamwork, and meeting customer requirements.

The process is like teaching the fundamentals to a baseball team. Learn what the fundamentals are for your company (Northern Trust's list is a good place to start), then teach those fundamentals to everybody in the company. With that foundation in place, use a variety of methods to continuously identify the additional training needs of departments, work units, teams, and individuals. The additional needs differ with each "player." In baseball, all pitchers run, to strengthen their leg muscles; they practice-throw in the bullpen, to work on their pitches and develop a rhythm; and they keep track of how other pitchers approach different hitters, to learn what will get those hitters out. The nonpitchers learn and practice other skills. Within the pitching group, each individual pitcher works on additional skills only he needs, such as developing a new pitch, improving a pickoff move, or changing speeds on an existing pitch. To improve the quality of the entire team, the team's coaches work with the pitchers as a group and with each pitcher individually.

The quality of a company, like the quality of a team, depends on the continuous improvement of every member. A training program that recognizes who needs what types of specific training has an advantage over any program that provides only one course in quality for all employees.

Because of its size, Globe is quick to respond when a single employee identifies a training need. "I step in to do one-on-one training immediately," says Jennings. "If an employee wants to make his or her job easier;

I'll offer some tools that may help. If someone needs insight into why a pattern on a control chart isn't random, I'll take 15 or 20 minutes to help them understand what could be going on.

"We don't put a lot of stock into evaluating this or that program," Jennings concludes. "We'd rather get out there and do things and learn on our own." A flat organization of Globe's size, dealing with an old technology employees know well, can afford to focus more on the immediate training needs of individuals and teams. Organizations that are larger, that are new to the quality improvement process, or that are involved in rapidly changing industries will need to first develop a quality training program that teaches the fundamentals to all employees, and then establish a mechanism, as Globe has done, that allows them to respond quickly to specific needs.

DELIVERING TRAINING

Preferring to train internally, Globe does not bring in consultants to conduct training programs. However, Globe does take advantage of training offered by its customers. "General Motors, Ford, Dow Corning, General Electric, and other customers have been very generous about training our employees," Jennings says. Whatever training is offered, the company is sensitive to the demands on its employees. "Our people won't sit still for a long time, maybe an hour or two at the most," says Jennings, "so we try to do our training on the fly. A half-hour to an hour training session is ideal."

Like Globe, Eastman does most of its training internally. Half of the training is done in the line units. The rest is handled by staff groups or outside trainers.

Northern Trust created a volunteer corps of 175 trainers drawn from its business units to teach the course on absolute quality. "All of them had to be certified to train," says Debra Danziger-Barron, senior vice president. "They each had 70 hours of preparation time, during which they attended class, studied absolute quality, and practiced being a trainer during videotaped sessions. They also spent about 100 hours each customizing the training materials for their business units." An *audit team* observes the training sessions to make sure the message is consistent and to help improve the training process.

Northern is now rethinking the extensive use of its volunteer corps. "People move to different assignments or companies, or you have small operations where it's hard for people to step out," says Danziger-Barron.

"We're looking at creating computer-based, interactive training to support the instructor-led pieces."

Customizing the materials for each business unit makes the information more relevant. Asking participants to apply what they are learning as individuals and teams helps them remember information. For example, one exercise in Northern Trust's "Training for Absolute Quality" course reinforces the steps in describing a problem. The exercise asks the participant to first "define a problem in one of your processes," and then to list key individuals or groups to be involved, current performance on key indicators, desired performance level, and a problem statement. A subsequent team exercise, after a section on identifying root causes, asks the participant team to choose one of the problems described previously and construct a cause–effect diagram to help identify likely causes.

Northern closes the loop with an "Action Guide" section that is rife with assignments on everything from conducting an internal partner interview to developing a plan for preventing service defects or assessing team information needs. "We're now looking to tie the tools piece to strategic issues," says Danziger-Barron. "Not everyone will go through the continuous improvement segment unless they get involved in some sort of process improvement."

The on-the-job application of knowledge and skills becomes more difficult when the training is more theoretical or general, or when immediate applications are not identified and monitored. Globe typically performs its training on the job. As Norm Jennings says, "If we're going to give training and take any time out of their day, we want them to be able to use it right away."

At Eastman, on-the-job application is part of the package when each line unit has its own training unit and is determining its training needs.

All three companies focus on quality during the orientation of new employees. One of the new projects for Eastman University is the development of a new employee orientation learning system called "Eastman Fundamentals." The new course will be a combination of orientation, Eastman's business, training in fundamental skills, and an introduction to quality.

Norm Jennings emphasizes quality system training for new Globe employees. "I describe the process from raw materials to finished product, then give them some background on the industries we serve and why." After the orientation, each new employee works with a production team for three months before working solo.

Northern introduces new employees to absolute quality in a letter they receive before they start work. A half-day seminar during their first week of work presents a more detailed description. Within their first two months, new employees attend a welcome assembly hosted by Northern's chairman. He talks about his career at the bank, how the new employees fit into the process, why they were chosen, and how they carry out the bank's quality mission.

EVALUATING THE EXTENT AND EFFECTIVENESS OF TRAINING

Evaluating the extent and effectiveness of training requires the identification and use of key indicators for each.

Extent is the easy one: How much of each type of training have your employees received? The number of training hours per employee varies considerably, even among quality leaders. Here are some guidelines:

- Motorola employees average about 40 hours.
- Marlow Industries employees average over 60 hours.
- Milliken associates average about 76 hours.
- Corning employees average more than 90 hours.
- Solectron employees average over 100 hours.
- Custom Research Inc. employees average over 130 hours.

The *effectiveness* of quality (and related) training is harder to measure. Many companies tie general improvements in quality to the completion of training. Other companies are measuring effectiveness through indicators more closely linked to the training—indicators that offer a more immediate and traceable footprint, instead of trying to extrapolate the impact of one quality contributor from that of the whole herd. Typical indicators come from:

- Surveys of employees, upon completion of a course, to measure such things as how appropriate the material was and how easy it was to understand.
- Surveys of employees, a few weeks or months after completion of a course, to determine the degree to which the course content has been retained and applied.
- Questions, in annual employee surveys, about training needs and effectiveness.
- Follow-up training sessions, some time after completion of a course, to discuss problems, obstacles, and successes.

- The development of measures that show the application of learned behaviors and skills on the job (statistical process control, for example).

Northern Trust surveys employees at the end of each module of the "Training for Absolute Quality" curriculum. It is looking at surveying employees again, six months after they complete the course, to check on how their new skills are being applied. The company also relies on its certified trainers for input. "We tap into them about every three months," says Danziger-Barron. "They've played a major role in helping us develop and refine the course for our nonmanagement employees."

For smaller companies, the measures of effectiveness tend to be more immediate. "We are beginning to utilize some measures of effectiveness now," says Globe's Jennings, "but we're so lean we can look at each other and know what areas need training. We don't need a lot of fanfare to make a change."

THE SHIFT IN THINKING

In the new business management model, a company is obligated to train its employees—to provide them with the intellectual arsenal they need to work in teams, collect and analyze data, initiate improvements, satisfy customers, and assume all the other responsibilities that come with empowerment and involvement. As the role models in this chapter and throughout this book prove, continuous improvement is possible only with the continuous and effective training of all employees at all levels.

The key to effective training is to truly understand your employees' and your company's training needs. Companies such as Globe, Eastman, and Northern Trust determine employees' needs through observation, surveys, testing, and listening. To find out where their employees and the company need to be, they listen to their customers, study their competitors, translate their short- and long-term goals into training needs, and solicit input from employees and teams.

Successful companies train all their employees in the fundamentals of quality as defined by their company's goals and objectives. They build on the fundamentals by tailoring more specific quality training to the needs of business units, divisions, departments, teams, and individuals.

Their training programs change constantly, to reflect and anticipate changes in customers' needs and expectations, new technologies, new markets, competition, and employees' capabilities. They change, but they never end, for individuals or for groups of employees. Improving your organization's "system" is a continuous process fraught with obstacles to overcome, challenges to tackle, and opportunities to seize. The people in the system are in the best position to make these improvements, but they cannot unlock the possibilities without knowledge.

At Eastman, one of the selling points for creating Eastman University was its role as an agent of change. "Our business is changing so much, senior leaders decided they wanted to keep an infrastructure in place that would promote employee development and ensure that we're doing this well as a company." The evolution of training from a *tactical response* to an urgent need and then to a *strategic initiative* designed to give a company a competitive advantage is just one more example of the dramatic shift in thinking the new management model requires.

8 REWARD AND RECOGNITION

Tennant Company

GTE Directories

Trident Precision Manufacturing

In the new management model, the role of employee rewards and recognition—such things as performance appraisals, compensation, recognition programs, and promotion systems—is to support the achievement of the company's goals. This aspect of the system is usually not among the first to receive attention, nor should it be when a company is still figuring out how to satisfy customers, manage processes, and involve employees. Besides, it is better to get the company's collective feet wet in the easy stuff before diving into the treacherous waters of reward and recognition.

The treachery lies in the common belief about what motivates people. Most managers and supervisors believe that pay is the prime motivator of performance. Research and surveys of employees suggest it is not. Traditionalists scoff at the need for pats on the back and thank-you, pointing out that people are paid well to do well. Surveys of employees and the experiences of a few companies, however, suggest that day-to-day recognition is a powerful motivator.

In an article in *Harvard Business Review*, former Baldrige judge Donald Berwick said, "Total quality comes not from contingencies set up by managers but from the native curiosity, pride, and desire for craftsmanship that are likely to be widespread in the workplace." The new management model supports the expression of curiosity, pride, and desire for craftsmanship because they are the attributes that make continuous improvement possible. At the same time, the new model supports the use of employee rewards and recognition—Berwick's "contingencies"—to attain the company's goals. As Berwick rightly claims, rewards and recognition will not produce total quality, but the lack thereof can produce the opposite: a steady erosion of an employee's belief in the real value of quality and of his or her contribution to improving it. A company's first charge when it does turn to this area is to bring its reward and recognition approaches into alignment with its new management system.

Of all the components of the new model, employee reward and recognition may have the farthest to go. Human resource and non-human-resource executives alike scratch their heads about how to send the right messages with their compensation and recognition programs. They are torn by opposing viewpoints:

- Performance appraisals help improve performance *versus* performance appraisals undermine performance.
- People focus on what they are paid to do *versus* pay is not a motivator.
- Formal recognition inspires quality improvement *versus* formal recognition is the least effective part of a total recognition program.
- Reward and recognition approaches should be in the domain of human resources *versus* employees should establish and improve these approaches.

In this chapter, we consider these viewpoints from the perspective of three models of excellence: Tennant Company, GTE Directories, and Trident Precision Manufacturing. They were chosen because they have aligned their reward and recognition systems with their quality improvement efforts. Each has a particular strength: Tennant, in the scope of its recognition programs; GTE Directories, for its individual and team recognition programs; Trident, for its reward and recognition strategy and plans. Yet none of the three is comfortable with leaving its program alone. "We realize we still don't have it right," says Rita Ferguson Maehling, Tennant's employee programs manager responsible for involvement and recognition, "and we need to step out of our own paradigms."

In this chapter, we challenge existing paradigms of pay and recognition by addressing three questions:

- How can we pay employees in ways that support the company's quality goals?

- How can we assess performance in ways that support the company's quality goals?
- How can we recognize employees in ways that support the company's quality goals?

MODELS OF EXCELLENCE

Tennant Company is one of the world's leading manufacturers of industrial and commercial floor maintenance equipment, floor coatings, and related products. It has approximately 1,700 employees and is headquartered in Minneapolis. The company's recognition program has an interesting historical/contemporary flavor. Although its profit sharing, service awards, and retirement parties have all been in place for more than 45 years, it has added a half-dozen new recognition programs in the past decade—all developed and run by employees.

GTE Directories is the largest directories publisher in the world. Located at Dallas/Fort Worth Airport, Texas, GTE Directories employs approximately 5,000 people and provides publishing, sales, and consultation services for nearly 2,400 directory titles throughout the United States, Canada, South America, Europe, and Asia. Among Yellow Pages publishers, GTE Directories ranks second in U.S. market share and has achieved a circulation of 80 million directories worldwide. GTE Directories won the Baldrige Award in 1994.

Trident Precision Manufacturing produces precision sheet metal components, electromechanical assemblies, and custom products, mostly in the office equipment, medical supplies, computer, and defense industries. A privately held company located in Webster, New York, it has grown from a three-person operation in 1979 to an employer of 180 people. Trident won the Baldrige Award in 1996.

HOW RECOGNITION PROGRAMS SUPPORT
THE NEW MODEL

When you think about recognition programs, what is the first type of recognition that pops into your head? Formal, right? Employee of the Month, maybe, or the company equivalent of the Academy Awards: the Chairman's Award, President's Award, or Company XYZ Quality Award.

If you were to ask a cross section of your coworkers the same question, you would get the same answers. If, however, you were to ask them what type of recognition they personally *value* most, you would probably find, as Tennant Company did, that the great majority prefer day-to-day thank-you's, praise, and pats on the back from their managers and coworkers.

In 1992, Tennant published a book titled *Recognition Redefined: Building Self-Esteem at Work.* In one chapter is a description of a survey of industrial employees conducted in 1946. Asked what factors provided the greatest job satisfaction, the workers ranked "full appreciation of work done" first. The same survey done again in 1981 and 1986 placed "full appreciation of work done" second behind "interesting work"—but still ahead of job security, good wages, good working conditions, and every other factor that contributes to job satisfaction. *Employees crave recognition.* Quality leaders take every opportunity to satisfy that craving with recognition for their efforts.

The distinction between rewards and recognition is that *rewards* are usually monetary, and *recognition* is an action or activity that is not monetary. Examples of rewards are bonuses, cash awards, trips, and merchandise. Examples of recognition are company awards, department or team awards and special events, individual awards, and personal thank-you's.

Based on research into human behavior and its own experiences and goals, Tennant created a *three-dimensional recognition model:* formal, informal, and day-to-day. To understand the benefits of each, Tennant identified a list of attributes that define a recognition program:

- It is *consistent*—delivered the same way every time.
- Some *cost* must be incurred.
- The recognition is *frequent.*
- The person providing the recognition uses *interpersonal skills* to give personal, specific information about the accomplishment.
- The recognition comes from *peers.*
- The goal is to recognize the highest *percentage* of total employees possible.
- Some *prestigious* awards are considered special and sought after.
- Public *display*—a high-visibility event—is involved.
- The recognition must be based on *sincere* trust and respect.
- *Specific feedback* is provided to show what the person did that was of value.
- The more people involved in the selection process, the more *subjective* their opinions and judgments become.
- The recognition comes from *superiors.*

- A *tangible reminder* is left behind to remind the recipient of the reason for the recognition.
- The recognition is *timely;* as little time as possible is allowed to elapse between the action and the recognition.
- The recognition is *win/win*—everyone is a winner.

Tennant then looked at each type of recognition offered—formal, informal, and day-to-day—and determined whether an attribute ranked high, medium, or low for that type. For example, with formal recognition the cost is high and the percentage of total employees recognized is low. Tennant divided the attributes into the three distinct continua shown in Table 8.1.

Table 8.1 reveals two insights: first, each type of recognition has different strengths, and second, all three types rank high in consistency, sincerity, and specific feedback. The first insight suggests that a three-pronged approach to quality recognition has a better chance of success than a program that provides only one type of recognition. The second insight suggests that consistency, sincerity, and specific feedback are critical to the success of any recognition program.

Formal Recognition

Like Tennant, most quality leaders begin with formal recognition. Intel, Carrier, IBM, Honeywell, and others have *corporate quality awards* based on quality and/or customer satisfaction measures. The awards have two primary goals:

1. To recognize employees for their contributions.
2. To communicate a commitment to quality and customer satisfaction at the highest levels of the company.

"We developed a reward and recognition strategy as a basis for performance management," says Joe Conchelos, Trident's vice president of quality. "The question is, how would you reward the actions you wanted?" Trident developed a reward and recognition plan that answers that question. The intent of the plan is to reinforce behaviors that contribute to achieving its goal of Total Customer Satisfaction.

GTE Directories designs reward and recognition programs to motivate employees to support its quality improvement efforts, and to encourage performance. Formal awards include the President's National Quality Team Award and the Award of Excellence.

TABLE 8.1.   Tennant company's recognition program attributes

Low	Medium	High
Formal Recognition		
Frequent	From peers	Consistent
Interpersonal skills	Subjective	Cost
Percentage of total	From superiors	Prestigious
Timely		Public display
Win/win		Sincere
		Specific feedback
		Tangible reminder
Informal Recognition		
Subjective	Cost	Consistent
	Frequent	Sincere
	Interpersonal skills	Specific feedback
	From peers	From superiors
	Percentage of total	
	Prestigious	
	Public display	
	Tangible reminder	
	Timely	
	Win/win	
Day-to-Day Recognition		
Cost		Consistent
Prestigious		Frequent
Public display		Interpersonal skills
Subjective		From peers
Tangible reminder		Percent of total
		Sincere
		Specific feedback
		From superiors
		Timely
		Win/win

Source. Tennant Company; used with permission.

Regional team finalists for the President's Award come to GTE Directories headquarters every October to share their processes and achievements with the Leadership Council, which selects one team to receive the Award. The winner receives no monetary award.

GTE Directories recognizes outstanding performance through Awards of Excellence, which honor individuals and teams for leadership, innovation, customer service, quality, and technology. Each winner receives a medal encased in wood and glass and a reward of $2,500.

Trident's formal awards include the President's Award and Employee of the Month Award. Each year, the CEO selects the person he feels has done the most for the organization. The President's Award winner, who receives $1,500 and a plaque, is honored at the company's year-end holiday celebration.

Employees of the Month are selected and nominated by employees and supervisors and chosen by management. Winners are announced at the monthly, companywide meetings. All Employees of the Month are eligible for the Employee of the Year Award, which also includes a $1,500 reward.

Tennant's first foray into quality recognition was in the formal arena. Candidates for the Formal Quality Recognition Award are nominated by their coworkers. The nominations for individuals and groups are reviewed and evaluated by a Recognition Committee, which is a cross-functional team of employees. Up to 25 individuals and 12 groups receive their awards at banquets in their honor.

To increase the number of employees recognized and to spread the honors throughout the year, Tennant introduced the *Koala T. Bear Award*. To qualify for the award, an employee must do one of the following:

- Exert extra effort to meet or exceed customers' needs.
- Go above and beyond job requirements in a small group or special project.
- Consistently meet job standards and have a positive work attitude.

Candidates are nominated in writing by their peers or managers. A cross-functional employee committee selects the winners. Each month, someone dons a koala bear costume, grabs a bunch of stuffed koala bears wearing Tennant Quality T-shirts, and surprises employees at all three of the company's Minneapolis facilities. Sounds hokey, right? Some employees thought so, causing the Koala T. Bear Award committee to get rid of the bear suit and just hand out the awards. But then a lot of employees asked where the costumed bear went. The committee brought it back.

Informal Recognition

The second dimension of Tennant's recognition program, informal recognition, took shape as the company sought ways to help managers and supervisors uniformly recognize groups. Informal recognition is given more frequently than formal recognition and less frequently than day-to-day recognition. According to Tennant's guidelines, it depends on:

- The amount of effort the group put into the project, beyond the members' regular job responsibilities.
- The amount of time expended to accomplish the task.
- The importance of the accomplishment to the entire organization.
- The ability of the group to set and meet goals.

The form of recognition usually falls into three categories:

1. Parties or gatherings (pizza parties, luncheons, or coffee and doughnuts).
2. Outings (tours of other companies, visits to customers or suppliers).
3. Gifts or giveaways (coffee mugs, pens and pencils, or gift certificates).

Managers decide what type of recognition to give. Each manager may access a corporate informal recognition fund equating to $15 per person per year. The most popular purchases include food, wearing apparel, and gift certificates.

Tennant's informal recognition program has had notable successes. One committee used informal recognition to encourage employees to wear their name tags. Employees whose names are randomly selected and who are caught wearing their name tags get a surprise visit from Name Tag Committee members, who give the name tag wearer a $20 gift certificate. As committee members walk through the facility to present the gift certificate, they often reward employees wearing their name tags with a candy bar, a can of soda, or a small gift. As a result, the number of employees wearing name tags doubled, from 30 percent to 60 percent, over a five-year period.

Tennant's informal recognition program for safety began in 1975. It includes cash awards, special dinners, small gifts, and internal publicity. The recognition helped Tennant to achieve one of the lowest workers' compensation rates in the country and to earn public recognition for its safety efforts.

Supervisors at GTE Directories recognize strong employee performance through discretionary awards of up to $450. All award winners are recognized in the monthly employee publication and periodic *Employee Bulletins.*

The focus of Trident's reward and recognition plan is on informal recognition. "We look at the entire organization as a team," says Conchelos, "and we have several awards for the company team. If we go an entire month without a customer complaint or rejected part, the employees select what they want for a extended lunch period. Senior managers may cook out. Lunch might be catered. Whatever the employees want. If we go six months with no more than two customer complaints, everyone gets a day off. And if we go 90 days without a recordable accident, we have a pizza party. We've had several of those."

Day-to-Day Recognition

The third dimension of Tennant's recognition program, day-to-day recognition, occurs when one employee thanks or praises another employee. The recognition can be verbal or written and can be used by any employee; it is not strictly a management tool. Research shows that people value such specific individual recognition more than any other type.

In *Recognition Redefined,* Maehling describes recent surveys that support this point:

- A study of 1,500 employees throughout the United States revealed that the most preferred recognition was "spur-of-the-moment" recognition from their direct supervisors.
- In studies of 5,000 employees and managers, conducted by recognition experts Kathryn Wall and Rosalind Jeffries, seven out of ten people said they wanted individual recognition for a job well done.

Maehling once asked over 400 people attending recognition training to rank the three types of recognition in order of importance to them. Two-thirds said day-to-day recognition was most important, 28 percent ranked informal recognition first, and only 6 percent put formal recognition at the top of the list. Asked to rank where the company placed its emphasis, 46 percent said the focus was on formal recognition, 44 percent said informal, and 10 percent said day-to-day.

"The surveys show that people crave day-to-day recognition but they're not getting it," says Maehling. "They want feedback. They can't function in a vacuum anymore. We need to change our culture so that regular; positive feedback is a natural reflex." Maehling intends to close the gap by increasing awareness of the value of positive feedback and by training more managers and employees in the skills they need to give and receive positive feedback. "One of our strengths at Tennant is our willingness as a corporation to do something about this," says Maehling.

Although it is not where it wants to be, Tennant is building on 14 years of attention to day-to-day recognition. The Operations Committee made positive feedback a priority in 1983 and, the next year, set up a Positive Feedback Committee to implement daily feedback. One of the committee's first acts was to introduce That-A-Way notes. Under a bold "That-A-Way" heading, an employee writes specific praise or thanks to another employee. Acceptance of the program is visible in the number of yellow That-A-Way notes people proudly display in their work areas. That-A-Way notes can also be sent by e-mail.

Like Tennant, many organizations are discovering the need for and value of daily positive feedback. Employees at Trident receive "At-A-Boy" and "At-A-Girl" notes from their peers and supervisors, and everyone who receives one is listed in the monthly *Trident Times*. GTE Directories' day-to-day recognition varies by department: Human Resources has its "Caught in the Act" program, Finance hands out more formal thank-you cards, and Publishing has the Penny Award. "People want managers and senior leaders to understand and appreciate the sacrifices they have to make," says Mike English, director of quality and customer services for GTE Directories.

As organizations listen to the "customers" of their recognition and reward programs and involve employees in improving them, the effectiveness of all types of recognition—formal, informal, and day-to-day—will grow in support of their quality and performance goals.

HOW PERFORMANCE REVIEWS SUPPORT THE NEW MODEL

Recognition and reward programs are generally accepted as valuable support for a company's agenda, but a consensus on performance assessments is not as easily achieved. Most businesspeople would agree that performance reviews conducted according to the principles of quality management fit neatly into the drive for continuous improvement. The prevailing opinion among quality experts is that performance appraisals support quality improvement under the following conditions:

1. *The performance appraisal must be separate from the compensation system.* The purpose of a performance appraisal is to improve performance through communication. Dangling pay like a carrot changes the emphasis from improving because it is the *right* thing to do to improving because it is the *profitable* thing to do.

2. *The performance appraisal must be based on observable, measurable behaviors and results.* The identification and use of key indicators is a principle of quality management that is just as valuable to an employee who is evaluating his or her performance as it is to an employee who is evaluating the performance of his or her punch press. In both cases, the goal is to improve performance, not to criticize the performer. And in both cases, the employee should help determine what to measure, then collect the data.

3. *The performance appraisal must include timely feedback.* Annual performance reviews are too infrequent to promote continuous improvement and defect prevention. Feedback should be specific, immediate, and positive, related to performance the employee can control.

4. *The performance appraisal must encourage employee participation.* The manager's role in a performance appraisal is to help the employee understand the assessment, to work with the employee to develop new goals and actions, to explore opportunities for career development, and to encourage the employee to provide feedback on the manager's performance as it relates to the employee. The employee is not a passive listener but an active participant.

This new way of reviewing performance is a natural extension of the principles that quality leaders have embraced. Employees are no longer commodities you do things to; they are *valued internal customers and suppliers* who are responsible for continuous improvement. A performance assessment that supports and encourages their contributions becomes an important tool for the quality improvement process.

HOW COMPENSATION SUPPORTS THE NEW MODEL

Most quality experts would agree with Dr. Michael Beer, a Harvard professor of business administration, who wrote in *Harvard Business Review:*

> Pay's function is to create equity and fairness. It should attract people to an organization and keep them there. Pay should not be an active ingredient in promoting teamwork and motivating performance.

To "create equity and fairness" while supporting the new management model, a compensation system should follow these key principles of quality management:

1. *Compensation should be customer driven.* Pay all employees for skills that matter to the company's external customers. Doing so requires a clear understanding of what customers need and expect, and what the company does to meet those needs and expectations. Internally, both employees and managers are "customers" of the compensation system. Their needs and expectations must also drive the compensation system.

2. *Compensation should be team-oriented.* Total quality management requires the extensive use of teams. If any compensation is considered "at risk"—dependent on performance or results—it should be based primarily on achieving team goals.

3. *Compensation should be measurable.* The measures used to determine any at-risk pay must be the observable results of team performance. Measures must be relevant, available throughout the process, focused on what is important to the customer, and established, collected, and controlled to a great degree by the team.

4. *The compensation system should have full employee participation.* As Berwick writes, "Knowledge is in the workforce." Employees, individually and in teams, must participate in setting meaningful goals, identifying key performance indicators, and monitoring and evaluating progress. The company must provide and encourage training to help employees master these tasks.

THE SHIFT IN THINKING

The shift in thinking about rewards and recognition reflects a shift in thinking about employees as a *resource,* not a commodity. The issue quality leaders are addressing is how to align their compensation and recognition programs with their new management model so that employees are rewarded and recognized for their achievements and motivated to do even better.

The best way to begin the alignment is by using the principles of quality management to assess and improve ongoing compensation and recognition programs:

1. Learn what the "customers" of the programs *need* and expect. You can develop effective programs only if they are based on the needs and expectations of all employees.

2. *Involve employees* in improving the compensation and recognition programs. The involvement may include:

   - Participating in opinion surveys.
   - Setting and tracking measures and objectives for any compensation tied to quality or customer satisfaction.
   - Creating new types and improving existing types of recognition.
   - Managing recognition programs.
   - Nominating other employees for awards.
   - Providing and accepting positive feedback.

3. Focus on recognizing and rewarding the achievement of *team* goals. The new management model relies on teamwork to succeed. Touting individual accomplishments when you are trying to encourage team-work can be destructive.

4. Make at-risk pay and formal recognition dependent on *measurable* performance. Even better, have the employees establish, collect, and control the measurements. And better yet, make the measurements measure team performance.

Finally, don't make your program worse. In your haste to improve quality, it is tempting to create a flashy Quality Award or a pay-for-quality plan that seems to promote exactly what you are looking for. Resist the temptation. Pay and recognition address some very basic human needs, such as security, acceptance, self-respect, achievement, and appreciation. You may introduce a new reward for all the right reasons, but if you have not talked to and involved employees in the process, it is likely to fail—or worse, it may leave employees feeling manipulated and controlled when you are trying to motivate and involve them.

If your existing reward and recognition programs are doing no harm, you may want to leave them alone until the new management model is in place. When your system is running smoothly, revamping or fine tuning the rewards and recognition can be just the booster needed to speed the company toward its goals.

9 EMPLOYEE FOCUS

Armstrong Building Products Operation

BI Performance Services

Ben & Jerry's

In the war between old and new management models, the attitude toward employees is surely the fiercest battleground. Old model advocates see employees as little more than commodities, "hired help" paid to do a job, expendable cogs in a corporate machine that barely notices their presence or absence. Such a view serves leaders who willingly sacrifice employee well-being for short-term financial results.

New model believers hold that employee satisfaction is a leading indicator of customer satisfaction, and that loyal employees develop loyal customers. As employee satisfaction increases, a company can expect its key customer satisfaction indicators to improve also, along with financial results.

These opposing views produce very different ideas about how a company should treat its employees. The transition from viewing employees as commodities to embracing them as partners in a shared mission continues to be slow. Competitive global markets have led many companies, including several of this country's role models, to demand so much of their people that stress has become a major problem for many employees.

Part of the employees' stress is fear of losing their jobs. A startling number of senior executives have turned to layoffs as the remedy for

111

mediocre financial performance. In a column for the Cox News Service, Dale Dauten blasts this "downsizing" trend:

> [CEOs who slash jobs] ought to be getting up and saying: "We did such a lousy job of planning and hiring that we have more people than we have work. And we are so broke and so dimwitted that we can't come up with any way to get more work, so our only choice is to send a lot of good people home. I am ashamed, and I am sorry."

Senior executives surely cringe at such harsh judgments. No doubt they can rationalize laying people off, but the rationalizations do not equal sound business reasoning. According to a study published by *US News & World Report,* a typical company's stock price rose by 10 percent after downsizing. Three years later, the stock had dropped by 35 percent.

Companies are learning that laying people off erodes their foundation. You cannot build teamwork when people feel they are expendable. You cannot expect people to give their best when they do not feel the company values them. You cannot rally the troops around a common vision of excellence when the troops know that the only excellence that really matters is profits to shareholders and bonuses to senior executives. Leaders need to understand that layoffs are counterproductive and can undermine the entire system.

Few leaders seem to recognize the contradictory nature of some of their actions. They say customer satisfaction is the primary goal, but make short-term decisions focused solely on improving the bottom line. They say that quality is an overriding value, but sacrifice quality when it threatens to cost too much. They say that the company's employees are responsible for the company's success, then lay them off. They say that the people who make the products and deliver the services and serve the customers are the most important people in the company, then pay themselves hundreds of times more than the people they are praising.

They don't get it. None of these contradictory messages is lost on employees. If senior management says one thing and does another, employees become distrustful, anxious, and cynical. They do not become satisfied. As leaders strive to align their management system, *they must also strive to align their messages.* If customer satisfaction is the primary goal, measure your success by customer satisfaction and retention. If quality is job one, sacrifice it for nothing. If your employees are responsible for your success, institute a no-layoff policy. If everyone is important, adjust your pay—including stock bonuses—to more equitable levels. And if you don't want to make such changes, don't make contrary claims.

In this chapter, we will look at how Armstrong Building Products Operations, BI Performance Services, and Ben & Jerry's focus on their employees. We will address three questions:

1. Why are our human resources so important?
2. How do we align human resources with the company's strategic plans?
3. How do we build employee loyalty?

The new management model is a people-focused system that is driven by customers and fueled by employees. As we saw in Chapters 5 and 6, a company must involve *all* its employees in meeting customers' requirements. Relationships grow in importance: the relationships between customers and employees, managers and employees, employees and other employees, employees and suppliers. Loyal employees do better in these relationships than dissatisfied employees. For that reason alone, it is in a company's best interests to produce loyal employees.

MODELS OF EXCELLENCE

Building Products Operations (BPO), a subsidiary of Armstrong World Industries, Inc., is the worldwide leader in manufacturing and marketing acoustical ceiling systems for commercial and residential markets. BPO employs approximately 2,400 people. Its headquarters is in Lancaster, Pennsylvania. Armstrong BPO won the Baldrige Award in 1995.

BI Performance Services develops, designs, and delivers program solutions that help its clients to improve the performance of their employees and distribution personnel, and to develop higher levels of consumer loyalty and frequency of purchase. BI has nearly 1,000 associates at its Minneapolis headquarters, its Eden Valley (Minnesota) facility, and its 24 sales offices, located in major cities throughout the United States. In 1994, BI became the first service company to win the Minnesota Quality Award.

Ben & Jerry's Homemade, Inc., was founded in 1978 in a renovated gas station in Burlington, Vermont. The company manufactures and markets super premium ice cream, low-fat and nonfat frozen yogurt, ice cream novelties, and sorbets, through supermarkets, grocery stores, convenience stores, and restaurants, and also franchises Ben & Jerry's scoop shops. It has more than 700 employees "dedicated to the creation and demonstration of a new corporate concept of linked prosperity" that includes "holding a deep respect for individuals inside and outside the company."

EMPLOYEE LOYALTY = CUSTOMER LOYALTY

BI Performance Services helps companies improve results by motivating employees to produce specific behaviors, an idea that built this incentive business. As the business matured, BI sought to prove the validity of that idea through statistical methods. It conducted studies with clients to see whether people respond better to cash or noncash incentives. Noncash wins every time.

BI also redefined the business by developing an integrated performance model focused on improving results. The performance model has four pieces—communication, training, measurement, and rewards—plus research. "We believe that, if you use all these elements, you can change people's behavior," says Mary Etta Coursolle, senior vice president at BI. "That changed behavior may or may not produce different attitudes, but it *does* produce results." BI draws from its model to shape performance improvement programs for its clients. It also applies the model to improving the performance of its own associates.

The elements of the performance model are evident in companies intent on creating a high-performance work environment. For example, Ben & Jerry's current human resource agenda includes:

- Distributing guides for managers and employees, called, respectively, *Coach's Guide* and *Player's Guide,* to *communicate* the principles behind the company's policies.
- Improving *communication* by having regular leadership meetings and making leaders responsible for relaying to their people the information shared at these meetings.
- Adding *training* on team and cooperative work skills.
- Enhancing *measurement* by improving the performance appraisal process.
- Introducing a new compensation system for production workers, to *reward* them for acquiring certain skills and competencies.

BI's performance model captures actions that any organization can take to improve performance. But what does improving performance have to do with developing loyal customers? One might assume that better performance means higher quality, faster delivery, or lower prices, but

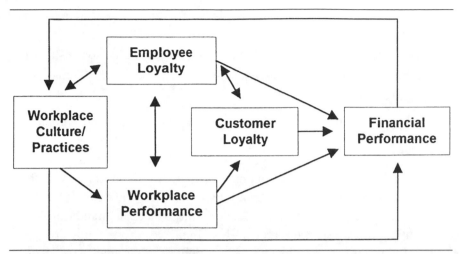

EXHIBIT 9.1. BI's loyalty model.

it could also mean more aggressive selling or working harder for longer hours. And if employees are working harder and longer, what does a model for improving performance mean to the employees being asked to improve?

To help answer these questions, two BI associates examined current performance models that link workplace practices with financial performance. Their goal was to develop a new model that is valid and useful, that offers insights into the dynamics of loyalty, and that shows the connections between workplace practices and financial performance. They called their new model the Loyalty Model.

As shown in Exhibit 9.1, the Loyalty Model identifies the sources of financial performance as workplace culture and practices, employee and customer loyalty, and workplace performance. Each area in the model has been identified by management experts and research as important, all areas have been measured, and all linkages are supported by research.

Workplace culture consists of the vision, values, and beliefs that define an organization. Employees who accept the culture translate its value to customers; employees who ignore or reject the culture create disconnects between what the company says it provides and what the customer receives.

Workplace practices are what employees do and how they do it.

Employee loyalty, as defined by BI, means that employees:

• Understand and commit to their organization's business goals and objectives.

- Make an active and ongoing decision to stay employed with the organization.
- Perform "above and beyond" behaviors to create value for customers.
- Modify their workplace behaviors to accommodate the demands of changing market environments.

Workplace culture and practices can help create or erode employee loyalty.

Workplace performance is the measure of how well products or services meet standards. (We talk more about this in Chapters 11 and 12.) Workplace culture and practices help set and communicate standards. Employee loyalty affects how well employees adhere to those standards. We'll look at employee satisfaction later in this chapter, but one study confirms the link between employee loyalty and product/service quality. AMP, discussed in Chapter 14, studied eight years' data on employee satisfaction scores and quality results. A correlation of the data showed that declines in employee morale led to declines in quality. Based on the study, AMP views employees' satisfaction as a leading indicator of quality performance.

Customer loyalty was discussed in Chapter 3. Why customer loyalty and not customer satisfaction? A study by Xerox found that totally satisfied customers (another definition of "loyal") were six times more likely to repurchase Xerox products than satisfied customers.

Higher rates of repurchase improve financial performance. As the model shows, long-term *financial performance* depends on workplace performance and the loyalty of employees and customers.

Develop loyal employees through the plans and actions we've discussed in Chapters 6 through 8. Promote trust and respect. Drive out fear. Give employees the responsibility and skills to do their jobs well. Recognize and reward their contributions.

None of this will happen by accident. To create loyal employees, you need a comprehensive plan that addresses every element that produces loyalty. Armstrong BPO provides an excellent example.

ARMSTRONG BPO: THE STRATEGIC MANAGEMENT OF HUMAN RESOURCES

BPO builds its strategic plans around what are called the Nonnegotiables:

- Increase the market share profitably.
- Be the best-cost supplier.

- Increase the flow of successful new products.
- Develop the human resource capability.

Each function within BPI, including the Human Resources (HR) unit, develops strategies that link to these Nonnegotiables. The functional leaders agree on global action plans, after which the members of each function meet to develop their own action plans, which include specific measures and goals.

The HR plans have five strategic components:

1. Safety.
2. Employee development/empowerment.
3. People development.
4. Recognition and reward.
5. Employee well-being and satisfaction.

"What I do in HR is not just on personal desires or whims but is directly tied to where we're going as a business," says Melvin Pugh, general manager of Human Resources for BPO. "We have a strategy for each component, and specific measures and goals for each. Most of the measures we track monthly, although recognition and reward are pretty much tracked quarterly, and employee well-being and satisfaction are tracked annually."

Specific strategies and action plans may be long-term, but HR must also have a short-term, tactical improvement plan for the next 12 to 18 months. BPO's overall HR strategy is:

- To provide the opportunity for employees to reach their full potential by developing a high-performance organization which supports the operation's Vision, Mission, and Goal. The behavior in deploying the strategy will be consistent with our corporate Operating Principles. [Editor's Note: This strategy confirms workplace culture and practices for BPO—the first element in the Loyalty Model.]
- To attract, develop, challenge, and retain a diverse workforce to ensure that we have the skills and organization to build our business.
- To involve and empower employees to improve processes and participate in decisions that affect the business.
- To recognize and reward performance that contributes to the business strategy and goals.
- To continuously improve those elements of the work environment that enhance employees' well-being, satisfaction, and productivity.

The long-term strategies and short-term plans contribute to exceptional financial performance, the final element in the Loyalty Model. In 1994, the year before BPO won the Baldrige Award, the company reduced its operating costs by a record $40 million. It set company and industry safety records, maintained or enhanced its leadership position in every market, and distributed its highest-ever gain-sharing and incentive payouts. Better yet, it did not produce these accomplishments at its employees' expense: BPO maintained or improved its already high levels of employee morale.

Armstrong BPO demonstrates, in myriad ways, that it values its employees. Empowering people; pay-for-skill and pay-for-knowledge systems; a three-pronged recognition approach based on the Tennant model (see Chapter 8); extensive training; a world-class safety record—all are part of a strategic plan that has produced higher customer satisfaction, greater market share, and improved financial and shareholder value. As BPO shows, employee loyalty equals customer loyalty—which equals improved financial performance.

FUN PLACES TO WORK

Empowerment, training, reward and recognition, and safety are essential to developing employee loyalty. More and more companies are also using another strategy: Lighten up, add a little joy to the workplace, *have fun!*

Jerry Greenfield, one of the cofounders of Ben & Jerry's, preaches a simple philosophy: "If it's not fun, why do it?" Acting on this philosophy, Greenfield created the Joy Gang to increase joy in the workplace. Among the Joy Gang's activities:

- *Name That Face Contest.* Employees brought in photos from their past. They were displayed on a bulletin board for other employees to guess who was who.
- *Barry Manilow Day.* To celebrate Manilow's birthday, Manilow tunes were played in the lunchroom, Manilow buttons were distributed, and employees voted on their favorite Manilow tune.
- *Jungle Party.* Employees dressed up in whatever jungle outfits they could find and went to a party featuring jungle music, limbo contests, and prizes.
- *Pizza & Puttin.* The Joy Gang sponsored a night out for employees at an indoor miniature golf course, and provided pizza during the putting.

- *Play Day.* The Joy Gang covered the lunchroom tables with white paper and left boxes of crayons, finger paints, and cans of Play-Doh for employees to enjoy.

The list is much longer, but the purpose is the same: *Increase joy in the workplace.* For companies that wish to improve service to their most valuable resource, increasing joy sounds like a good place to start.

At BI Performance Services, the equivalent of the Joy Gang is the Fun QIT, a group of volunteers dedicated to bringing more fun to the workplace. BI has about 200 associates signed up as "fun consultants" eager to help the QIT with its events, which include a Valentine candy exchange (an associate buys candy for any other associate, and the Fun QIT delivers it), a book fair, May Daffodil Day, and a Dunk the Director party (music and a disk jockey, lunch, and a big dunk tank for game senior executives).

"It's all done in a tongue-and-cheek way," says Coursolle, "because everyone knows this isn't how you have fun." Work is work, after all, and the *real* fun comes from learning, working as a team, doing a job well, reaching a goal, and being recognized for your accomplishments.

DETERMINING EMPLOYEE SATISFACTION

In the new management model, relevant information is required to improve the system, not to fix blame. If a process goes out of control, information about that process is used to bring it back into control, not to seek out the responsible people and chew them out. This is true whether the process involves manufacturing a widget or managing people. It is the reason companies that embrace the new model need to do a better job of collecting information about employee satisfaction.

Consider the parallels to customer satisfaction. Companies have always assumed that they knew what their customers required. However, when they were forced by competition and other pressures to get closer to their customers, they quickly discovered that their understanding was only skin-deep. Companies such as Solectron, IBM Rochester, Xerox, and Staples now work hard to stay on top of customer requirements because they know those requirements drive their business—and the requirements change.

We can apply the same shift in thinking to employee satisfaction. Companies have always assumed that they know what their employees require. However, as they are being forced to involve all of their employees in meeting customer requirements, they are discovering that their understanding is very shallow. Companies that believe that employee satisfaction is an indicator of customer satisfaction know that they must do a better job of understanding and meeting their employees' requirements.

Most companies determine employee satisfaction through an employee survey. Ben & Jerry's conducts a survey roughly every other year; BI has an annual survey. Both companies communicate the results to all employees/associates, analyze the results, and develop and implement improvement plans. For example, one of the lowest-scoring statements in BI's 1995 survey related to training in the company's different products and services. A Quality Improvement Team was formed to respond. As a result of monthly training sessions and a self-study product guide, the score on the statement rose 38 percent in 1996.

An infrequent survey creates two problems: (1) an absence of data much of the time, and (2) an abundance of data and improvement activities once a year or so. During the course of a year, the attitudes of employees may change significantly, but management will not be able to measure those shifts or respond appropriately until the survey results are available.

One solution to this problem is being introduced by GTE Directories, which will soon begin surveying one-twelfth of its employees every month. Each month's results will be added to the previous 11 months' results to produce a rolling 12-month score for all survey items. The monthly surveys give the company more timely data about employee attitudes, but each employee completes the survey just once a year. In addition, human resource issues receive ongoing attention rather than the burst of activity that typically follows the annual survey.

Another solution involves using other means (in addition to surveys) of assessing employee attitudes, such as focus groups and interviews. Armstrong BPO has an employee survey, but its best source of information about how employees feel is its confidential, one-on-one employee interviewing process, which the company has relied on for more than 20 years. The interviews are staggered over 12 months (soon, 18 months) and include all salaried personnel and at least half of the nonsalaried employees at all sites. All employees who volunteer to be interviewed are accepted. The interviews are conducted by the industrial relations manager responsible for a site, and by a corporate organizational development person.

"It's a neat process because it doesn't presume that we know the right things to ask on a survey," says Pugh. "People will come into the interviews with notes already prepared and we basically just write. We're not in there prompting or trying to steer the discussion. We only ask questions to clarify."

The results of the interviews are aggregated, analyzed, and used to initiate improvements. "We put the information into a report that normally breaks down into six or seven different categories," says Pugh. "The interview process says we care and we're asking what we can improve on."

By demonstrating their concern for how employees feel, Armstrong BPO creates loyal employees: the annual turnover rate is less than one quarter of one percent.

THE SHIFT IN THINKING

In the new management model, *employees make the system work.* They interact with customers, translate customers' requirements into products and services, manage and improve processes, work with suppliers, determine and use measurements, compare their processes to others, contribute to their communities, and perform all the other tasks that turn a building filled with equipment into a successful business.

In this respect, the new management model heads in the direction laid out by economist Lester Thurow, who has written that, "in the twenty-first century; the education and skills of the work force will end up being the dominant competitive weapon." Thurow wrote this prophecy in his book, *Head to Head* (William Morrow and Company, 1992). He pointed out that individuals, companies, and countries become rich through some combination of four factors: more natural resources, more capital, superior technologies, or more skills. Comparing the economies of the United States, Japan, and Europe, he states:

> New technologies and new institutions are combining to substantially alter these four traditional sources of competitive advantage. Natural resources essentially drop out of the competitive equation. Being born rich becomes much less of an advantage than it used to be. Technology gets turned upside down. New product technologies become secondary; new process technologies become primary.

And the new process technologies depend on people who are empowered, trained, recognized—and satisfied with their work.

The shift in thinking in this area is as dramatic as any required by the new management model. If a company truly succeeds or fails because of its human resources, *it must always act as if employees are its most important asset.* Management must serve the workforce, in the sense that it must help people learn, grow, contribute, and excel.

More than 20 years ago, Robert Greenleaf wrote an essay called "The Servant as Leader." A line from that essay captures the new management model's employee focus:

> The business exists as much to provide meaningful work to the person as it exists to provide a product or service to the customer.

10 CUSTOMER CONTACTS

Solectron

Randall's Food Markets

Thomas Interior Systems

"Satisfied employees produce satisfied customers." In the old style of management, the one or two people who actually believed this statement interpreted it to mean that happy employees cared more about the quality of the widgets they were assembling than disgruntled employees did. The warning never to buy a car built on a Monday was offered as proof.

In the new management model, the connection between satisfied employees and satisfied customers is much broader. Companies intent on tracking their customers' changing requirements and improving their service are encouraging more and more employees to interact with customer representatives on a regular basis. As competition neutralizes the distinctions among products, companies vie to differentiate themselves through the quality of their service.

Several years ago, MetLife developed a personal quality training program and identified six personal attributes that contribute to solid customer relationships:

1. Treat customers as you want to be treated when you are a customer.
2. Take personal responsibility to see that customers' needs are met.
3. Constantly seek to improve by learning as much as possible about your job so as to serve your customers more effectively.
4. Share your knowledge, skills, and time with others, offering help and assistance to customers and coworkers.

5. Have a positive outlook and be persistent in meeting customers' expectations.
6. Communicate effectively with customers and fellow employees.

With this list, MetLife recognized the power of personal contact. In fact, the attributes would be equally valuable in any type of relationship. It is striking to notice the similarities between MetLife's attributes of personal quality and the ways quality leaders such as Engelhard-Huntsville and Ben & Jerry's relate to their employees (see Chapters 5 and 9) or how Bose relates to its key suppliers (see Chapter 13), or the ways USAA and IMC relate to their communities (see Chapter 16). MetLife's attributes have the feel of universal truths, like the behaviors that contribute to a good marriage or the wisdom we wish to pass along to our children, yet they were the result of an extensive study of *customer expectations. As the foundation for solid customer relationships, they are the point where intuition and intellect meet.*

If all of this sounds too touchy-feely, too bad. You can either work hard at relating to your customers on a personal level, or you can watch them run off with the first company that does. Successful companies in all types of industries are doing everything they can to bring their customers into their organizations. They are reorganized to be:

- Customer-focused, not function-focused.
- Driven by customer requirements, not operational requirements.
- Relationship oriented, not product or service oriented.

For example (as discussed in Chapter 2), FedEx has three cardinal rules for achieving a quality perspective:

1. We must take the customer's viewpoint.
2. We must emphasize the emotional issues by making the product or service emotionally attractive.
3. We must look at everything that affects the customer.

These are all *relationship* issues. In this chapter, we will look at how three companies improve their customer relationships. As in any relationship, the success of a customer relationship depends on how well you answer these questions:

- How do we define and carry out our roles and responsibilities in this relationship?
- How do we communicate with our customers?

Implicit in both questions is the need to continuously improve. Solectron, one of this chapter's role models and a 1991 Baldrige Award winner, has one of the best systems we have seen for staying close to its customers. It is aggressively seeking a better way, by updating and modifying the questions it asks *all customers, every week.* Solectron understands what all of us need to learn: A customer relationship is a dynamic process that needs constant care and attention.

MODELS OF EXCELLENCE

Solectron operates one of the world's largest surface mount facilities for the assembly of complex printed circuit boards and subsystems. Its customers include manufacturers of computers, workstations, disk and tape drives, and other equipment. It has 6,000 employees in Milpitas, California. In 1990, Solectron won 11 superior performance awards from its customers. In 1991, it won the Baldrige Award. The Milpitas facility won the California Governor's Golden State Quality Award in 1994. In 1996, Solectron's Austin facility won the Texas Quality Award, the Charlotte plant won the North Carolina Quality Leadership Award, and its Panang (Malaysia) facility won the Quality Management Excellence Award in Panang. The Panang plant won the Prime Minister's Quality Award, a Malaysian award similar to the Baldrige Award, in 1997.

Randall's Food Markets, Inc. has more than $1 billion in sales annually from 48 supermarkets, 46 of which are in the Houston area. Its 12,000 employees serve more than a million customers each week. Randall's customer service orientation has helped it grow and flourish for 27 years, despite the up-and-down Houston economy.

Thomas Interior Systems provides office planning and furnishings services to organizations of all sizes, through two locations in the Chicago metropolitan area. It has 70 employees. The goal of the company is to be the leader in its industry, a goal it intends to reach by providing value-added office, environmental, and business tools that enhance the business productivity of its customers.

IMPROVING CUSTOMER CONTACT

A common problem for large companies with multiple business units is having to implement by persuasion rather than mandate. Smaller companies can standardize their approaches more quickly and implement them throughout the company. At Solectron, the standards for contact with customers are listed in a *Customer Service Guidelines Manual.* Compared to MetLife's general attributes, Solectron's specific standards sound arbitrary and rigid. However, each company's standards reflect the expectations and requirements of its customers.

Solectron's 120 original equipment manufacturing customers are served by plants in the United States, Mexico, South America, Europe, and Asia. With such a small customer base, Solectron's employees constantly interact with the same customers. Solectron has translated its customer service requirements into *standards* that include:

- If unexpected problems occur, notify the customer as soon as possible; identify the problem and its impact, and propose an action and scheduling.

- Answer phone calls within four rings; respond to messages from customers within two hours.

- Acknowledge receipt of customers' problems as soon as possible; respond within twenty-four hours with a solution, an action plan, or a date for a plan.

- When a customer calls to complain, listen carefully; do not argue. Encourage the customer to talk, apologize for any inconvenience or misunderstanding, give assurance for satisfaction, ask for suggestions, and take action immediately. Follow up by calling back within four hours.

- Any Solectron person contacted by a customer represents Solectron. Do not blame Solectron's problems on any individual or department within Solectron. Resolve the issue internally and apologize to the customer on the company's behalf.

- All ongoing customer partnerships must have weekly formal exchanges with the customer.

Listen. Act. Take responsibility. Meet expectations. Be courteous. Communicate. The essence of Solectron's standards fits well with MetLife's attributes of personal quality. The definition of the standards varies with customers' expectations and the organization's structure.

Randall's Food Markets, a 48-store company, is as adamant as Solectron about anticipating and meeting customers' requirements. For example, Randall's does not have a set of standards it imposes on every new store it opens. Instead, it surveys the area where the new store will be built, in an effort to understand the people it will serve, then sets up the store based on its potential customers' preferences. As the store's relationship with its customers matures, it changes to more accurately respond to customers' needs. "It takes a couple years for a store to adapt to its community," says R. Randall Onstead, Jr., president and chief operating officer.

Randall's is very relationship oriented. Its employees are trained and encouraged to listen to and assist customers. For example, when a customer asks a Randall's stock person where to find an item, the stock person will not rattle off an aisle number or point the customer in the general direction. The response these employees have been trained to give is, "Let me show you where that is." Another example: Employees at the checkout counter have been trained to listen carefully to customers while they work because "They're the ones who seem to hear everything," Onstead says. If the customer has any concern or question, the employee calls over a manager to handle it on the spot.

All this listening helps store and company management stay close to their customers' changing needs. Do they want their groceries bagged for them? Do they want them carried out to their cars? Do they want to be able to rent videotapes or fill prescriptions at the store? Customers are quick to tell Randall's employees their likes and dislikes, in large part because Randall's has a reputation for listening and responding. "My job is to give the stores the tools they need to be successful," says Onstead. "We're in the business of giving people what they want."

Treat customers as you would like to be treated when you are a customer. Successful companies understand that the "golden rule" is just as golden for business relationships as it is for personal ones.

COMMUNICATING WITH CUSTOMERS

Good relationships require constant communication. Randall's is quick to point out that an important part of communication is active listening. "What differentiates us from our competitors is that we're better listeners," says Onstead. "If we didn't have a reputation for listening, we wouldn't get near the response we're getting."

In addition to the daily feedback it gets from on-site customers, the company receives about 20 letters a day. It responds to every letter. About half are complimentary. The rest are requests to add, change, or fix something, or complaints. The chairman personally responds to those customers who are upset about something.

Good relationships also require close contact. Randall's maintains that contact because of the nature of its business, but it trains its people to take advantage of the contact by listening and assisting. Companies that do not enjoy such frequent interaction can still make it easy for their customers to stay in touch. Many give their customers lists of key employees' telephone and pager numbers. They equip their customer-contact personnel with pagers, car phones, portable computers with fax capabilities, and access to e-mail. They encourage their customers to contact them by setting up direct numbers, "800" numbers, voice mail, and conference calls.

At Thomas Interior Systems, only about a half-dozen employees do not have direct, daily contact with customers. With such broad exposure, the company recognizes the need for employees to be generalists, familiar with customer requirements and with every element of Thomas's business. It responds to the need through its customer focus process, which includes 40 hours of training a year in such subjects as product lines of and programs with major manufacturers, specifications for major lines (i.e., carpeting, panel systems, electrical), project management, delivery and installation, estimating, design, computer issues, and business math.

All training is managed by employee teams—the units through which Thomas operates. Each team has a weekly meeting to focus on customer and operational requirements and performance. Team administrators meet weekly to coordinate activities across team lines and to share learning.

In 1991, Thomas decided that some extra face-to-face contact with customers would help both sides better understand the other while helping Thomas Interior Systems improve its service. Every person in the company visited a customer. Employees did not visit customers they normally served. Each associate spent time at a customer's facility and asked three questions about how Thomas Interior Systems could improve. "We got a lot of good information from this," says president Thomas Klobucher. "We took the top five expectations and revised our customer satisfaction survey to reflect them."

To capture customer feedback, Thomas relies on its customer satisfaction surveys and on employee participation in weekly team meetings. The company sends surveys to customers after every delivery. About one-fourth are returned. Every employee either reads or hears about every response. Results for each question on the survey are compiled and tracked monthly.

Employees bring issues raised by customers to weekly team meetings for discussion and action. All action items are addressed at the team level first, then across teams as necessary, before they are elevated to the management level.

Solectron relies on a more formal process to communicate with its customers. It surveys every customer every week, and its executive staffs at every plant meet weekly to review the results. Before a customer is surveyed, Solectron finds out who, in the customer's organization, has the best information on how Solectron is performing. That person is asked to reply to the survey. The company faxes its one-page Customer Satisfaction Index (CSI) survey to these key people every Friday. The form asks one question each about quality, delivery, communication, and service. Customers respond with a letter grade (A–D) and any comments, then fax the completed form back, usually within a day.

The CSI coordinators who receive the completed surveys at Solectron know from experience when a response suggests a problem. The coordinators immediately contact the responsible division to advise it of the problem so that a plan of action can be discussed during the weekly executive meeting. Solectron also enters all the weekly survey information into a database, to track numbers and plot trends by customer, category, division, and so on. On the evening before the executive meeting, the coordinators usually crank out a pile of overheads on this information for the next morning's presentation.

The weekly meetings typically include senior executives and customer-contact people. Each meeting starts with a corporation-wide summary of the previous day's quality results, then turns to a review of the week's performance and enlists the stack of overheads for illustration. Depending on the number or severity of the issues, managers spend a total of about a half-hour describing the problems, analyzing the causes, and proposing solutions. The purpose is not to put managers on the spot. but to make customer issues highly visible. "We want our customers to tell us weekly about anything they are dissatisfied with, and it doesn't matter whose fault it is," says Sae Jae Cho, director of customer satisfaction. "We want to make the problems visible to the management at this company. Not many problems last more than a week or two."

Solectron has found that most problems are caused by poor communication. The solution is usually as simple as contacting the customer to make sure everyone agrees on the problem, then changing the communication process so that the lapse does not happen again.

As with all parts of the customer relationship, communication is the key to making customer surveys work. Companies that tried to increase the frequency of their surveys were usually deterred when the customers complained about how much work was involved—or refused to complete the surveys. Solectron has encountered similar resistance. To persuade customers to participate, it invites them to attend the weekly meetings. "When they see that they aren't filling out a form just to fill out a form, and that the information they send back is used to improve, they tend to become believers," says Cho. If a customer still resists, a division vice president visits the customer's president to explain the value of the process. The fact that every Solectron customer participates in the weekly survey suggests that customers believe the value outweighs the minor hassle.

Solectron's goal with every survey is "straight As." Any grade of B or worse on a customer survey is considered a complaint and is formally logged into the company's system. Solectron sends an acknowledgment to the customer that it has received the complaint and is addressing it, then pursues one of two problem-solving modes:

- If something is out of control in the process, the company does whatever is necessary to bring it back into control. It then goes through a formal process to find out what happened and to take steps to prevent it from happening again.
- If the process is in control but the customer is unhappy, it tightens the tolerance limits on the process, using statistical tools.

All complaints are tracked until they are closed. Although customers are encouraged to communicate and complain in any way they choose, this is the formal process for handling complaints.

The survey is only one of many ways Solectron stays close to its customers. Customer focus teams review quality and current delivery schedules during weekly meetings. Its customer's executives make presentations at Solectron's weekly Tuesday morning forums. Each quarter, a team headed by the senior executive who represents the customer's interests at Solectron visits the customer to discuss ways to improve existing projects, and plans for future projects. Customer executives are surveyed twice a year, and an annual third-party survey provides objective data for comparison.

As Solectron shows, constant communication and close contact are essential to building and maintaining sound customer relationships. Solectron began its weekly customer satisfaction index in 1987. In the course of five years, it raised its average score from 86 percent to 96 percent. To understand how impressive that 96 percent is, consider the scoring valves:

$$
\begin{aligned}
A &= 100 \text{ percent} \\
A- &= 90 \\
B+ &= 85 \\
B &= 80 \\
B- &= 75 \\
C &= 0 \\
D &= -100
\end{aligned}
$$

It would not take many Ds to bring the average down. By surveying its customers weekly and acting on their concerns immediately, Solectron prevents Bs from turning into Ds, retains satisfied customers, and gains new customers through referrals. As a result, the company has grown at an average annual rate of 60 percent since 1991.

THE SHIFT IN THINKING

In the new management model, companies work very hard at bringing their customers into their organizations. They have learned from experience that constant communication solidifies customer relationships, and that such communication is much easier when:

- Customer contact is continuous.
- As many employees as possible are involved.
- A variety of communication vehicles are used.
- Formal processes are established for listening and responding to customer concerns.

The contact occurs at many points in the new model. Leaders are making it a part of their job to regularly visit their peers at key customer companies. Many executive staff meetings now include time for the executives to share what they learned from their recent customer visits. A broader range of customer data is used to guide decision making.

Some companies are including customers in their strategic planning process. They invite customer representatives to participate in discussions about current and future customer requirements because they understand that such requirements drive the planning process. They also encourage customers to review the plans and suggest ways they could be improved.

Many companies are setting up teams to work closely with customers on designing and manufacturing the customers' products and services. The teams interact with their customers on an ongoing basis, establishing relationships that blur the lines between customer and supplier. Customers feel that they are part of the process, welcome at their suppliers' facilities, and valued for their ideas and guidance.

Successful companies use every opportunity to learn more about what their customers need and want. At Solectron, Randall's Food Markets, and Thomas Interior Systems, there are many different methods for staying close to customers. To the extent that you use different methods in an organized, long-term way, and your people who have contact with customers practice the attributes of personal quality, your company will develop a customer focus and will strengthen the relationships that are critical to sustained growth and profitability.

11 DESIGN OF PRODUCTS AND SERVICES

Intel Corporation

American Express Financial Advisors

Custom Research Inc.

The design of products and services is the most customer-focused activity your company undertakes. In the design process, external requirements are translated into internal requirements, and customers "throw the switch" that activates your business. The design process constantly forces companies that are truly customer-driven to reevaluate customer requirements and their response to those requirements. It is a cauldron of opinions and ideas stirred by customers, suppliers, and employees throughout the company.

Popularly known as "concurrent engineering," this process encourages everyone involved in product development—designers, engineers, customers, and suppliers—to contribute *simultaneously as a team*. The traditional method passes the baton from one group to the next in relay fashion. The sequence looks something like this:

- Sales and marketing identify a customer need and define the requirements to meet that need.
- They tell engineering what they want.
- Engineering develops a product in a series of steps that can take several years.

- When engineering finally has a model that marketing is happy with, it "tosses it over the wall" to manufacturing.
- Manufacturing figures out how to produce it.

This *serial design process* is lengthy and fraught with opportunities for miscommunication and reworking. Decisions are made at various stages without the benefit of valuable input from affected parties. When this input is finally received, designs must be reworked, new models created, new tests ordered, and new production schedules arranged. By comparison, companies that use *concurrent engineering* find that it typically cuts the time from conception to production in half, reduces costs, and improves quality.

Intel's CEO, Andrew Grove, in a *Fortune* article, said, "When companies lose their proprietary advantages, speed seems to be what matters most." Intel introduces new microprocessors on a regular basis, but it continues to work on its next three generations of product at the same time. We will look at Intel's design process in this chapter.

Involving all relevant departments simultaneously also cuts costs. Although only 5 percent to 8 percent of a product's cost is spent in the design phase, the designers' decisions lock in 60 percent to 80 percent of the total costs. A change in the design that may cost $1,000 early in the process can cost millions as production nears.

Concurrent engineering improves quality by "building it in" in the early stages of development. The design process takes into account the manufacturability of products and the deliverability of services; it anticipates quality issues and initiates corrective action *before* the design is completed. This proactive, prevention-based approach has proven to be a far more effective way of improving quality than fixing problems along the way. Judith Corson puts it succinctly: "Quality pays and it's more fun. Doing things over is not." She is one of two partners who founded Custom Research, which is another model of excellence in this chapter.

Through concurrent engineering, companies strive to involve customers in every stage of the development cycle. If the goal is to translate customer requirements into products and services, it makes sense to keep customers close so that the design team can run new ideas and changes past them. The improved communication among all those involved in the design process is one of the key reasons that concurrent engineering works.

The idea of forming cross-functional teams to design products and services is equally applicable to service companies. They too share the goals of reducing cycle time, cutting costs, and improving quality. The primary difference is that the variability of a service is often in the hands of the person or team providing it. For example, if a customer sits down with a bank's loan officer to talk about borrowing money, the loan officer determines from the customer's requirements what type of loan to recommend. Through the relationship with the customer, the loan officer learns what the specific requirements are, then translates those requirements into a loan package that is most appropriate for the situation.

The loan officer chooses from a list of options the bank has generated during its loan design process, which may have used an approach similar to concurrent engineering. However, the officer's relationship with the customer is often more important to satisfying and retaining that customer than the loan itself. As this chapter's third model of excellence, American Express Financial Advisors, has discovered, its clients' primary requirement is a long-term relationship with one financial planner. The company has redesigned its entire organization to improve this relationship.

In this chapter, we will use the experiences of three models of excellence—Intel, American Express Financial Advisors, and Custom Research—to look at the design process in the new business management model. Each enterprise offers new insights into key questions:

- How do we translate customer requirements into product and service design requirements?
- How do we ensure design quality?
- How do we reduce design-to-introduction cycle time?
- How do we improve the design process?

We will answer these questions a little differently here than in other chapters. Because each of our three models has a distinctive design process, it would be confusing to jump from one to the other in order to draw general conclusions. Instead, we will present Intel's process first, followed by American Express Financial Advisors' process and Custom Research's process. Although we cite Intel when we discuss translating customer requirements into design requirements, all three of our models address this critical point. All three also touch on achieving design quality, reducing cycle time, and improving the design process. These connections are noted throughout the chapter.

MODELS OF EXCELLENCE

Intel Corporation is the world's largest semiconductor company. Approximately 80 percent of the personal computers in use around the world are based on Intel architecture microprocessors. Headquartered in Santa Clara, California, Intel employs more than 49,000 people. In 1996, Intel's market value more than doubled—to $111 billion. Intel invested more than $1.8 billion in research and development in 1996.

American Express Financial Advisors offers financial planning and other investment advisory services to individuals and businesses across the United States. Its products include more than 100 financial and investment choices, including mutual funds, life insurance, annuities, and securities brokerage services. It employs 5,000 people at its headquarters in Minneapolis and at its regional offices, and it supports 8,000 advisors—independent contractors who sell the company's products. Total assets owned or managed by American Express Financial Advisors exceed $133 billion.

Custom Research Inc. (CRI) provides marketing research services to Fortune 500 companies. Custom Research professionals work with their client counterparts to design research projects that will provide information the clients need to make good business decisions. Most of the projects deal with new product research and development, including testing new concepts, products, packaging, advertising, and pricing. Headquartered in Minneapolis, Custom Research has approximately 100 employees. CRI won the Baldrige Award in 1996 and the Minnesota Quality Award in 1995.

INTEL: DESIGNING TO CUSTOMER REQUIREMENTS

When Intel introduced the Pentium processor in 1993, experts hailed it as the most important product in the company's history. The company's previous generations of chips are being used by 100 million people worldwide, and its product lead time requires continually working on the next three generations of chips, so "most important" is a transitory title. Intel is like a pro football coach who depends on his star quarterback for the current schedule but has his eye on a few college prospects who, he feels, could be the key to his team's future. The star is the star until someone better is developed. And someone better *will* be developed.

Intel develops its next stars through a design process that relies heavily on input from three sources: the people who use computers run by Intel chips; customers; and the architects, engineers, marketing people, and other experts at Intel.

The company has a formal process for soliciting the views of its end users: a consortium, consisting primarily of information systems managers, meets every four months in the United States and Europe, and every four to six months in Asia. "We ask them what they are looking for in their products, what they are looking to do with their computers, and what applications they're going to be using," says Pamela Olivier, strategic planning process manager for Intel's processor products group.

Intel talks to its customers constantly. "We believe in treating our customers as full partners," says Michael Wood, field product planning manager. "We directly contact a reasonable percentage of customers to determine such things as their distribution channels, geographic considerations, the ways they sell their products, and other critical information, because we want to find out what their needs are and why they're important."

Intel's internal experts combine this customer and end-user input with their own experience and knowledge to brainstorm possible design solutions. "At first, we tend to float our ideas past our field applications force," says Wood. "Most of them have computer science or electrical engineering degrees with at least five years' design experience. All of them work closely with our customers. We'll talk to them to get their opinions about how they think customers will respond to our ideas."

Intel begins the design process by posing open-ended questions to its assembled experts. As their ideas are narrowed to specific types of products, Intel begins to bring customers back into the design loop to test the experts' perceptions. "We are very hesitant, early in the planning stages, to take ideas out to our customer base," Wood says. "The issues we are dealing with are so advanced that most of our customers haven't usually thought about them yet." Having said that, Wood is quick to point out that Intel takes new product ideas to its customers earlier than it used to, citing customer involvement early in the development of the Pentium processor.

Involvement with key customers occurs at many different points within Intel. *Everyone* who is participating on a product design team has direct responsibility for dealing with the customers that have been pulled into the process. "In our industry, we need to limit the number of customers involved in the definition phase, but then deal with them in a very open and closed-loop fashion," says Wood. "This helps maintain very strong customer relations, which is extremely important to us."

Intel involves customers and end users in *establishing* their requirements, then involves them again in *evaluating* Intel's responses to those requirements. Companies with less sophisticated products and services tend to involve their customers at every phase of the design process, from conception to production, in order to improve communication, keep the focus on customer requirements, and add a valuable outside perspective to the process.

High-performance companies are also bringing more internal groups into the design process. At Intel, "Everybody gets involved in the definition of a product," says Olivier. "If a product crosses into other organizations, they become part of the product development team." Companies striving to create more horizontal organizations call this "laying the silos on their sides," because the first time a company does it, it must overcome the functional "silos"—the marketing department, the engineering department, the manufacturing department, and so on—that have traditionally dictated how the company operates. Some companies pull together people from these different silos into one physical area to work on a specific product, product line, or service. For manufacturing design, these cells become the hub for the company's concurrent engineering activities.

Intel does not directly involve suppliers in the product definition phase. However, if a new technology is involved that affects a supplier's capabilities, the supplier's voice is brought into the team via an internal supplier who works with the external supplier. Other companies are making external suppliers full members of their product development teams (for more information on this, see Chapter 13).

Once a product has been defined, Intel moves to the design phase, which follows a product implementation plan (PIP). The PIP identifies the critical steps of the development cycle, including design completion, customer samples and approval, and product certification. Designs are reviewed regularly: weekly by the design team, monthly by management, and quarterly or semiannually by the executive staff. An ongoing review makes sure the product continues to meet specifications, is still manufacturable, and will still perform as expected, so that when it is actually produced, it will meet all customer and internal specifications.

Intel relies on a team to improve its design process by reviewing and marrying the definition and design phases. After a product is introduced, it conducts regular postmortems to check the design process as well as the new product. The teams involved in these activities include people from marketing, design, the field, and management.

Intel benchmarks other companies to spur improvements in its design process. "I think there are people at Intel who are better at bringing the voice of the end user to the process. Strategic planning is trying to figure out how to learn from that," says Olivier. "I think we're very good at bringing Intel's ability to innovate to the process."

The results with its generations of Pentium processors indicate that Intel is rapidly improving its design process. When the first manufactured Pentium processor was plugged in and "booted up," the process took only ten minutes, compared to five days for its predecessor; the Intel 486.

Despite these advances, Intel is working hard to improve the process for the next generations of chips. "We are the most highly self-critical company I've seen," says Wood. "We're working to understand the changes we make, to measure them, and to assess their implications. You can be sure that whatever we have in place now will be improved next year."

AMERICAN EXPRESS FINANCIAL ADVISORS: IMPROVING DESIGN QUALITY AND REDUCING CYCLE TIME

Whereas Intel has a cultural propensity for change, American Express Financial Advisors (AEFA) is in the final stages of a project so sweeping that its goal has been to create a new company that could put the old one out of business—before a competitor tries to do just that.

Financial planning is a relationship-oriented activity in which people trust the achievement of their financial goals to an AEFA advisor and the company that supports that advisor. AEFA knew as early as 1986 that it needed to focus on this relationship to succeed. It got serious about it in 1990.

By then, the company had made several sincere efforts to improve its client relationships, but none had taken root, and although it was good by industry standards, it was not as good as it wanted to be. Senior management decided that the only way to break through the barriers to change was to redesign the entire system, and the best way to drive the change was through a new cross-functional team created solely for this purpose.

The 31-person team focused on four objectives:

1. Retain 95 percent of clients.
2. Retain 80 percent of financial planners who had four years of service and 97 percent of veteran financial planners.
3. Achieve annual revenue growth of 18 percent.
4. Bolster the company's position as industry leader.

The team spent about a year interviewing clients, advisors, management, and staff to find out more about the existing system. They benchmarked companies such as Motorola, Microsoft, and Wal-Mart to find out how other firms handled similar processes. When their research was completed, they developed a list of process- and system-oriented recommendations, most of which have been implemented.

The recommendations focus on serving the needs of clients. AEFA asked advisors to form groups that would make a broader level of knowledge available to clients. Each client still has a primary advisor, but if the client needs more specialized information about a particular topic, such as taxes or education funding, the primary advisor can bring in from the group another advisor who has that expertise. When the primary advisor is not available to assist the client, someone else from the group can take over and provide the assistance required.

To support the groups of advisors, AEFA reorganized its field management, which had a traditional hierarchical structure, into coordinating teams. The company formed 44 coordinating teams based on geography, demographics, and number of clients. A group vice president leads each team, which is responsible for supporting its assigned advisors across all market groups and for all specialties.

In 1996, AEFA began forming process committees responsible for the company's six key processes, which include technology, marketing, and acquiring and developing advisors. Each process committee includes members of the coordinating teams and is led by a senior vice president with field responsibility. One of these committees is looking at the design, production, and delivery of AEFA's products.

To serve field managers' and advisors' needs for information, AEFA has been working on identifying almost everything an advisor needs to serve clients, and then placing these resources at the advisor's fingertips. Previously, advisors could not perform basic service functions, such as name or address changes. They had to complete forms and forward them to headquarters, then wait for the change to be made. That information, and the ability to change it instantly, is now available on-line to advisors, who have the technology to access it. Once it is entered, the advisor does not have to reenter the same information for subsequent transactions.

The technology also gives the advisor the flexibility to tailor a financial plan presentation to the client's preferred way of receiving information. By pressing a key, the advisor can choose to present information using numbers or pie charts and graphs, to use longer or shorter explanations, to add information in an appendix, or to employ other options that make it easier for clients to understand their financial plans. AEFA expects to have the technology fully implemented in 1998.

With the reorganization of the company, every advisor became a designer and gained the authority to bring other experts into the design process—other advisors, or headquarters personnel. AEFA provides the necessary tools and support, but it is the advisor's role to understand a customer's requirements and to define and design a plan that will meet those requirements.

Much of the necessary support comes from the field managers, whose revised role has them working with their planners to understand their needs and find ways to assist.

AEFA also redesigned its processes and products to improve service to its clients and advisors. Client service processing is an example. AEFA used to have a different service area for nearly every type of product it sold. If clients or planners had questions, they might be passed to several departments before they got one that could help. To improve service, the company looked at this process from the client's perspective, then created service teams that could answer all product service questions from clients and planners in one call. It also organized its coordinating teams around a specific geographic region so that each team's operating hours match the region it serves.

In addition to its functional silos—marketing, finance, legal—AEFA also has *product silos*. The life insurance group develops its own products, as do the annuity group, the mutual fund group, and the other product groups. The reorganization changed the way the company designs its products: the product design people from these various groups are brought together to form a team responsible for designing all products. The design team uses client information gathered from surveys, focus groups, planners, and other listening posts to develop products that meet the requirements of AEFA's target markets.

All these major changes were driven by the company's desire to satisfy client requirements. In the process, AEFA redesigned not only its processes, products, and services, but the entire company and culture. "The objectives of the reorganization were client retention, advisor retention, revenue growth, and image in the industry," says Ora Kaine, director of National Implementation and Quality of Advice (an initiative to measure the quality of advice given to clients). "We have found that the redesign has improved all four areas. As with any massive change, the results dipped early, in 1995. In 1996, leaders pointed out that we were seeing improvements not in spite of the reorganization, but because of it. The coordinating teams get a lot of credit for that."

CUSTOM RESEARCH: IMPROVING THE DESIGN PROCESS

According to independent surveys, Custom Research Inc. (CRI) is a leader in its industry. Unlike American Express Financial Advisors, however, it has no plans for a major redesign of its organization. It has been customer driven since it was founded in 1974, and that customer focus permeates its design process.

Like many small companies, Custom Research is responsible for a piece of a much larger organization's process. In CRI's case, that piece frequently fits into the client's design process. Custom Research does market research for large companies that want to find out more about their customers' preferences before they make any expensive decisions. CRI's clients have four key requirements: they want their research to be accurate, on time, and on budget, and to meet or exceed their expectations. For every research project it accepts, the project team assigned to carry it out works with the client to define what these four criteria mean for the project.

Almost all of Custom Research's work involves custom-designed research. It is the service company equivalent of a "job shop." Because each project is unique, each project's design phase is critical to CRI's clear understanding of its clients' requirements.

The design begins when a senior executive and the account manager who works directly with the account meet with the client to find out specifically what the client expects in the relationship and how it prefers to work with CRI. A summary of the meeting is circulated to the team members who will work with that client. The senior executive also summarizes the client's requirements in a letter that is sent to the client for verification. The letter (revised if necessary, to reflect client feedback) becomes the basis for planning and action by the project team and for the team's service standards and account plan.

Communication between customer and supplier is nothing new, but, for small service companies like Custom Research—law firms, advertising agencies, and medical practices, to name a few—defining specific client requirements on paper and verifying their accuracy with the client are rarely done with any consistency. CRI does it every time; a *project design,* based on the client's expressed requirements, will then guide the project team's efforts.

Those requirements are translated into a more detailed project design by the account manager and project team. They prepare a *plan of action* that includes the research design, questionnaire design, data collection, data tabulation, statistical analysis, report, timetables, responsibilities, and cost estimate.

A critical element in the success of the research process is the design of the questionnaire. The project results are useful only if the client knows they accurately reflect what the target audience thinks and feels about the subject. Custom Research uses templates to ensure consistent design, then checks proposed questionnaires with computer-generated responses. "We've identified four to eight fatal flaws that can render the project useless," says partner Jeffrey Pope. "We have checkpoints that will reveal if any of these flaws are present."

Questionnaires are also pretested with a small sample of people to evaluate the effectiveness of the design—especially, whether the methodology can be implemented and whether the questions solicit the necessary information. Clients review proposed questionnaires and offer their suggestions. "We have a lot of checks and balances built into the design process," says partner Judith Corson, "such as having the client review the questionnaire, determining how to code any open-ended questions, and finding out what the client wants in the survey report."

When the data collection has been completed, CRI makes sure that the accumulated data are correct, then generates reports directly from those data, to avoid rekeying errors. The account manager presents the reports to the client and refers to the plan of action generated earlier to find out whether the reports and CRI's performance met customer requirements.

Every quarter, CRI's steering committee compares the company's performance with its clients' four key requirements. Account teams review performance on key accounts quarterly. This relentless drive to measure and analyze its performance, together with the company's constant communication with clients, has produced exceptional customer satisfaction. In CRI's fiscal year 1996, 97 percent of its projects met clients' requirements, and 73 percent exceeded those requirements.

Custom Research's experience offers three lessons for similar firms:

1. *Be explicit about what your clients expect.* "We've sat down purposefully and periodically with our clients to discuss their requirements. It's rare they don't tell us something we need to learn," says Pope.

2. *Measure customer satisfaction.* CRI sends a short questionnaire to every client on every project, asking about the client's overall level of satisfaction, and conducts a telephone survey of major clients.

3. *Tie internal measures to customer requirements.* CRI has established such internal measures as Project Quality Recap Reports. On each project, every team member documents problems or errors on questionnaires, data tables, reports, and timing. Similar companies (law firms, ad agencies, etc.) like to claim that what they do cannot be measured. Custom Research shows that it can. (For more discussion about this topic, see Chapters 5 and 14.)

THE SHIFT IN THINKING

In the new business management model, the design process has been commandeered from the hands of an elite corps of engineers and delegated to a host of internal experts. People from marketing, engineering, manufacturing, and other rapidly disintegrating silos come together during the design process to address every aspect of design, production, delivery, and service. They invite customers into their teams to better understand what customer requirements really are and how well their ideas are responding. They pull key suppliers into the process, to benefit from their special knowledge and to assess their capabilities. The new design process is *a freewheeling exchange of information and ideas* that has some very specific goals: meet or exceed customer requirements, design quality in, and get the new product or service to customers faster than before.

American Express Financial Advisors and Custom Research are achieving these goals by putting the responsibility for service design in the hands of the people who work with the clients. The advisor or project team uses information gathered directly from the client to shape the service. The design process is repeated for every client, and each plan is unique to that client. Compared to the traditional "one size fits all" mentality, the new design process is able to translate individual customer requirements into products and services that meet those requirements *exactly*.

This type of process is not limited to service companies. For example, in Japan, a cyclist in the market for a new bicycle can go to a local bike shop and get fitted for the exact bicycle the cyclist wants. More than 11 million variations on 18 different models are available. The National Bicycle Industrial Company can build any bike to a purchaser's requirements in three hours.

Meeting customer requirements. Improving quality. Reducing cycle time. In the new management model, the design process has the most critical role in achieving these goals.

12 PROCESS MANAGEMENT

Raytheon TI Systems

New England Mutual Life Insurance Company

Wainwright Industries

In the late 1980s, when the New England Mutual Life Insurance Company ("The New England") decided to look for a program that would help it improve quality, the company's focus was on providing full financial services. It thought of itself as a *full financial services company*. As its pursuit of quality led it to understand that quality is a business strategy, not a program, the company's focus changed. The New England is now a *customer-responsive company*.

The difference in focus is much more than a few words. As a full financial services company, The New England organized employees with similar skills into functional groups that produced, delivered, and supported its services. As a customer-responsive company, The New England organized employees around key processes that respond to customer requirements. One is vertical—the "silos" we discussed in the previous chapter. The other is horizontal—cutting across the vertical silos, as in The New England's case, or laying the silos on their sides, as American Express Financial Advisors has done.

This move from vertical to horizontal is an essential part of the new business management model. As The New England discovered, it is very difficult to serve external customers well when the company is organized to serve internal managers. The *customer driven* company has no choice:

It must look at itself from the customer's perspective, then reorganize to improve the processes that feed the customer's requirements.

In this chapter, we look at how three companies—Raytheon TI Systems, The New England, and Wainwright Industries—satisfy their customers through *process management*. In all three companies, process management and improvement is a cornerstone of their continuous improvement processes.

The New England fell in love with process improvement at first sight. "It was a no-brainer," says James Medeiros, vice president of quality commitment. "Process improvement fit into the strategy we were trying to shape, it was quick to install, and we got immediate results. I think process management is the key to the whole thing." Robert Shafto, the company's chairman and CEO, concurs. At a speech to the Canadian Life Insurance Association, Shafto identified seven key premises of The New England's quality improvement efforts, the first of which was: "All work is a process, and by definition, processes cut across vertical slices of the functional organization. To succeed in quality, an organization has to determine what are its core business processes that add value to customer satisfaction, and improve their effectiveness." Some have called this "process innovation," "core process redesign," or "reengineering." By whatever name, process management affects every person in a company and every task performed.

MODELS OF EXCELLENCE

Raytheon TI Systems (RTIS) designs and manufactures advanced defense systems and electronics technology for the U.S. Department of Defense. Formed during World War II, it has grown to become the country's eighth largest defense electronics contractor. Employing approximately 12,000 people, the company operates eight manufacturing, testing, research, and distribution facilities in north and central Texas. As Texas Instruments Defense Systems & Electronics Group, the organization won the Baldrige Award in 1992.

The New England has approximately $60 billion in assets under management. Founded in 1835, The New England was the nation's first chartered mutual life insurance company. It offers a broad array of insurance and investment products and services to individual and business customers through a national distribution network of 3,000 representatives. It also has thirteen regional Employee Benefit offices for sales and service of its group life, health, and pension product lines. The New England has approximately 2,600 associates at its Boston headquarters.

Wainwright Industries is the sole producer of piston inserts for automobile manufacturers. Wainwright also manufactures a broad range of high-volume, close-tolerance metal stampings and assemblies for automotive and nonautomotive customers. Located in St. Peters, Missouri, Wainwright is a privately held company with approximately 300 employees. It won the Baldrige Award in 1994, was honored as one of *Industry Week's* ten best plants in 1996, and received QS-9000 certification in 1997.

IDENTIFYING A PROCESS

Before examining how our three benchmarks manage and improve their processes, we need to be clear about basic terms and concepts. By definition, a process is a group of related tasks that yields a product or service to satisfy a customer. Demonstrated graphically, a process would look like Exhibit 12.1, the COPIS model. The acronym is in reverse order to emphasize how the model is customer driven: *Customers* → *Output* → *Process* → *Input* → *Suppliers*.

RTIS visualizes the process in another way (see Exhibit 12.2). It encourages all employees to implement this model in their jobs.

Unlike The New England, RTIS began working on process management after it was well into its quality improvement process. It was turned onto the concept when it completed its first Baldrige Award application. "We were cocky," Emery Powell, process strategy manager, remembers. "We thought we were different, that this didn't apply to us." They learned differently. "All the management practices now being recognized as best practices follow the same basic approach: identify what is important to the customer, identify your approach, and measure the results." That's process management, and although it may sound like a pretty common-sense

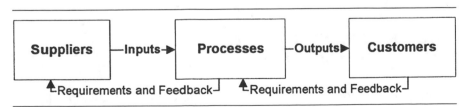

EXHIBIT 12.1.   The COPIS model: How processes satisfy customers.

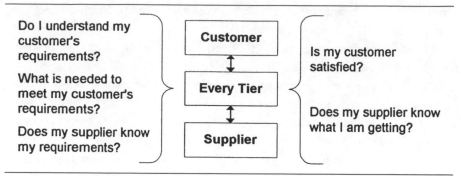

EXHIBIT 12.2.   The customer–supplier relationship at RTIS.

approach, it generates large amounts of resistance among businesses, functions, and individuals.

"It doesn't really matter what function it is: all functions resist change," says Powell. "All elements of a business resist change, which is why companies need to apply change management before process management." Based on RTIS's experience, Powell believes that the effort most companies go through to identify, map, benchmark, and plan improvements to their key processes is less than one-fourth of the effort required to dramatically improve a process. "It takes three or four times that effort to deploy the new approach," he says. "We found that it typically takes two to three years to be halfway deployed in an organization our size."

To help manage change, RTIS created a Black Belt Network of internal specialists in quality, cycle time, and cost reduction methodologies and techniques. The specialists are operational employees who have gotten their managers' commitment to make them experts in these areas.

RTIS also established Center for Excellence owners responsible for building improvement skills in their functional areas. "One of the lessons we've learned is, if you want to make significant improvement in these areas, you've got to dedicate resources to them," Powell says. "Another lesson is that it takes years of constant management attention to deploy a major change."

PROCESS IMPROVEMENT AT WAINWRIGHT INDUSTRIES

Management attention has never been lacking at Wainwright. The problem was, all the attention focused on financial results and not on the people and processes that produced those results. Once senior leaders decided to create an environment that reflected a "sincere trust and be-lief in people," their attention shifted from the results of their processes to the processes themselves.

It all begins with the vision and purpose of the company, what plant manager Mike Simms calls the "master goals." "We have established mas-ter goals which all processes flow toward," says Simms, "because until you get a master alignment, an understanding of what you're in business for, all the smaller processes fall apart."

These are Wainwright's master goals:

Safety first.

Employees second.

Customers third.

Quality is job four, not job one.

Net income last.

The order of Wainwright's goals affirms its "sincere trust and belief in people." "It's amazing how, with safety first, employees second, and net income last, the numbers keep going up," says Simms. As of July 1997, the company's St. Peters plant had gone 36 consecutive months without a workers' compensation claim. Customer service and quality have im-proved just as dramatically. Through process improvement, Wainwright cut the lead time for making one of its principal products—drawn hous-ings for electric motors—to 15 minutes from the previous 8.75 days, and reduced defect rates tenfold. For customers, the benefits translated into an on-time delivery rate of nearly 100 percent (compared with 75 percent previously) and a 35 percent reduction in product cost. Sales rose from $20 million in 1990 to $28 million in 1995.

As a Baldrige Award winner, Wainwright holds regular workshops for people who want to learn more about the company. To illustrate the criti-cal need for "master goals," presenters refer to the 1997 floods in Grand Forks, North Dakota. "What you saw in all the reports on the floods were natural work teams—sandbaggers—focused on two visual goals that gov-erned all their work: the level of the water and the level of the sandbags," says Simms. "Now what happens if you bring in a performance appraisal process and start grading people on the number of sandbags filled? The process falls apart because you've shifted from the common goals to 'how many sandbags I can fill.'"

Wainwright avoids this problem by keeping all processes focused on its master goals. Mission Control and its customer satisfaction indexes trigger process improvements.

Mission Control is a conference room at the company's St. Peters facility that displays quality and performance charts and graphs for each customer, monthly satisfaction index scores, stretch targets, and weekly customer feedback reports. All indicators link to the company's master goals. Every customer has a "champion." Within 48 hours of a customer's complaining or expressing a concern, the champion will form a team of people who are most knowledgeable about the customer and/or the process. Depending on the size of the issue, the team takes quick corrective action or initiates a more significant process change effort. The team lets the customer know what's happening throughout the improvement process.

All key processes at Wainwright have been mapped, and the requirements for each have been identified. All employees have been trained in root cause analysis, the tool used to evaluate and improve key processes.

Trends in external and internal customer satisfaction indexes often spawn process improvements. For example, the internal index showed dissatisfaction with the payroll process. The human resources manager championed a process improvement team that dramatically improved the payroll process.

Wainwright looks at process improvement as two separate vehicles: one is part of everyone's daily job and the other is the more formal team activity. Wainwright manages its process through standard control methods, such as statistical process control, and through the strong desire of its people to improve. The company *currently averages 1.5 implemented improvements per employee per week*—an amazing number when you consider that most American companies average one improvement per employee per year.

Through its effort to improve processes and the insights of its employees, Wainwright is working cheaper, faster, and better in pursuit of its master goals.

CHEAPER-FASTER-BETTER AT RAYTHEON TI SYSTEMS

In 1992, the focus of process improvement for RTIS was quality—specifically, achieving Six-Sigma. The company then turned its attention to cycle time and to cost reduction, before realizing that all three elements are integrated. "You can't do one exclusive of the others or you suboptimize the system," says Emery Powell. "You have to look at how to reduce cycle time, improve products, and reduce costs, and you have to look at all three as objectives."

Six-Sigma is a process for improving processes. *Sigma* is the measure of a process's capability to perform *defect-free work.* The sigma value indicates how often defects are likely to occur. The higher the sigma value, the less likely a process is defective. RTIS's goal is to achieve Six-Sigma quality, which roughly translates into no more than 3.4 defects per million opportunities. The group's approach to process improvement is based on six steps to Six-Sigma:

1. Identify the product you create or the service you provide. *What do you do?*
2. Identify the customers for your product or service, and determine what they consider important. *For whom do you do your work?*
3. Identify your needs to provide a product/service that will satisfy the customer. *What do you need to do your work?*
4. Define the process for doing the work. *How do you do your work or process?*
5. Make the process mistake-proof, and eliminate wasted effort. *How can you do your work better?*
6. Ensure continuous improvement by measuring, analyzing, and controlling the improved process. *How perfectly are you doing your customer-focused work?*

The purpose of this process is to help employees define, measure, control, and improve their processes. However, even after a process has been improved, it is still subject to significant variations known as "out-of-control occurrences." To bring the process back into control, RTIS applies a process called the *QC Story.* Companies worldwide use this eight-step process to identify the root cause of a problem and implement improvements. The process is:

1. Select the problem.
2. Understand the current situation.
3. Identify the root cause.
4. Plan improvement.
5. Execute improvement.
6. Confirm results.
7. Standardize the improvement.
8. Study remaining problems/make future plans.

RTIS applied the six steps to Six-Sigma and the QC Story to its major processes and subprocesses. In 1995, changes in the industry demanded that RTIS rethink its business strategies, including the role of quality improvement. The result was a business model built around three key strategies: customer, process, and people. The new model is shown in Exhibit 12.3. "The customer strategy defined for us where we need to go. The process strategy defined what we need to do to get there. The people strategy defined how we use our people to do the work," Powell says. "When you address all three, they give you a pretty complete business strategy."

RTIS then broke the process strategy into two elements: managing the processes and executing the processes.

Before it could manage the processes, RTIS had to identify which processes were most important to: (1) provide its customers with competitive (cheaper, faster, better) advantage; and (2) provide RTIS with competitive advantage. "We identified a set of processes we're going to invest in to provide us with competitive advantage for the next five years, including such processes as our process focus, easy access to information, and our integrated design and manufacturing capability," says Powell.

The second element involves managing to the process. "If we're going to have a competitive advantage, we need a process that delivers a solution

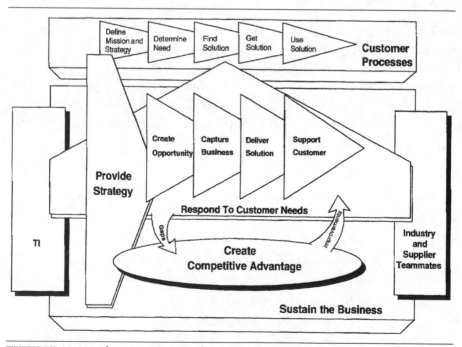

EXHIBIT 12.3.   The systems group business process map.

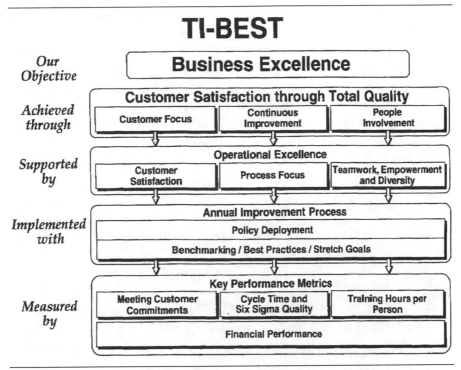

TI-BEST

Our Objective	**Business Excellence**	
Achieved through	**Customer Satisfaction through Total Quality**	
	Customer Focus	Continuous Improvement	People Involvement
Supported by	**Operational Excellence**	
	Customer Satisfaction	Process Focus	Teamwork, Empowerment and Diversity
Implemented with	**Annual Improvement Process**	
	Policy Deployment	
	Benchmarking / Best Practices / Stretch Goals	
Measured by	**Key Performance Metrics**	
	Meeting Customer Commitments	Cycle Time and Six Sigma Quality	Training Hours per Person
	Financial Performance	

EXHIBIT 12.4.   The TI-Best system.

to the customer," says Powell. "We told our operational managers that we're going to measure their performance by how well they execute the process to its full capabilities."

RTIS also initiated an annual process (called TI Best) to define what constitutes business excellence. The performance of its processes is compared to that standard. Exhibit 12.4 shows how RTIS's customer, process, and people strategies are cascaded throughout the organization. "It's a rigorous process," says Powell, "that starts with the leadership team. We look at your objectives, how well you are doing, and your improvement plans. It all comes down to the same basic, fundamental idea: You've got to get started, understand where you are, do something to improve, and assess your progress." In a nutshell, that's process management.

IMPROVING PROCESSES AT THE NEW ENGLAND

One of The New England's first steps was to identify its core processes. At the same time, the company trained 75 associates in a nine-step process analysis technique methodology and gave all 2,650 associates four days of quality core training.

The New England uses two types of teams to improve its processes: *process analysis teams* (PATs) and *quality improvement teams* (QITs). PATs address *horizontal* processes, core processes, or *subprocesses* that cut across divisional and departmental boundaries. It calls these "value-adding delivery chains." QITs primarily focus on subprocesses within one of these chains and on tasks typically performed within a specific division or department. Exhibit 12.5 shows how PATs and QITs interrelate.

Process Analysis Teams

Process analysis teams use a nine-step process divided into three phases:

A. *Commitment*
   1. Decide to form a PAT.
   2. Identify the boundaries of the process.
   3. Write a document stating objectives, methodology, and schedule.
B. *Information Gathering*
   4. Understand the existing flow of work activities.
   5. Meet to share information.
   6. Interview task experts throughout the process.
C. *Analysis and Implementation of Revisions*
   7. Analyze the existing process and look for improvement opportunities.

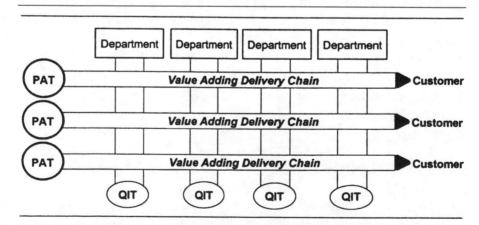

EXHIBIT 12.5.   The New England's quality improvement process.

8. Test the revised process.

9. Decide to implement.

The process can take anywhere from 8 to 20 weeks, depending on the complexity of the analysis. For its first PATs, The New England turned to the core process map it had developed, and chose two areas primarily because the managers of those areas recognized the value of process analysis. One of the areas was New Business, the core process that involves responding to applications for insurance. The cross-functional New Business PAT included 11 associates. Its major objective was to improve agent satisfaction with the New Business process.

The team had its work cut out for it. Agents—the primary customers of the process—had been complaining that New Business was not easily dealt with and that the process was taking at least two or three weeks longer than it should. New Business had valid reasons for this, but, as John Small, senior vice president in charge of New Business, points out, "The bottom line was, 'So what'; our customers were not happy!"

Before forming the PAT, Small and his staff studied the problem. First, they considered that the problem might be in the customers' minds, but realized that too many complaints were coming from too many people, both external and internal. Next, they wondered whether the problem might be with New Business personnel, but more than 30 of its people had won the company's Extra Mile Award for extraordinary service, and the field claimed that the personnel were holding the place together. They then turned their attention to the New Business process. At this point, the PAT took over.

"We started saying we should do a New Business PAT," says Maura Howe, senior issue consultant and a member of the PAT. "It took us about a week to decide it should be broken down." From this initial experience, The New England learned to narrow the scope of its PATs. "For the first PAT, you should pick something critical to the company, then get buy-in from the CEO and other leaders," says Scott Andrews, quality commitment consultant. "Start small, though, not with sixteen processes."

The New Business PAT used the quality improvement model shown in Exhibit 12.5 to identify regions as the vertical "departments" and Large Amount, Regional Underwriting, Fast Track, and Pension Issue as the horizontal "value adding delivery chains." It then identified the points where the process broke down and established goals, measures, and actions for those points. Maureen Leydon, second vice president of New Business Services, describes the results of a PAT recommendation to put the variable life product on Fast Track. (Fast Track is a process by which an application that meets certain criteria can be approved within 96 hours of receipt.) "We couldn't do that because we needed a registered signature approving the application, which usually meant a senior vice president—and they weren't always available. The PAT said someone *should* be available. The solution was to register one of our Fast Track underwriters—and now the product is on Fast Track."

The PAT completed its work in five months. New Business continues to implement the team's recommendations. Major achievements to date include:

- *Fast-track processing.* Percentage of qualifying cases improved from 14 percent to 22 percent, with a goal of 30 percent.
- *Nonfast-track processing.* Percentage of successful laboratory tests matching on the first try increased from 50 percent to better than 70 percent.
- *Large amount processing.* Average speed of processing time improved by more than 20 percent.

"What the PATs have done best is crystallize the process by mapping it out," says Scott McInturff, second vice president and actuary, "and they have required managers to change their approach to one of management, not decision making. Managers don't make all the decisions, as they did in the past. Now it's the associates who make decisions, and the managers facilitate that process. We manage the process, and associates are responsible for the results. Our role now is to set expectations for such things as deliverables and dates, meet with the associates to make sure they are clear about the expectations, then hold people to them."

Quality Improvement Teams

The New England also uses quality improvement teams to manage and improve its smaller department-level processes. In the case of New Business, the PAT recommendations led to the creation of 21 QITs.

QITs follow a process that is similar to the PATs. For example, in July 1991, Michael Bachand, second vice president of office services and printing, formed an Image Scanner and Output QIT to address a problem with his department's image-scanning process. "They initially spent a lot of time on discovery and getting buy-in before looking at the whole process," says Bachand. "Everybody on the team was apprehensive going in, but now they're very proud of their finished document." The document is a 19-page report that traces the process the team followed: identifying the problems; deciding on the methodology to use to arrive at its recommendations; the recommendations and action plan. The document reflects the team's understanding and use of statistical tools:

- A fishbone diagram shows the problems that were identified.
- A Gantt chart shows who was responsible for what activity and when.
- A process map defines the interdependent components of the image-scanning process.

Bachand and his staff began implementing the recommendations and action plan at the end of 1992.

As The New England's PATs and QITs have touched more and more of the company's processes, functions, and tasks, the company has moved from a vertical organization focused on satisfying the boss to horizontal process management focused on satisfying the customer.

THE SHIFT IN THINKING

A customer-driven company must be organized around the *core processes that meet customer requirements*. As our role models show, such an organization depends on:

- Understanding customer requirements.
- Defining the processes that serve those requirements.
- Identifying process owners and teams.
- Mapping the process.
- Establishing measures.
- Bringing the process under control.
- Developing and implementing a plan to improve the process.

The new business management model demands *process-oriented thinking*. It forces companies to ask what their processes are for understanding customer requirements, communicating customer and quality requirements throughout the organization, determining and tracking key measures, strategic planning, involving employees, managing processes, measuring and improving customer satisfaction, and all other key elements that define the company's "work."

How do you do what you do? What's the process? The new model asks these questions relentlessly. In our experience, only those companies that think in terms of processes and that have identified and sought to improve their processes are capable of providing answers.

Such a shift in thinking ripples throughout the organization. Because all work is part of at least one process, a process orientation changes how people think of their work. Employees need to be trained in this new model. They need to learn the team and problem-solving skills required to manage and improve their processes. Leadership must empower them to apply their new skills and align the reward and recognition programs to support their efforts. Leadership must also direct their efforts, using its vision of the company's future to prioritize the company's process improvement initiatives.

Finally, the company must understand its customers' requirements. Core processes aim at the bull's-eye of customer satisfaction and operational performance, or what Wainwright calls "master goals." Remove the bull's-eye, and process management becomes a hit-or-miss proposition.

13 SUPPLIER QUALITY

Bose Corporation

Sprint

Ames Rubber Corporation

A critical part of process management is *managing the handoffs,* those points at which a person, team, or department completes its work and passes it along to the next unit. Companies seek fewer, faster, defect-free handoffs, from supplier to customer or until the process is complete. As the previous chapter concluded, such handoffs must first be identified, then refined relentlessly to improve quality.

This chapter is also about supplier-to-customer handoffs, except that the suppliers we are talking about are external. The good news is that identifying the handoffs is much easier because they exist wherever an outside vendor provides a product or service. The bad news is that improving the handoffs—as well as the quality of the products and services being provided—is often more difficult because you are dealing with another company.

High-performance companies attack this problem by blurring the lines between supplier and customer. Bose Corporation brings supplier representatives right into its plants and empowers them to act as buyers for Bose. Sprint provides its key suppliers with well-defined, written requirements and monthly operations reviews. Ames forms close partnerships with its key suppliers that are characterized by open, honest relationships. As discussed in earlier chapters, quality leaders rely on training, recognition, teamwork, and empowerment to dramatically improve quality and performance. The role models in this chapter show that such initiatives are equally effective with suppliers.

The importance of improving supplier quality and performance grows as companies pare down to their core competencies. Companies that want to be lean and nimble in ever-flatter organizations strive to do only what they do best and to outsource the rest, without sacrificing quality, schedule, or cost. This is possible only when a company abandons its adversarial relationship with suppliers and establishes long-term partnerships. We will describe how three successful companies are doing just that.

We invite those who cannot shake their preoccupation with price to consider how improving supplier quality inevitably leads to lower prices— or to steady prices for higher-quality goods. "Our goal is to drive costs down every year," says Lance Dixon, executive director of Bose's Just in Time (JIT) II Education & Research Center.

To find out how Bose, Sprint, and Ames improve supplier quality and performance, we will address two questions:

1. How do you define your requirements, communicate those requirements to your suppliers, and make sure they are being met?
2. How do you improve your purchasing/supplier processes?

This chapter focuses on the relationship between a company and those who supply it with products and services. All companies have such relationships; however, some companies have other relationships that could be classified as supplier relationships, including those with distributors, dealers, contractors, franchises, and strategic allies. They can be thought of as suppliers because they supply goods and services during some stage of production, delivery, and use of a company's products and services. We have chosen not to address issues specific to these types of suppliers because a narrower range of companies is affected by them and because the general ideas and strategies presented in this chapter apply equally well to all types of suppliers.

MODELS OF EXCELLENCE

Bose Corporation designs and manufactures high-quality audio products for home and commercial use. Founded in 1964, the company has more than 3,500 employees at manufacturing locations in Massachusetts, Arizona, South Carolina, and Michigan, and in Canada, Mexico, and Ireland. It has approximately 450 suppliers. The concept of JIT II, described later in this chapter, originated with Bose, which created the JIT II Education & Research Center to help companies learn about and apply the concept.

Sprint is a global communications company and the world's largest carrier of Internet traffic. Sprint built and operates the only nationwide, all-digital, fiber-optic network in the United States, and is the leader in advanced data communications services. The company services more than 16 million business and residential customers.

Ames Rubber Corporation produces elastomeric products, primarily elastomeric rollers used in office machines such as copiers, printers, and typewriters. All of its products are made to order to customers' design specifications. The company, which was founded in 1949, is located in Hamburg, New Jersey. It has more than 400 employees. Ames won the Baldrige Award in 1993.

TELLING SUPPLIERS WHAT YOU WANT—AND GETTING IT

Sprint buys products and services from thousands of suppliers. For this chapter, we're going to focus on suppliers of internal services to employees, such as travel, forms and records management, and printing services. These suppliers are managed by the Business Resources department, and it's no small task: Sprint spends $50 million each year on air fares alone.

Business Resources oversees many small suppliers, but it focuses the majority of its attention on key suppliers of travel services, warehousing and distribution, and records management. To choose key suppliers, Business Resources follows a rigorous process that includes these steps:

1. Involve key user groups in establishing requirements.
2. Identify companies that could handle the scope and volume of work.
3. Gather information about the candidates (through trade publications, Internet sites, and so on).
4. Request general information from potential suppliers.
5. Narrow the list to about a half-dozen candidates.
6. Initiate a formal RFP process.
7. Using matrix management, narrow the list to two finalists (matrix management involves identifying key criteria, assigning a value to each, then scoring each candidate for each category, to arrive at a total score).

8. Invite the finalists to give face-to-face presentations.
9. Choose a supplier.

Once a supplier is selected, Sprint specifies what it expects. "We don't necessarily provide our service requirements in the RFP," says Margie Linck, director of Business Resources, "but we ask the suppliers what they provide, then negotiate those requirements. Once we've chosen a supplier, the requirements are extremely well-defined, and they're written so there's no misinterpretation."

To communicate performance to requirements, Linck has monthly operations reviews with the three key suppliers. "We look at how we're doing on service and customer perception based on phone statistics, error rates, and customer surveys and feedback," she says. "We have very specific performance requirements that the supplier has to meet."

At Ames, specific requirements are given: "We're a job shop," says Ed DiPetrillo, Ames's purchasing manager. "We're always building to somebody's blueprints." In addition to the job specifications, Ames measures suppliers on quality and delivery. "We have a department goal for where we want suppliers to be by category, such as metal and components and raw materials. The goal is to hit 99 percent, a single number that is 60 percent quality and 40 percent delivery."

Ames tracks supplier performance on quality and delivery and sends the tracking data to suppliers monthly. It relies on suppliers to give their best price. Ames has benchmarked pricing to get an idea of what the market is charging, but it doesn't play one supplier off another just to get the lowest price. "We are a very open, honest company," says DiPetrillo. "We treat people the way we want to be treated. By having that open relationship, we expect to get their best price."

Ames has built such relationships with 18 key suppliers, down from 42 in 1990. The company made a deliberate effort to slim down its key supplier base in order to:

- Increase its clout (major customers get more attention than the rest of the pack).
- Simplify the interaction ("It's easier to deal with one person versus ten," says DiPetrillo).
- Reduce costs (as volumes go up, prices go down).
- Build partnerships.

"We take partnering very seriously," says DiPetrillo. "We're running a major project right now that I've involved two of our key suppliers in.

They came into the project at its inception. The agreement was that we would split the business evenly between the two. They both know of each other and they've both been in the same meeting. They know what we know. No secrets."

Companies that want to develop partnering relationships with key suppliers often fear that proprietary information will be compromised. In the next section, we will describe how Bose is dismissing that fear through its JIT II concept. However, even companies that do not implement JIT II are able to build partnerships with their suppliers if, as Ames has shown, they are open and honest.

Openness and honesty do not exist automatically. Partnerships between companies take time to develop, and customers must be careful about whom they select to partner with and what the boundaries of that relationship are.

Ames is able to build these relationships because of its culture and because of the technical knowledge of its purchasing department. "One of the unique things about our department is that we are staffed by technical people. I was a machinist and I'm a certified quality engineer. When you have that background, it's very easy to talk to machine shops. We've even set up statistical process control programs for them from the purchasing department. Our suppliers tell us they like to call purchasing and get answers rather than getting referred to other departments," says DiPetrillo.

By involving suppliers in projects at their inception and bringing technical expertise to the purchasing department, Ames improves communication between the company and its key suppliers. That is also one of the great benefits of JIT II.

BRINGING SUPPLIERS IN-HOUSE

One of the leaders in redefining supplier partnerships is Bose Corporation. In 1987, Bose began using a concept it called *JIT II*. "For eons there have been sellers selling and buyers buying, and it's basically been adversarial. For me to win, I had to pull on my end of the rope," says Lance Dixon, executive director of Bose's JIT II Education & Research Center. "We determined that we had sellers selling to us and they weren't really selling; we had been sold on their companies for years. And we had buyers who weren't really buying. I knew there had to be a better way to do this."

Dixon's better way was to have representatives of key suppliers work full-time in Bose's facilities. The representatives operate at the buyer level and are empowered to use Bose's purchase orders to place orders at their own companies. They are invited to attend any design engineering meetings involving their companies' product area, with full access to Bose's facilities, personnel, and data. JIT II eliminates the buyer and salesperson. The in-plant representative becomes the link between Bose's planning department and the supplier's production plant. Dixon calls it "insourcing."

The only limitations on these in-plant representatives are the same limitations placed on Bose's own buyers. They place orders for standard cost items whose price has already been calculated, and each representative has a purchase limit. Orders above that limit require a signature from a purchasing supervisor. As Dixon points out, "The normal controls that the typical purchasing systems and purchasing manager place on a buyer function quite well."

Bose is currently using JIT II with nine suppliers. These suppliers provide twelve in-plant employees and are responsible for 30 percent of Bose's outside purchases and 65 percent of its transportation expenses. Bose implements only one JIT II supplier per commodity, although it continues to have competing suppliers in the same commodity. The indicators that suggest a supplier may be a candidate for JIT II status are:

- General supplier excellence: the best in a given commodity.
- Dollar volume over $1 million.
- Good quality already being achieved.
- Good delivery record.
- A substantial number of purchase order transactions.
- Evolving technology, but not at a revolutionary pace.
- Good cost levels already being achieved.
- Operations in a Bose area that does not involve key trade secrets or sensitive technologies.
- Good engineering support already being provided.

Both Bose and the supplier receive incentives for beginning a JIT II relationship. The participating supplier's business with Bose typically increases by 35 to 45 percent, and Bose's savings in overhead alone are about $1 million a year. For example, when Bose moved from a JIT relationship to a JIT II relationship with one supplier, it reduced inventories to one-eighth of the already low levels achieved through JIT.

The key to making JIT II work is the in-plant representative. As part of Bose's system, the rep spends much of the time getting information, analyzing and critiquing Bose's plans, and working with Bose's engineers on product development. Dixon calls the reps "a living, breathing standards program," because they are constantly pushing standard parts and processes with the design engineers.

"You want engineers to design state-of-the-art, innovative, exciting products using routine, standardized parts, which goes against human nature. The idea of calling in suppliers to contribute to concurrent engineering also goes against human nature, because engineers get busy, they move fast, and sometimes they don't take the time to talk to outside people. And if you bring in the suppliers too late, it's not concurrent engineering. Now imagine a dozen people, all experts in their given commodities, roaming engineering and offering their assistance." As an example, Dixon points to one in-house supplier that Bose asked to evaluate the design for a speaker-enclosure. The supplier suggested a resin change that saved Bose $50,000 annually.

After Bose established its in-plant representatives, it discovered that they improved not only purchasing, but also planning, engineering, importing, and transportation. For example, Bose's three JIT II transportation suppliers give it access to their computer systems controlling material movement. For 98 percent of manufacturers, material en route to their factories is considered material in the pipeline. Bose considers it inventory, because it can track that material anywhere in the world. As Dixon says, "When material flowing toward Bose from locations offshore can be located and routinely accessed, the material functions as inventory, just as effectively as such inventory in our plant or warehouse."

At the other end of the pipeline, suppliers who used to keep secret piles of buffer inventory have gotten rid of it because their in-plant representatives know exactly what is needed, when.

Bose's success with JIT II has generated a great deal of interest. Most of its suppliers use it in their marketing with other customers. Companies such as Honeywell, Intel, Ford, AT&T Bell Labs, and DuPont have already implemented it with key suppliers. Bose estimates that more than 150 companies are now using JIT II. The academic community, including Harvard and MIT, are using Bose as a case study. Professional societies have endorsed JIT II as a leap ahead in customer–supplier relationships.

Companies that take the leap can look forward to a host of benefits, as outlined by Dixon in *JIT II: Revolution in Buying & Sellling* (coauthored with Anne Millen Porter; Cahners Publishing Co., 1994). Benefits for the customer include:

- Direct and indirect cost reduction.
- Inventory reduction.

- Improved human resource utilization.
- Improved purchasing support to internal customers.
- Concurrent planning with suppliers.
- Improved information management and communication.
- Improved purchase order placement.
- Concurrent engineering at the earliest stages of design.
- Perpetual value analysis.
- An ongoing standards program.
- Enhanced control over inbound and outbound freight.

Benefits for the supplier, as described by Dixon in an article in *Purchasing* magazine, include:

- It eliminates the sales effort (although the cost is offset by having a full-time person at the customer's location).
- Communication and purchase order placement improve dramatically.
- The volume of business increases at the start of the program and is ongoing as the in-plant person gets involved with new products.
- The agreement is an evergreen contract—no end date and no bidding.
- The supplier can sell directly to engineering.
- Efficient invoicing and payment administration are achieved.
- On-site personnel have a dual career path: They can advance in their own company or at Bose after one year.

Dixon and his colleagues continue to expand the JIT II concept, which Bose has trademarked. The current focus is on logistics. "We've built a command center tying together the computer systems of all key suppliers to create a functional inventory," Dixon says. "It's on trucks. It's in containers. We can pick off material as we need it for tight inventory deadlines. Managers at Bose have the authority to divert shipments to their lines in a timely fashion. We can now get material on our assembly line from anywhere in the world in 26 hours."

IMPROVING BOTH ENDS OF THE CUSTOMER–SUPPLIER PIPE

Bose's in-plant supplier representatives do not blur the lines between customer and supplier; they obliterate them, setting aside "the pipe" in favor of working side-by-side on issues of mutual interest. They redefine customer–supplier partnerships by the levels of trust, cooperation, and empowerment both sides need and expect. As the widespread interest in JIT II suggests, many high-performance companies recognize it as another step in the unavoidable progression from adversarial relationships to partnerships.

However, most suppliers will not qualify for JIT II status. Bose has only nine out of hundreds of suppliers, and purchases 70 percent of its materials from non-JIT II suppliers. For these suppliers, "the pipe" still exists, and quality leaders are working just as hard to improve their own procurement activities as they are to improve supplier performance.

For example, Sprint's Business Resources department has created what it calls a "360 questionnaire," a one-page document given to internal customers and suppliers to grade performance on everything from quality to ordering, distribution, and communication. "The supplier provides information back to us to tell us how we did and we do the same for them," says Margie Linck. "We've pulled the results together in a database by category so we can identify gaps."

Linck also decided to lead a joint process improvement effort with the company's travel services supplier. "If we don't improve our processes," she says, "we never get out of firefighting."

Ames is currently evaluating ways to expand its supplier certification program, which it has been piloting for the past year. "We have to build a database to see how our suppliers are doing," says DiPetrillo. "Once the process settles, we'll be able to identify candidates for 'dock-to-stock' status."

Another way companies improve the customer–supplier relationship is by including suppliers in internal activities. Ames has an internal recognition called "Atta Boys," which are heartfelt thank-you's for exceptional performance. Ames extended the recognition to suppliers in the form of an award or certificate that may be given by nonpurchasing people (the source of recognition suppliers covet most).

Ames also includes suppliers in its seminars; local suppliers are called to see whether they're interested in attending. The company has conducted formal quality seminars in the past, but has not done so recently because the key supplier group has not changed.

In the summer of 1997, Sprint Business Resources organized its first workshop for its three key suppliers and others, such as its car rental supplier and preferred airline. The focus of the workshop was on improving relationships, quality, managing to the data, strategic thinking, and process management.

THE SHIFT IN THINKING

One of the characteristics of the new business management model is its *universality.* Strategic planning guides and permeates all activities; continuous improvement in any area depends on employee involvement; process management techniques work for any type of process; employee satisfaction is linked to customer satisfaction. The basics of improving quality and performance remain the same, regardless of the issue or people involved.

On a macro level, your company's management model whirs and buzzes and spits out products and services through the ongoing efforts of employees, customers, and suppliers alike. Poor connections between or within these groups sabotage the system and impede improvement.

On a micro level, the attributes of personal quality—treating people as you want to be treated, taking responsibility, improving yourself, sharing your knowledge, having a positive outlook, and communicating effectively—apply whether you are dealing with other employees, customers, or suppliers. You cannot succeed with one set of values for customers, another for employees, and yet another for suppliers. Your values for all people in and affected by your company must be consistent, or the disparity, like poor connections, will sabotage the system.

Suppliers have borne the brunt of any disparity, but, as our role models show, that disparity is waning. The lines between customer and supplier are blurring as companies get horizontal; their focus on core competencies elevates suppliers' roles and importance. The very term *partnership* implies equality, the sharing of risks and rewards, a focus on mutual goals. You cannot create an adversarial partnership.

That is a shift in thinking, in the same way that high-performance companies are shifting their thinking about their employees. Suppliers, like employees, are not commodities to be handled as you please. They are not children to be bribed, chastised, threatened, and punished. They are *partners in a joint venture,* members of a bigger system, allies armed with technology, knowledge, and insight your company can use to improve.

Like your company, your suppliers must be on the leading edge of their businesses to compete, and you can benefit from that. Like your company, they read books such as this to learn more about improving their systems and their relationships with their customers. Like your company, they are committed to continuous improvement and are aggressive about meeting and exceeding their customers' expectations. In fact, your best suppliers are so much like your company, they tend to make excellent partners.

14 DATA COLLECTION AND ANALYSIS

Carrier

Kennametal-Solon

AMP

CIT Commercial Services

In the first chapter, we talked about the tse-tse fly's inability to "see" zebras. If we were tse-tse flies and we wanted to avoid being trampled, we would need to find a way to get that information to our brains. Special glasses, maybe. Spray paint the zebras. Hire another bug as our "seeing eye fly."

The same idea holds true for our businesses. With "zebras" running wild in our processes, we must find a way to "see" them, to get the information we need to identify problems, take action, and measure results. That is why we collect and analyze data.

The "brain center" of the new management model is a comprehensive data and tracking system that produces actionable data that are easily accessible to those who can use the data to improve. High-performance companies understand that they can manage only what they can measure—and that is as true for such areas as marketing, administration, and legal as it is for manufacturing. As Fred Smith, chairman and chief executive officer for FedEx, said, "We believe that service quality must be mathematically measured." The better the measurement system, the better the quality.

This chapter's role models use excellent measurement systems to acquire company-level data, which they then use to:

- Translate customers' requirements into process parameters.
- Monitor key processes.
- Identify problems.
- Analyze trends.
- Observe the impact of improvements.
- Delight customers.

From the perspective of our new management model, *the measurement system helps them align and integrate their quality systems.* As Joseph M. Juran wrote, "Once we have established a system of measurement, we have a common language or metric. We can use that language to help us at each and every step."

But first we need to understand the steps to establishing an effective measurement system. We will use the experiences of Carrier, Kennametal-Solon, AMP, and CIT Commercial Services to address these questions:

- How do you know what data and information to collect?
- How do you know they are accurate, reliable, and useful?
- How do you aggregate and analyze these data to improve customer satisfaction, quality, and operational performance?
- How do you institutionalize your new measurement system?

MODELS OF EXCELLENCE

Carrier is the world's leader in heating and air-conditioning products. The company's founder, Willis Carrier, started an industry when he invented an "apparatus for treating air" in 1902. Carrier is a subsidiary of United Technologies and is headquartered in Farmington, Connecticut. The company has 28,000 employees and maintains manufacturing operations in 17 countries.

Kennametal's Solon, Ohio, plant manufactures high-quality tool holders for customers who machine metal. Nearly 500 employees work at a state-of-the-art facility Kennametal built in 1988. The new plant combined two existing operations (neither of which was doing very well) into one facility organized into manufacturing cells that are run by *self-managed work teams.* This team approach has produced significant improvements in on-time delivery, cost reductions, and shorter lead times.

AMP is the world's largest producer of electrical and electronic connecting devices. Its headquarters are in Harrisburg, Pennsylvania. AMP has more than 46,000 employees in close to 50 countries. It has had several years' experience with collecting measures and aggregating them on its Quality and Delivery Scorecards.

CIT Commercial Services, a wholly owned subsidiary of CIT Group Holdings Inc., specializes in credit protection, asset-based loans, and bookkeeping and collection services, and is one of the world's largest factory companies. Its 700 employees are located at its New York City headquarters and at offices in Charlotte, Los Angeles, Miami, Dallas, and Hong Kong. An operations center is located in Danville, Virginia.

DETERMINING WHAT DATA AND INFORMATION TO COLLECT

A company's measurement system, like its entire management system, must be driven by its customers. As you determine your customers' requirements (see Chapter 3) and decide how you will meet those requirements (Chapters 4–13), you will want to construct a measurement system that aligns all activities with improving customer satisfaction.

One of the most popular approaches to measurement system construction is the Balanced Scorecard. Conceived by Robert Kaplan and David Norton, the Balanced Scorecard is a measurement system to guide current performance and target future performance. As coauthors Kaplan and Norton write in their book, *The Balanced Scorecard* (Harvard Business School Press, 1996), "The Balanced Scorecard translates an organization's mission and strategy into a comprehensive set of performance measures that provides the framework for a strategic measurement and management system."

Larry Marsiello, president and CEO of CIT Commercial Services, learned about the Balanced Scorecard from Kaplan during an advanced management program at the Harvard Business School. His senior people discussed the concept in 1992, but the approach was put on hold while CIT acquired a company and consolidated operations. CIT Commercial Services then turned its attention to how it would improve performance.

"We had employee surveys that showed improvement, but it wasn't what we had hoped to see," says Marsiello. "We were disappointed because we had invested a great deal of effort. I thought the Balanced Scorecard was the most pervasive because it touched on the alignment of people, value for the client, and improved profits."

The first step was to create a sense of urgency, which Marsiello says "came from our concern about a nontraditional competitor appearing in the market and that improvements were dwindling even though the efforts of senior management were rising."

The next step involved achieving consensus among senior management about the vision, mission, and key strategies of the company. "I thought we were a very tight management group, but we ended up spending three or four days over a two-month period coming to agreement," says Marsiello. "Are we a market driven or product driven company? That decision in and of itself gave us direction."

Once agreement among senior managers was reached, the company translated the mission and vision into 22 strategic performance measures in four categories (or "buckets" in Balanced Scorecard-ese):

1. Market drivers and outcomes.
2. Employee drivers and outcomes.
3. Process outcomes.
4. Financial outcomes.

With these categories and measures in place, the company identified 50 to 60 "agents of change" who would take the vision, mission, and strategic performance measures and build functional linkages between them and daily operations. The change agents led the charge to identify measures within their functions and across functions with both short- and long-term goals. Alignment was gained in two ways: through review by senior managers and through interfunctional meetings.

"Our strategic performance measurement system is not a quantitative game where everything is measured," says Marsiello. "It's very important not to fall in love with the idea of measuring for measurement's sake. The heart of the issue is the degree of learning that takes place and changing behaviors."

Historically, service companies have had weak measurement systems, that focused almost exclusively on financial indicators. As Marsiello says, "Financial services companies have always had well-developed financial measures. The issue is how can we develop other sets of measures that tell us how employees and clients are doing." Even manufacturing companies with strong production metrics have failed to measure nonmanufacturing processes. The problem is not that these processes cannot be measured, but that people have not tried to measure them. As Patrick Mene, corporate director of quality for Baldrige Award-winner Ritz-Carlton, said,

"People who haven't measured, haven't even tried. They're making excuses." (For more about what Ritz-Carlton measured, see Chapter 5.)

When Kennametal's Solon plant got serious about measuring, it actually created the opposite problem: The plant started with too many measures. It got rid of irrelevant measures by focusing on customers' requirements and expectations. The Solon facility now has approximately 50 key performance indicators (KPIs) in use throughout the operation, including support functions such as human resources.

Business unit teams select their own measures. A coordinator keeps track of all the measures and works with the teams on identifying, establishing, and tracking them. Every measure must have a goal. "Measuring without a goal doesn't accomplish anything," says Paul Cahan, former plant manager and director of global steel operations. "Through the use of measures and realistic goals, you can improve performance."

Like Kennametal-Solon, Carrier has its business units use measurement to identify and solve problems. "The kind of reporting I see is each business unit identifies its top five problems, where they are in solving them, implementing action, and standardizing procedures so they don't recur," says Larry Sweet, vice president of operations at Carrier. "From a corporate point of view, we're driving a culture of consistently focusing on relentless root cause."

Like CIT Commercial Services, Carrier has constructed a corporate scorecard that covers what it considers its core business processes. The key "buckets" in Carrier's scorecard are:

- Engineering productivity (metrics associated with the product development process).
- Product reliability (measures such as customer failure rate and warranty costs).
- Product quality (measures such as factory defects and supplier defects).
- Product delivery (measures along the whole supply chain).
- Customer satisfaction (annual survey of dealers and distributors).
- Employee satisfaction (annual survey).
- Cost productivity (total cost of purchased material, which includes such things as logistics).
- Financial (traditional measures of financial performance).

"Some of these buckets are mature, with four- to five-year trends," says Sweet. "Others are newer, such as product delivery and cost productivity.

We've done pilots on them to prove that the metrics are effective in help-ing with implementation. We look at metrics in three stages: implementa-tion, process, and financial."

Sweet points out that Carrier has moved away from a focus on aggre-gating measurements at a corporate level. It focuses on producing mea-surements that help key process owners drive improvement. Global councils play a major role in identifying metrics and using them to im-prove global, cross-functional processes.

Carrier's most encompassing corporate metrics are the Baldrige cri-teria, which it uses to assess business units that compete for the Willis H. Carrier Global Quality Award. Unlike most companies that are using the Baldrige criteria in a formal program, Carrier developed a short diagnos-tic questionnaire to make the criteria and the assessment process more accessible. (For more information about the Baldrige criteria as a system assessment tool, see Chapter 17.)

MAKING SURE THE DATA AND INFORMATION ARE USEFUL

Once you have systems in place for collecting and analyzing key quality and performance measurements, the next step is to communicate the measurements to the people who can use them. Skimping on this step is like buying a sleek sports car without the key; it's a great-looking system, but it's not going to get you very far.

One of the best systems for communicating key data quickly has been developed by AMP, which introduced its Quality Scorecard system in January 1993. Employees can turn to their computer terminals and call up a matrix that shows quality, delivery, value, and service down the ver-tical column, and suppliers, internal AMP, and customers across the hori-zontal line. A number in each box shows the month-to-date measure of quality. For example, the box at the intersection of "Internal AMP" and "Delivery" might show 95 percent, which would represent AMP's on-time delivery percentage. Put the cursor inside a box, hit "Enter," and you have the detailed system of measures that produced that single number. You can further pursue measures that compare divisions, measures for a par-ticular division, measures for locations within a division, all late orders, and performance (by customer). The online data are updated daily and will soon be available to AMP employees around the world.

"We've taken all of our global metrics and put them on an online global system," says Dick Hoffman, director of information and analysis of Customer Satisfaction/Business Effectiveness (CSBE). "It's a system that any executive around the world can access to see monthly performance results of all measures." The move to a global system responded to customer requirements. "We're dealing with more global customers now, so we must look uniform and consistent around the world," says Dean Hooper, vice president of CSBE.

AMP also has a Delivery Scorecard and is in the process of developing a Balanced Scorecard that will build on the Quality and Delivery Scorecards.

AMP trains employees in how to maneuver within the systems to find the data they need to improve quality and customer satisfaction. Employees learn to zero in on systemic, not individual, areas for improvement. AMP sells 65,000 different parts in 400 product families. Chasing individual events would be like bailing water from a boat with a thimble. Employees use Pareto analysis (the 80/20 rule) to identify such things as the five tools a division is having the most trouble with, locations that are struggling, or the ten customers that need immediate attention.

As powerful as this system is, AMP is working hard to improve it. It has added the ability to look at shipments to internal as well as external customers. It has made the data available in tabular form, showing year-to-date and current performance trends. It has introduced variable standards for such measures as on-time delivery: A "customer variable window" allows different units to define the shipment window for specific accounts.

Since 1993, AMP has refined the Quality Scorecard as a proactive tool for continuous improvement. Employees use this comprehensive measurement system daily to monitor performance and initiate improvements. In many companies, people resist measuring what they do because they fear the measurement will be used to criticize their work, punish them, or control them. Quality leaders use measures to evaluate a process or system, not a person. "We don't use measures to tell people they're not performing," says Kennametal's Cahan. "We use them to tell people what's important and why."

At Kennametal's Solon plant, measures of key performance indicators are posted in highly visible areas where the people who use them are located. The measures are updated weekly; typically, they show a year's worth of history in monthly and weekly increments.

AMP makes its measurements available online, but it also publishes hard copies and posts them in its plants for review by employees who don't have easy access to a computer terminal. The goal is to put the data, as quickly as they become available, in front of the people who can influence them. AMP also decided to change how trends are presented, to make movement in a measurement more apparent. "All of our charts showing quality, delivery, and cost measures now move down and to the right," says Hooper. "We do that because you get more amplification on the chart and because stating it as a weakness allows you to move into structured problem solving."

USING DATA AND INFORMATION TO IMPROVE

In 1996, the Kennametal Solon plant reorganized into four business units within the facility, while implementing new business systems in order processing and accounting. These radical changes had an impact on performance—and on Kennametal's measurement system.

"What we're doing now is relearning what performance measures we need to make improvements," says Chris Lowe, Solon plant manager. "We don't think the indicators we had before are sufficient to drive changes from this point on, so we're looking at adding performance indicators that isolate where we're having problems adjusting to the new system."

At the Solon plant, supervisors work as facilitators with their business units, discussing how they can improve performance to reach the goals they have set. The key performance indicators (KPIs) help promote continuous improvement because the employee teams want to meet their goals and move the trends in the right direction.

In addition to monitoring production activities, KPIs can be used in almost every part of a business. The first step is to identify the process or procedure to be improved, then communicate the data to the people who can improve it, establish measures and goals, and empower those people to use the data to improve.

At the corporate level, companies need to aggregate and analyze a wide variety of data if they are to make wise decisions. This is one of the most difficult tasks a company faces. It must identify what information it needs, pull that information together in a timely manner; compare the data to determine what is happening (making sure they're comparing apples to apples), and put the data and analyses in the hands of decision makers in a format they can use to assess cause/effect connections and resource and financial implications, and to initiate improvement. And that improvement often means significant change.

"I feel very strongly that the Scorecard approach helps drive change," says CIT's Marsiello. "As business conditions change, we're using our strategic performance measures to see if we remain consistent with our strategies. The measures help us avoid becoming too tactical, avoid incremental thinking. They help us focus on building future capabilities, competencies, and disciplines."

Every quarter, at CIT Commercial Services, senior management and managers responsible at the functional level review all 22 strategic performance measures by functional area. The review helps leaders focus attention and resources on key areas for improvement. The company has linked the strategic performance measures to its performance management program and is currently tying them to its reward and recognition policies.

AMP aggregates and analyzes the data it collects—some cover eight or more years—to help leaders understand their business better. Recent analyses include:

- The development of a new customer survey to determine which attributes are important, with the goal of converting satisfied customers into loyal customers.

- The correlation of attributes rated important by customers with employees' perception of what is important to customers. The results of the correlations have been statistically significant, causing AMP to focus on communication and awareness.

- A comparison of employee morale and the quality of AMP's products. A study that compared eight years of AMP quality results to employee opinion survey results indicated that employee satisfaction is a leading indicator of quality.

Carrier's focus has gone in the other direction, away from aggregating at the corporate level, and toward disaggregating to drive continuous improvement. "We stopped collecting measurements on a business unit basis and now collect on a product line basis," says Sweet. "What's very important is to get people involved in improving quality."

INSTITUTIONALIZING THE NEW MEASUREMENT SYSTEM

All areas of a management system are constantly changing, but the area of data collection and analysis is surely one of the most dynamic. Every company in this chapter—and probably every company in this book—speaks about measurement and change in the same breath. Every leader talks about wrestling with what to measure, how to align measures, and how to get employees involved in measuring and improving. For companies steeped in financial measures but often lacking in any others, the idea of developing a unifying measurement system that supports and serves their visions and strategies is both attractive and frightening.

"Managing a measurement system is a different kind of management," says Marsiello. "Once you start these processes, you have to follow through. Senior management has to have the conviction that this is worth the pain of change, because it's hard to win the hearts and minds of your employees."

THE SHIFT IN THINKING

In the new business management model, management acts on the basis of reliable information, data, and analysis. For managers who already believe they are "managing by fact," the data systems of companies like AMP and CIT Commercial Services provide a reality check. The data come from all parts of a company and from customers, suppliers, competitors, and other sources. The data are aggregated, analyzed, and used for a variety of company purposes, including process management, planning, improving customer service, and empowering employees.

Successful companies establish internal performance indicators that reflect the factors that produce customer satisfaction and quality improvement. Kennametal's Solon plant has nearly 50 key performance indicators. They were chosen by the teams that can affect them, and they are tied to customer requirements. CIT Commercial Services has 22 strategic performance measures. As the Baldrige criteria state, "A system of indicators tied to customer and/or company performance requirements represents a clear and objective basis for aligning all activities of the company toward common goals."

To develop such an integrated data strategy, consider the following Measurement Norms (in italics), taken from a 1993 Carrier communication. Our commentary follows the statement of each norm.

- *Customer-focused on our performance vs. their expectations.* Measuring for measurement's sake has no value. The best measures are customer-focused and goal-oriented. Only measure what you can control.
- *Easy to collect, report, and understand the data.* Charts and graphs help people understand trends at a glance. Electronic communication,

like AMP's Quality Scorecard, provides instant access and the ability to seek further detail.

- *Managers initiate, expect, and review the data.* Those who make decisions about improvements in the system and in processes must want, expect, and use the data that will help them evaluate and improve.

- *Work group and/or individual develops and reports the data for ownership.* The people closest to the process are in the best position to identify and gather the data. They are also in the best position to use the data to improve their process.

- *Data will be used for process improvement and not to spear the messenger.* Nothing will sabotage a measurement system faster than using data to evaluate an individual's performance. Data are indicators of a process's performance, not of people's performance.

- *Rewards by management for progress and permanent solutions.* Whether the rewards are monetary bonuses, team celebrations, or pats on the back, progress on key performance indicators needs to be appreciated.

15 BENCHMARKING

Alcoa

Ameritech

Seitz Corporation

Seitz Corporation makes the gears and bearings that move paper in such things as printers and copiers. When its largest market shriveled up in the mid-1980s, Seitz lost two-thirds of its workforce and saw annual sales drop from $12 million to $5 million. It turned to benchmarking to overhaul its business. By 1996, sales had grown to $30 million, and its benchmarking process was well entrenched. Teams of employees were benchmarking everything from manufacturing automation and customer service to safety procedures and employee cafeterias.

Ameritech defines benchmarking as "the identification and implementation of best practices to achieve superior customer results and business performance." It has been called a power tool of quality because it can generate significant improvements in a company's key business processes.

Benchmarking itself is a process. You do not use it to prove you are best at something, but *to learn how to become the best.* Benchmarking, by itself, does not improve performance; it provides information you can use to improve. It is a discovery process aimed at exceeding customer expectations.

Alcoa built its quality improvement process on tools, one of which was benchmarking. The company made benchmarking a primary tool because it believed benchmarking could help it progress farther, faster, and more efficiently toward its goals. As Alcoa sees its benefits, the benchmarking process:

- Helps identify the topics that are most valuable to benchmark, and learn ways to improve performance through internal and external study.
- Reveals the strengths and weaknesses of significant operations, activities, and technologies.
- Improves understanding of latent business threats and competitive positioning.
- Better prepares Alcoa to meet its customers' requirements.
- Helps identify opportunities to improve current processes, eliminate unnecessary processes, and create new products and services.

Seitz was ahead of the game when it recognized these benefits in the mid-1980s; most companies have been considering the concept only in the past few years. Many credit the Baldrige Award program with bringing benchmarking to people's attention. The Baldrige criteria ask how your quality and operational performance results compare to those of competitors and world-class companies, and how you use benchmarking to encourage breakthrough approaches. Early Baldrige Award winners (Motorola, Milliken, and Xerox) showed how companies could "borrow shamelessly" from world-class benchmarks to meet ambitious "stretch" goals.

Alcoa defines such benchmarks as "models of excellence." In this chapter, we will use Alcoa, Ameritech, and Seitz as our models of excellence in the area of benchmarking. All three use this power tool to energize their efforts to improve quality, productivity, and customer satisfaction. As you will see, size and type of business do not preclude the successful use of benchmarking: Alcoa and Seitz are manufacturing companies; Ameritech is a service company. Alcoa and Ameritech have about 65,000 employees each; Seitz has around 200.

We will use our three quality leaders to answer these questions:

- How do we prepare for a benchmarking project?
- How do we gather benchmarking information?
- What do we do with the information we collect?

The questions cover all the steps in the benchmarking process. (The number of steps tends to vary from company to company.) Xerox's process, probably the most copied process in the country, has ten steps. A team at Alcoa spent several months studying the Xerox process, and others, before developing its six-step process:

1. Decide what to benchmark.
2. Plan the benchmarking project.
3. Understand your own performance.
4. Study others.
5. Learn from the data.
6. Use the findings.

By comparison, Seitz presents its process as a flow chart consisting of fourteen steps, and Ameritech's benchmarking process has four phases and eight steps:

Phase 1: Project conception and planning:

  Step 1. Project conception.

  Step 2. Project planning.

Phase 2: Internal and external data gathering and partner selection:

  Step 3. Defining internal processes and performance.

  Step 4. Selecting benchmarking partners.

  Step 5. Collecting benchmarking partners' data.

Phase 3: Analysis and assessment:

  Step 6. Comparing internal processes with partners' processes.

Phase 4: Recommendations and action:

  Step 7. Recommendations and implementation.

  Step 8. Recalibration.

Regardless of the number of steps, all formal benchmarking processes reflect the three activities we will address in this chapter:

- Getting ready to benchmark.
- Conducting the site visit.
- Using what you learn as the basis for improvement.

Informal benchmarking may skip the first and second activities, but its goal is still to improve. Informal benchmarking covers a range of activities that includes reading about similar processes or results in trade publications, talking to competitors or peers at other companies about shared issues or problems, checking out the competition during trade shows, and asking customers and suppliers to compare your performance to that of others. Although informal benchmarking does not require the same degree of planning and execution as formal benchmarking, it can benefit from a similar process: Know your product/service/process; find out what other companies are doing; compare and identify gaps; and initiate improvements.

MODELS OF EXCELLENCE

Ameritech, headquartered in Chicago, is a regional Bell operating company that offers local area telecommunications services to people in Indiana, Illinois, Michigan, Ohio, and Wisconsin. The company also has publishing, mobile telephone, security monitoring, and corporate international groups. It has nearly 68,000 employees. Ameritech is a founder and active participant in the Telecommunications Industry Benchmarking Consortium, a group of 18 telecommunications companies (representing 98 percent of the North American telecom industry) formed to use benchmarking to improve quality.

Alcoa is one of the leading aluminum companies in the world, with 159 locations in 22 countries. Its products are used in beverage containers, airplanes and cars, commercial and residential buildings, chemicals, and an array of consumer and industrial applications. With headquarters in Pittsburgh, Alcoa has more than 65,000 employees in 22 business units.

Seitz Corporation is an injection molder, assembler, and contract manufacturer of thermoplastic components. Its headquarters is in Torrington, Connecticut, and its manufacturing plant is in Rockford, Illinois. The family-owned business employs 230 people. The company's sales increased from $5 million in 1986 to $30 million in 1996. In 1992, it won the State Blue Chip Enterprise Initiative Award as "the best example of a small business that effectively used resources to overcome adversity and emerge stronger." Seitz attributes its improvement to benchmarking.

PREPARING FOR A BENCHMARKING STUDY

Before employees can conduct a study, they need to know what benchmarking is, believe in its benefits, and feel empowered to invest the time such a study takes, and then act on their findings. Alcoa met these needs by making benchmarking a part of its culture and a requirement of its planning process. "Our culture is very 'can do' and 'invented here,'" says Martin Leeper, former manager of corporate quality. "We wanted to counteract that, so we made benchmarking one of our first three quality improvement tools, along with effective teaming and our eight-step problem-solving process. These three tools drive every quality project at Alcoa."

Alcoa did a great deal of training in effective teaming and the eight-step process, but chose not to train people in benchmarking, except for two-hour presentations on the subject. "The benchmarking process is fundamentally easy to understand. We decided to postpone training because otherwise people believe they can't do it until they take a course. We wanted them to get into benchmarking right away." Corporate quality provides support by facilitating, coaching, and counseling the benchmarking teams.

Ameritech has created a Benchmarking Resource Center, which provides internal teams with the benchmarking methodology and process, site visit advice, contacts, and other assistance.

Seitz includes benchmarking in its 33 hours of quality training, then reviews the steps when a team begins a benchmarking project.

Benchmarking projects can be divided into two types: internal and external. External projects are either competitive ("industry best") or functional ("best-in-class"). "We do a lot of internal comparisons at the department or work group level to gain 20 to 30 percent improvements," says Alcoa's Leeper. "But when it comes to breakthrough leadership and looking for 40 to 70 percent improvements in cycle time, quality, and cost, that comes from looking outside the company."

Obtain Management Commitment to Benchmarking

According to Leeper, the biggest problem people face when it comes to benchmarking is, "Where do we start?" As with any long-term management initiative, *the place to begin is with senior management.* "Most managers have a misconception about benchmarking, whether it is comparing companies and numbers or understanding processes," says Ameritech's Brown. "The whole thrust of our breakthrough leadership initiative is radical change. Most leaders understand this means radical changes with limited resources, based on comparisons with external, world-class companies. Benchmarking has helped our leaders become more externally focused."

Senior managers' support is critical because they must commit time, allocate resources, remove roadblocks, and reward the effort. Benchmarking teams that proceed without this support expose themselves to second-guessing about how they spend their time, a lack of funds to complete the project, insurmountable objections by other managers and departments affected by the study, and little or no action on their recommendations. When the senior staff endorses benchmarking, these obstructions can be removed.

Senior management can also make sure the company's benchmarking efforts are coordinated. Companies that have identified their key business processes usually have a good handle on what a particular benchmarking study will do to other parts of the system. Communication among the areas affected by the study helps prevent interdepartmental conflicts and bottlenecks.

Finally, it is important for senior management and benchmarking teams to remember that a formal benchmarking study typically takes around six months to complete. There are no shortcuts. "The biggest problem is finding the time to do a study," says Leeper. If changes need to be made quickly, you will be better off choosing other tools.

Identifying What Should Be Benchmarked

So you have senior management buy-in and six months to get the job done. How do you decide what to study?

"Customers will tell you when you're messing up. They're a great place to start a benchmark," says Sharon LeGault, marketing manager at Seitz. "Internal and external salespeople can also see differences. Another source is people who recognize a problem: 'We're losing money because of. . . . '" Seitz does benchmarking in response to a gap, a suspected gap, or a problem. Once the need is identified, Seitz's senior staff recommends forming a team to address it, after which the team takes the leadership role.

Alcoa identifies benchmarking opportunities through its planning process and as teams work through its eight-step problem-solving process. Two questions the teams must answer are:

- Has anyone ever faced a similar problem before?
- What did they do about it?

Benchmarking is an obvious tool for finding the answers.

Alcoa uses the following criteria to decide whether a topic is relevant and valid as a benchmarking subject:

- Is the topic important to our customers?
- Is the topic consistent with our mission, values, and milestones?

- Does the topic reflect an important business need?
- Is the topic significant in terms of costs or key nonfinancial indicators?
- Is the topic in an area where additional information could influence plans and actions?

The first question is undoubtedly the most important. *A benchmarking study must have clear and accurate objectives based on customer requirements.* "Some of our studies get customers involved, either through phone calls, focus groups, or bringing them on the site visit, to help us understand their requirements," says Brown. "Another advantage of involving customers is that, when it's time to implement the team's recommendations, they are based on clear, accurate customer requirements."

Topics for benchmarking studies cover any process that is critical to customer service and the company's success. Ameritech is currently conducting studies on product development cycle time, operational efficiency in its buying organization, human resources staffing processes, and financial operations. Seitz has benchmarked tooling, customer service, accounting practices, safety, and bar coding. Answering Alcoa's questions, listed above, will tell you whether a topic makes good benchmarking material.

Creating a Benchmarking Project Plan

The next step in the process involves creating a plan of action. Ameritech calls this the project plan and suggests covering the following areas:

- Goals and objectives.
- Scope and resources.
- Key players.
- Critical success factors.
- Roles and responsibilities.
- Milestones and deliverables.
- Performance measures.
- High-level process flows.

Seitz asks its benchmarking teams to select who will be leader, process guide, scribe, and timekeeper. The leader leads. The process guide maintains the rules (e.g., no evaluating during brainstorming; and everyone is to be involved in the discussions). The scribe records everything and distributes meeting minutes. The timekeeper keeps meetings within time limits and makes sure the team is progressing as planned.

The teams use *statistical problem-solving tools* to develop their proposal. They begin by brainstorming to make sure the perceived problem exists. If it does, the team uses a fishbone diagram to identify the reasons for the outcome, does a Pareto chart to determine the primary opportunities, then creates a flow chart to map the process under study. "Once the team puts the brainstorming, fishbone, and Pareto together, the team's senior staff member brings the proposal to the senior staff with a request for resources, including money, to implement the study," says LeGault.

Many benchmarking efforts fail because teams do not understand their company's process first. It is like deciding to buy new office furniture without finding out what employees are currently using, what they need, what existing furniture will be kept, where it will be put, what the work environment is like, how it is changing, and so on. *You cannot ask intelligent questions or collect meaningful information without a clear understanding of the existing process you wish to improve.*

Alcoa describes this step in its benchmarking booklet as follows:

> Teams examine the factors that influence performance and learn which characteristics are most important and which are less important. They also learn what data relate to important characteristics and how to collect and measure that data. In addition, the collection of internal data and the analysis of limits to performance may reveal new ways to overcome specific barriers. Finally; this internal collection of performance data creates the baseline and structure for benchmarking comparisons.

The easiest way to make comparisons is by developing *a common set of metrics* that define key elements of the process. Ameritech seeks metrics that are driven by customer requirements, as a way of keeping the focus on improving the process, in order to improve customer satisfaction. Benchmarking teams often encounter a different set of metrics in use at the company being benchmarked. "The problem is getting an apples-to-apples comparison," says Brown. "We've been able to avoid the problem by asking, 'This is what we're looking for. How would you map to that?' It's not always easy, but it hasn't been a significant problem."

Identifying Companies to Use as Benchmarks

Once the project proposal is written and approved, the next step is to identify benchmarking prospects. Teams often struggle with this step; either they do not have a clue where to find such prospects, or they have one or two companies they have heard about and that is their list.

Ameritech encourages its teams to brainstorm until they have at least 30 potential companies. Among the sources or places to look for leads are:

- Process owners.
- Internal and external customers.
- Professional organizations.
- Trade shows and seminars.
- Professional and trade publications.
- Newspaper and magazine articles.
- Industry experts.
- Industry studies.
- Suppliers.

Small companies often have trouble finding benchmarking partners. Seitz focuses on companies of similar size, getting most of its leads from customers, newspaper and magazine articles, and conferences and trade shows. It has tried benchmarking large companies, but team members came back overwhelmed, and Seitz discovered that it could not afford to implement what the larger companies were doing.

The goal of the search is to find companies that are satisfying the same customer needs as the ongoing internal process, and are doing it with a high degree of success. "You can identify similar . . . , but better-than-you is the trick," says LeGault. "Our people make up a short questionnaire they use to ask potential companies leading questions. We try to come up with a long list of 15 companies, call them, then pick the top three or four to benchmark." The questions are specific and qualifying. Team members record the responses and ask whether the target would be willing to participate.

Ameritech uses the following criteria to help determine appropriate partner companies:

- Companies that have received quality or business awards.
- Top-rated firms in industry surveys.
- Success stories published in periodicals.
- Statements of pride in business articles.
- Companies with excellent financial results.
- Feedback from internal and external experts, customers, suppliers, and business partners.

To narrow its list of 30 to about a dozen, Ameritech uses these questions:

- For what quality process or result is the company known?
- What evidence exists to confirm the partner is an industry leader in the area of interest?
- What is the level of customer satisfaction?
- What is the company's profitability?
- What is the company's market share?
- Has the company made any contributions to the state of the art in its industry? Any new technology impacts?

Once it has a dozen or so qualified prospects, Ameritech uses a comparison matrix to cut that list down to six to eight partners. The company's benchmarking manual includes the generic sample shown in Table 15.1.

Some of the matrix can be completed with information already collected. The rest comes from phone interviews with the potential partners. Brown has found that he usually has the name of someone he can call, identified through his own networking, the quality department, or the industry benchmarking consortium to which Ameritech belongs. He tries to initiate all contacts because most companies prefer a single point of contact.

Companies deluged by benchmarking requests appreciate such courtesy. Quality leaders, such as those who have won Baldrige Awards, have been very visible benchmarking targets—to a point where two winners, Milliken and Westinghouse Commercial Nuclear Fuel, are accepting requests only by customers and suppliers (which is why they are not in this

TABLE 15.1. Ameritech's benchmarking partner criteria matrix

Criteria	Co. A	Co. B	Co. C	Co. D	Co. E
1. Quality-oriented					
2. Successful product/service reputation					
3. Service-oriented					
4. Excellent cycle time					
5. 100% reliability					
6. 25% improvement yr.-to-yr. sales growth					
7. 25% improvement yr.-to-yr. profitability					
8. More than 20,000 employees					

book). However, many will still agree to participate, especially if they can learn something in return.

"Companies realize they have to have their processes identified and that you're going to be in their plant for three hours. That's a lot to ask for some companies," says LeGault. "Others say they're not familiar with benchmarking and don't have the resources to deal with it. Out of our short list, 50 to 75 percent will agree to participate."

GATHERING BENCHMARKING INFORMATION

For companies willing to participate, you should agree on: the time frame and length of the site visit, an agenda, your benchmarking practices, and the questions you will ask. Seitz faxes its questions to its partners so that they can review them before the site visit and eliminate any they do not want to address. In its benchmarking guide, Ameritech suggests the kinds of questions a team might ask, to learn more about a process:

- Does the company have a defined, documented process?
- How is the process communicated to the process customers and users?
- How are the users kept up to date on the process changes?
- What is the management system of the process?
- What aspects of the process are considered to be world-class?

At Seitz, team members decide who will go to which companies, usually in groups of two or three. "We'll go in with 20 different questions and write comparisons side-by-side to see the differences in time and benefits," says LeGault. Team members are encouraged to ask anything and everything, but only if they are questions that Seitz would be willing to answer itself. In fact, the team members should have the answers for their own process written down so that they can use them for comparison during the visit. Seitz offers to share the results of its project with all partners. Most companies are willing to share their results, although some ask for confidentiality, which Seitz respects.

The act of opening up one company's facilities and processes for another company to scrutinize carries with it the potential for abuse. Many companies are adopting a benchmarking code of conduct, to govern their activities and reassure their potential partners. Ameritech is a member of the Strategic Planning Institute's Council on Benchmarking, which created and adopted the following *code of conduct:*

1. Keep it legal.
2. Be willing to provide the same information that you request.
3. Respect confidentiality.
4. Keep information internal for your use only.
5. Initiate contact through benchmarking contacts.
6. Don't refer without permission.
7. Be prepared at initial contact.
8. Have a basic knowledge of benchmarking, and follow the process.
9. Have determined what to benchmark, and complete a rigorous self-assessment.

The effectiveness of a site visit depends primarily on how well prepared both sides are. If both companies understand their processes and if the benchmarking team knows exactly what it wants to learn, most visits proceed fairly smoothly. During its ten years of benchmarking experience, Seitz has encountered four common problems:

1. *People are not prepared to actually compare gaps.* As a result, they gather information not pertinent to the project. Teams must be careful not to become tourists during the site visit.

2. *People take poor notes.* "We recommend that every employee in the group has a copy of the same questionnaire. When the question is asked, everyone writes down the answer they hear," says LeGault.

3. *People do not understand the purpose of the study.* LeGault talks about how one site visit backfired when a team of toolmakers returned saying they were underpaid, the target company had better equipment, and they liked their landscaping very much.

4. *Senior management doesn't want to be bothered to participate on the teams.* If senior staff personnel do not show interest, people on the team do not think it is important either.

Another problem, mentioned earlier, is finding information and data in a form you can use. "When making comparisons, the best way is to roll it up to a level where you get an apples-to-apples comparison, which is hard because people generally migrate to lower levels of detail," says Brown. "I've found myself making repeated calls to try to understand the data I've gotten." Developing a good relationship with your benchmarking partner makes this ongoing exchange of information possible.

WHAT TO DO WITH WHAT YOU LEARN

At Alcoa, teams analyze the data they have collected, quantify performance gaps, explore the implications of those gaps, and identify which pieces of information might help improve performance. They then work with the project sponsor to determine how to use the findings.

Ameritech talks about segmenting the gap between current and proposed performance into strategic and tactical actions necessary to close the gap. *Tactical changes* result in minor productivity gains. *Strategic changes* are major changes required to close the gap.

At Seitz, the benchmarking teams fill out comparison charts to clarify the differences on key points. Table 15.2 is an example from a team's study of Kanban. The study led to a new inventory system at Seitz, reduced work in process (WIP) in the assembly area by 15 to 20 percent, and depleted 90 percent of the inventory on the floor, allowing the company to add one-third more assembly line.

After the teams complete the comparison charts, they pull in people from other departments to review what they learned and to develop a list of recommendations, including any savings of time and money. "If changes are in order, our employees are empowered to make the changes they think they need," says LeGault. "The only time they have to go to upper management is when they need to spend more than $500."

Companies involved in achieving ISO or QS-9000 certification, and companies that have achieved a certification, need to be careful that process changes learned through benchmarking don't conflict with their documentation—or they must change the documentation to reflect the process changes. "When changes affect procedures defined by ISO or

TABLE 15.2.   Sample of a Seitz information comparison chart

Question: When issuing an order, how much work is delivered to the department?			
Seitz Full order amount	*Company A* 1 day's work is issued	*Company B* 1 week's work is issued	*Company C* 2 days' work is issued
Results —WIP is high —Taking up large space for material storage	—No WIP —No space needed	—Lower amount of WIP —Small area for material storage	—Low WIP —Very small area for material storage

WIP = Work in Progress

QS-9000 criteria," says LeGault, "the process owner must participate on the team and then become responsible for formally documenting the new process, including training and verification of efficacy."

Not every study results in change. "At times, the results are too expensive or don't work for you, so you do another type of problem-solving process," LeGault says.

One way to improve the odds of getting benchmarking results you can use is to benchmark more companies. "In the majority of benchmarking studies, we find that three or four of the companies we've benchmarked can give us 40 percent-plus improvement," says Ameritech's Brown. "We typically include a half-dozen companies or more because there will be some companies we don't learn much from. We generally don't get all our improvements from one company, although there have been a few times when we've gotten a fair amount from one source."

Implementing Changes That Result from Benchmarking

Ameritech recommends the following steps to implement the changes needed to close the gap:

- Select implementation alternatives.
- Assign resources and create a schedule.
- Establish goals.
- Develop a monitoring plan.
- Gain appropriate approval to alter the current practices.
- Implement the plan.
- Communicate the benchmarking findings.

After the plan is implemented, the processes it affects must be *measured* and *monitored* to see whether they are performing as expected and to continue to improve them. The final point in Ameritech's list is also important: Information gained from benchmarking is often valuable to other parts of the organization, especially in larger companies. At Alcoa, benchmarking teams are asked to identify others in Alcoa who might benefit from the work they have done. The corporate quality unit maintains a *benchmarking database* that lists topics and organizations that have been benchmarked, and business units aggregate and share relevant information.

Ameritech's final step is *recalibration*, the reevaluation process. This is not a review of how the plan has worked, but the beginning of a new benchmarking process that will repeat all eight steps. As Brown points out, "The ultimate goal is for benchmarking to be institutionalized throughout the organization, to ensure its continued success."

THE SHIFT IN THINKING

The new business management model promotes *systems* thinking, in terms of understanding both the internal systems around which a company is built and the external systems that affect it. In previous chapters, we have examined the links with customers and suppliers. In the next chapter, we will look at a company's responsibilities to its communities. These external influences force a company to constantly review the premises and processes on which it is based.

Benchmarking enables you to improve your internal systems by learning from external resources. As we have seen in this chapter, it is a process of discovering exactly what you are doing, what the best inside and outside your company are doing, how they compare, and what you can do to improve.

Our three models of excellence follow formal benchmarking processes, although all three processes differ slightly. The important points are: each follows a well-defined process, and the process does not always have to be so formal. For example, Alcoa's senior management was concerned about improving in one of its values: promoting the health and well-being of employees. It already had the best safety record in its industry, but it did not consider itself good enough and it was not improving. "We took our corporate and human resource leaders and national union leaders and did a week-long study mission. The participants learned that you manage safety like you manage quality," says Leeper. "The process opened up a dialogue among these leaders that led to common knowledge and acceptance. We emphasize that this is a mutual learning process."

Considered a power tool for quality, benchmarking is an indispensable tool for the learning organization. Without it, you will never know how your company stands relative to competitors and world-class performers; you will miss out on new ways of thinking that are needed to achieve breakthrough improvements; and you will have no way of gauging the effectiveness of your processes or imagining how good they can be.

In the new management model, benchmarking is used to find out what is best and to guide process improvements that will make your company the next model of excellence—all with the goal of developing loyal customers.

16 CORPORATE RESPONSIBILITY AND CITIZENSHIP

3M

USAA

Insurance Management Company (IMC)

For many people, the connection between *business management* and *corporate responsibility and citizenship* is vague. What does business ethics have to do with quality? What do environmental issues have to do with improving performance? What is the value to our company of promoting community involvement?

When quality leaders answer these questions, their responses tend to fall into two categories: (1) you do it because it is profitable; (2) you do it because it is the right thing to do. An example of the first response is 3M, which has saved an average of $4 million every year for two decades through its Pollution Prevention Pays program. An example of the second is the USAA Volunteer Corps, which helped more than 4,400 USAA volunteers contribute over 190,000 hours to their communities in 1996.

Every organizational "system" functions within, affects, and is affected by many other systems. Customers and suppliers have their own business systems. Markets are systems. The communities in which we work are systems. These systems are the focus of this chapter; they define a business's relationships with the community at large, whether local, state, national, or global.

First, we need to distinguish between company responsibility and company citizenship. *Company responsibility* refers to basic public expectations, such as conducting business ethically and protecting public health and safety and the environment. *Company citizenship* means leading and supporting publicly important purposes, such as education, community services, industry and trade practices, and quality improvement.

In this chapter, we will look at how three companies—3M, USAA, and IMC—take the lead in corporate citizenship and in their responsibilities to the public. We will use their experiences to clarify the connections between the new management model and a company's public responsibilities, as we answer these questions:

- How do we address corporate responsibility and citizenship in our business?
- How do we improve the ways we meet our public expectations?
- How do we lead as corporate citizens?

The purpose of this chapter is not to sell you on the merits of acting more aggressively in these areas, although our three quality leaders do present compelling arguments. Like the decision to make quality improvement a corporate priority, the decision to make public responsibility and citizenship a priority requires *enlightened leadership* and an ongoing *cultural transformation.* Your company must determine for itself what it can and will do for the public good. As our benchmarks show, what is good for the public can also be a good business strategy.

MODELS OF EXCELLENCE

3M manufactures more than 50,000 products for industrial, commercial, health care, and consumer markets around the world, including pressure-sensitive tapes, photographic films, recording tapes, coated abrasives, and insulating materials. 3M employs nearly 75,000 people in 60 nations. Its headquarters are in St. Paul, Minnesota.

In 1922, twenty-five Army officers founded the United Services Automobile Association, better known as USAA, to provide themselves with competitively priced auto insurance. Today, USAA is the fifth largest personal automobile insurer and fourth largest homeowners' insurer in the country. It has over 16,000 employees. In addition to auto and homeowners' insurance, USAA offers life insurance, health insurance, annuities, mutual funds and discount brokerage services, full banking and credit card services, auto leasing and buying services, cruise services, and a retirement community. It sells virtually all of its products by telephone and mail. USAA received Baldrige site visits in 1990 and 1991. In 1995, Arthur D. Little, Inc. recognized USAA as one of its "Best of the Best" process management practitioners. In 1997, *Fortune* selected USAA as one of "America's most admired companies."

IMC, which was established in 1933, is a third-generation, family-owned business specializing in providing quality risk management and insurance brokering services. IMC serves nearly 150 clients in 19 countries and 42 states. In 1996, 90 percent of its clients rated IMC outstanding or world-class. IMC is located in Erie, Pennsylvania, and has 28 associates. It won the Erie Quality Award in 1993 and the Keystone level of the Pennsylvania Quality Award in 1994. In 1996, second-generation owner Bill Bloomstine received the Edward C. Doll Community Service Award for personal philanthropy and volunteerism.

INCORPORATING RESPONSIBILITY AND CITIZENSHIP

The process of incorporating public responsibility and citizenship is not unlike the way a company incorporates quality improvement. It begins with an understanding of customer requirements, then translates those requirements into a *vision*, a *mission*, and *goals* for the company.

The major difference is in the need to have the definition of "customer" include all of an organization's stakeholders: the people who buy its products and services; stockholders, employees, and suppliers; and the people in the communities in which the company is a "citizen." Employees also live in these communities, so a company that pays attention to its responsibilities to the community is actually attending to a part of itself. Separating work and home, business and nonbusiness activities, is tired thinking. The new management model takes a more *holistic view* of employees' roles in their company and community—and of their company's role in the community. Such a view challenges businesses to listen and be responsive to a broader range of needs and opinions, but it also rewards them by acting in and for their employees' best interests.

Concern for the Environment

In the next section of this chapter, we will introduce 3M's innovative program, Pollution Prevention Pays (3P). Tom Zosel, who manages the program, emphasizes how the program takes advantage of people's desire to care for the environment. "I think the biggest hook in the entire program is giving people the opportunity to bring their environmental activism to their jobs. If you went out today and surveyed 3M employees and asked if they considered themselves environmentalists, I'd be surprised if you got less than a 90 percent positive response."

3M's corporate values reflect its employees' values by including a commitment to "respecting our social and physical environment." The goals 3M has identified to carry out this value are:

- Complying with all laws, and meeting or exceeding regulations.
- Keeping customers, employees, investors, and the public informed about operations.
- Developing products and processes that have minimal impact on the environment.
- Staying attuned to the changing needs and preferences of customers, employees, and society.
- Bringing uncompromising honesty and integrity to every aspect of the organization.

In the year 3M started its 3P program, the board of directors adopted the following *corporate environmental policy*:

3M will continue to recognize and exercise its responsibility to:

- Solve its own environmental pollution and conservation problems.
- Prevent pollution at the source wherever and whenever possible.
- Develop products that will have a minimum effect on the environment.
- Conserve natural resources through the use of reclamation and other appropriate methods.
- Ensure that its facilities and products meet and sustain the regulations of all federal, state, and local environmental agencies.
- Assist, wherever possible, governmental agencies and other official organizations engaged in environmental activities.

To turn the policy into action, 3M's senior management created specific policies, objectives, and implementation standards. The policies include going beyond regulatory requirements, preventing pollution at the source, conducting detailed environmental audits, and phasing out all ozone-depleting chemicals and PCBs. "Environmental concerns are considered at every step in the development and manufacture of our products," says chairman L. D. DeSimone. "This assures upper management that our goals of environmental protection are being met."

3M's goals and policies respond to the perceived requirements of its customers, employees, shareholders, and communities. Companies that put their values down on paper communicate their thinking about their communities. For example, Corning's purpose is "to deliver superior, long-range economic benefits to our customers, our shareholders, our employees, and *the communities in which we operate.*"

Attention to Business Ethics

Business ethics is an area that every company says it promotes, but few can say how. For companies like IMC and USAA, *ethics is ingrained in the corporate culture.* At USAA, new employees are first exposed to the company's position on ethics during orientation. They are further exposed during training courses that have ethical considerations embedded in their curricula. With employees currently receiving an average of 55 hours of formal training per year, reinforcement is frequent and consistent. In addition, the Leadership and Organizational Development Department offers tailored sessions for each company, and will bring them to a work area at the company's request. In 1996, Robert Herres, USAA's CEO, decided to introduce a more formal process into the ethics of the association. He guided the development of a new USAA Code of Ethics and established an ethics coordinator and a USAA Ethics Council chaired by a USAA senior officer.

USAA keeps people focused on corporate responsibility and citizenship by making it part of the company's planning process. USAA has identified six key result areas (KRAs): (1) service, (2) financial strength, (3) product value, (4) relationship building, (5) strategic assets (people and technology), and (6) public outreach. By including public outreach as a KRA, along with other company priorities, USAA establishes its importance for all employees. By then developing five-year and annual plans to achieve its public outreach goals, USAA translates those goals into measurable actions and objectives—the surest way to make corporate responsibility and citizenship a part of the company's culture.

ADDRESSING THE RESPONSIBILITY TO PRESERVE THE ENVIRONMENT

Where public responsibilities are concerned, business ethics and public health and safety are basically no-brainers. Regardless of a company's management philosophy, it should conduct business ethically and do everything possible to protect public health and safety. From a new management model perspective, that means:

- Establishing the company's expectations for these areas.
- Training employees to understand and act on their responsibilities.
- Identifying and measuring the appropriate indicators of responsible behavior and actions.

The area of public responsibility that causes companies the most anguish is the environment. Faced with the "greening" of America, more and more businesses are boarding the environmental bandwagon with no clear sense of where it will take them. By contrast, quality leaders are grabbing hold of the reins and steering their companies toward environmental leadership by applying the principles of quality management to pollution prevention. The application is so appropriate that it has spawned a new name: *total quality environmental management* (TQEM).

The Global Environmental Management Initiative (GEMI) is credited with coining TQEM. GEMI was founded in 1990 by senior environmental health and safety professionals from several major U.S. companies, including Procter & Gamble, AT&T, Eastman Kodak, and Florida Power & Light. Its goal is to provide an exchange of information on the most advanced environmental management techniques. In a speech at GEMI's first conference, Gerald Kotes, director of the Environmental Protection Agency (EPA) office of pollution prevention, said, "A basic premise of total quality management is, if a firm doesn't build waste into its product, then it doesn't have to pay to take the waste out. With pollution prevention, the premise is very similar. If the firm doesn't generate waste in the first place, then it doesn't have to pay to manage it."

3M's Zosel puts it this way: "Pollution is a defect. The goal of total quality management is to eliminate defects." 3M focuses on waste reduction to reduce defects, to cut the amount of pollution being generated. It does this by involving every employee in the effort. "To do pollution prevention," says Zosel, "you must get into a total quality management mentality—give people a goal and a method for achieving it, then let them do it."

The goals are part of 3M's global strategy for achieving excellence in every 3M business and support unit. The strategy, called Q90s, is based on the Baldrige criteria, which means it includes an assessment of how each unit improves in the areas of corporate responsibility and citizenship. Most business units have been through two or three assessments using the criteria, in addition to several mini self-audits. "As a result, our business assessment process is being integrated into the business planning process," says Ron Kubinski, quality manager. "Quality and business are becoming one plan focused on 3M's primary goals: listening to the voice of the customer, reducing time to market, and reducing cost."

3M has more than 7,000 core manufacturing processes based on about 100 core technologies. It is a customer-focused, technology-leveraged company that thrives on massive sharing about how units use the core technologies. The size and nature of its business present many opportunities for protecting the environment. 3M seized these opportunities in 1975, when it initiated an industrial environmental program called *Pollution Prevention Pays* (3P). At that time, applying pollution prevention companywide through a globally organized effort—and recording the results—had not been done by any major American corporation.

"What we did with Pollution Prevention Pays parallels the entire total quality management process," says Zosel. "When we looked at all the regulations that were coming, we knew we couldn't do it all from the end of the pipe, with pollution control. We had to design out the environmental problems, which means we had to build a pollution prevention ethic into the corporation."

Zosel and his environmental cohorts presented 3M's management with two choices: (1) You can spend this much for pollution control, or (2) you can tell people to prevent the pollution by design, up front. Management took the second choice, in part because innovation and change are 3M strengths. "We wanted to be proactive on it, to address regulations in a way that is environmentally efficient and cost-effective," says Zosel.

How 3M Implements Its Pollution Prevention Programs

The basic concept and goals of the 3P program have remained constant since 1975. The program is run by a 3P *coordinating committee,* which represents 3M's engineering, manufacturing, and laboratory organizations and the corporate Environmental Engineering and Pollution Control unit. The committee establishes criteria for 3P participation and recommends employee recognition.

Most 3P projects are initiated when employees recognize a specific pollution or waste disposal problem. A cross-functional team is formed to analyze the problem and develop solutions. The team submits a proposal to the affected operating division, which decides whether to commit funds, time, and other resources to it.

Employee involvement is key to the program's success. A 3M plant in Aberdeen, South Dakota, provides an example. The plant makes round respirator masks out of square fabric; one-third of the fabric ends up as waste that used to be carried to local landfills. A team of process engineers recognized the waste problem and tackled the issue with the goal of *zero* waste. Such a goal forces new thinking, because even the most efficient use of fabric will still produce waste. The team changed its thinking and targeted the waste as a supply of raw materials. It then reformulated the product so that the fibers in the waste could be used for a new line of 3M products for hazardous waste cleanup. The goal of zero waste was achieved. As one engineer said, "Our goal is that everything that comes into the plant goes out as a useful item."

Such ambitious thinking is common throughout 3M. In the first 17 years of the 3P program, 3M cut its pollution in half (by more than 1.3 billion pounds) and saved 3M approximately $650 million. Similar reductions in pollution and costs continue today.

In addition to tapping into people's desire to protect the environment, 3M motivates participation through *recognition*. To qualify for formal recognition, a 3P program must meet the following criteria:

- Prevent pollution, not control it.
- Offer some other environmental benefit besides preventing pollution.
- Save money for 3M.
- Include a technical accomplishment.

3P doesn't exclude innovative improvements that are not technical, or new programs that prevent pollution but cost money; however, they are not formally recognized. Depending on the innovative nature of their accomplishments, people get 3P awards, plaques, or certificates. In the program's first 14 years 2,511 projects received formal recognition.

The Pollution Prevention Pays program also makes *monetary rewards* available to anyone who runs a 3P project. To avoid competition, the name of every person who participates in a 3P project is put into a hat. Ten percent of the names are drawn, and those people receive $500 gift certificates.

In 1988, 3M expanded its 3P program to address pollution prevention in a more structured way. *Pollution Prevention Plus* (3P+) encourages technical innovation to prevent pollution at the source—through product reformulation, process modification, equipment redesign, and resource recovery. 3P+ emphasizes that, with or without cost savings, 3M will spend whatever amount is necessary to protect the environment.

Waste minimization teams have been established in every 3M product operating division, to identify source reduction and recycling opportunities, and to develop plans to address them. A pollution prevention staff within the corporate environmental organization makes 3P+ happen, by monitoring and reporting progress to management, encouraging the sharing of ideas, monitoring legislative and regulatory activity, and administering the award program. The objective of 3P+ was to reduce all hazardous and nonhazardous releases to the air, land, and water by 90 percent, and to reduce the generations of waste by 50 percent by 1995, with 1990 levels as baselines. Chairman L. D. DeSimone has been quoted as saying that, by achieving this objective, 3M has "significantly cut the inflation-adjusted cost per unit of most products."

Many successful companies have stumbled onto the fact that pollution prevention can save significant amounts of money. Time after time, manufacturers change a process because it is environmentally better, and then discover that it is also economically better. To paraphrase Kotes, if you don't generate waste, you don't have to pay to manage it.

Successful companies recognize that *waste minimization and quality are two sides of the same coin.* Japanese companies surpassed American companies in the quality of their products during the 1970s and 1980s. The by-products of their quality improvement were: better utilization of resources, and reduction of waste. Japan uses 50 percent less material and energy than the United States does to produce one unit of GNP, which gives many Japanese products a 5 percent cost advantage—in addition to their quality advantage. All these economic benefits result from the quality improvement process.

Companies fail to meet their public responsibilities when they look at them as costly activities delegated to a few people to control and clean up. 3M approaches its environmental responsibilities from a new management perspective: they are opportunities to satisfy customers and reduce waste and costs. It then uses a total quality management approach of involving everyone in identifying and acting on those opportunities. The results it has realized suggest that this is an effective approach to addressing public responsibilities.

BECOMING A MODEL CITIZEN

Although many companies question the extent of their public responsibilities, many more wonder about their roles as corporate citizens. They know they have to satisfy their customers, reduce waste, and cut costs to succeed. They understand that, in the new business management model, success means understanding customer requirements, involving people, and managing processes. But what does corporate citizenship have to do with any of these corporate goals?

Our quality role models believe that taking the lead in publicly important areas is an essential part of a successful system. These areas include supporting education, volunteering for and funding community services, contributing to industry and trade activities, and promoting quality improvement.

3M actively encourages and supports employee involvement in all these areas. "In the process of giving, you get," says Kubinski. "It makes good corporate sense for us to be good corporate citizens."

The fact is, whether the motives are financial or altruistic, the results of being community leaders tend to be the same: The more you give, the more you get in return. And among the returns with immeasurable value are the pride and satisfaction for each individual who contributes.

USAA: Encouraging Volunteer Service in the Community

At community activities in the San Antonio area, it is easy to spot USAA employees by the special shirts they wear. "People talk to our employees about how wonderful their company is and how much they appreciate the employees' being there," says Paul Ringenbach, assistant vice president in the Office of Corporate Communications. "It builds pride, and they bring that pride back here, so they want to do a better job. They bring something back they didn't leave with."

USAA has a corporate culture that puts superior service to its members and customers first—but being a good neighbor in its communities is close behind. The motivation for participation at USAA stems from this culture and from its chairman and chief executive officer, retired Air Force General Robert T. Herres. Herres believes strongly in support of the community. He organized all community support activities, including philanthropy and volunteers, under a vice president of community relations who reports directly to him. In addition, he personally sets an example and participates in community efforts. He was chairman of National Junior Achievement in 1997.

The USAA Volunteer Corps matches USAA employees with community nonprofit agencies that need additional helpers to achieve their humanitarian goals. In 1996, more than 4,400 USAA volunteers contributed over 190,000 hours to their communities. Over 350 initiatives began in San Antonio alone. Employees are notified of opportunities by newsletter.

They volunteer hours to whatever activities they wish to support. A computer database tracks the numbers of volunteers and the hours they expend. One of the more popular volunteer projects has been Habitat for Humanity. In 1997, about 80 volunteers helped build a house for a San Antonio family.

USAA's community educational programs—including its nationally recognized mentor program, Junior Achievement; math tutors; and pen pals—make a significant contribution to the San Antonio community. The educational program provides one-on-one mentoring and Junior Achievement classroom instruction to over 1,000 at-risk students in a number of San Antonio elementary, middle, and high schools. Through USAA's example and training, 68 groups of other volunteers from military bases, businesses, and government offices provide an additional 2,700 mentors to the city's students.

The most significant USAA corporate good citizenship effort directed nationally was the Arnold Shapiro documentaries sponsored by the Association. The series of programs that had begun in 1988 with *Raising Good Kids in Bad Times* continued to focus on improving the quality of life for children and their families. In 1994, Walter Cronkite hosted *Victory Over Violence,* which suggested ways for communities to reduce violence in their neighborhoods. One columnist reported that Vice President Al Gore praised the documentary lavishly around the White House. *Scared Silent,* hosted by Oprah Winfrey, dealt with physical, emotional, and sexual abuse of children. This pioneering special appeared on all four major networks (NBC, ABC, CBS, PBS) and was the most watched documentary in television history, attracting an estimated 56 million viewers. The production generated over 110,000 telephone calls to the National Child Abuse hotline during the show alone. Calls to the hotline tripled the normal amount for more than nine months, and are still running double the former average rate. Winfrey called it the most important show she had ever done on television. Since its initial airing, *Scared Silent* has appeared in over forty nations worldwide.

When child abuse agencies asked for something on abuse that could be shown to children, USAA sponsored *Break the Silence.* Hosted by Jane Seymour and aired on CBS, the documentary won the George Foster Peabody Award for Broadcasting in 1995. Other recent USAA-sponsored documentaries included *Bad Dads,* hosted by heavyweight boxing champion George Foreman on the FOX network, and *Everybody's Business,* carried by NBC and hosted by Katie Couric of *The Today Show.* Designed to encourage businesses to increase their efforts to help children in their own communities, *Everybody's Business* was also distributed to Chambers of Commerce across the nation.

Support for Charities from USAA

In 1996, USAA employees donated $3.6 million to United Way. USAA then provided an additional $2 million in matching corporate funds, bringing the total to $5.6 million. Although USAA comprises less than 2 percent of the workforce in San Antonio, USAA's United Way contributions accounted for one out of every six dollars of the total monies donated in the community in 1996, or 17 percent of the total contributions.

USAA has become a community leader because it is committed to service and has organized internally to provide that service. The organization helps identify opportunities for service, and gives employees a simple way to find out what needs to be done and to volunteer their assistance. Supported by a corporate culture that values community service, USAA employees choose to look outward and to give freely of their knowledge and skills. The difference is one of *attitude:* Either a company believes it must serve its community or it does not. If it believes it must lead and support publicly important purposes, it must find ways to identify those purposes and to facilitate corporate and employee involvement. As USAA has shown, an *organized approach to community service* targets the areas of greatest need while attracting the largest number of volunteers.

IMC: A Culture of Caring

As a small company, IMC enjoys the same sense of community that exists in small towns. Associates know and care about each other and their community. "Everybody here realizes that they owe their success to the community," says John Bloomstine, president of IMC. "Our clients are all basically within a 50-mile radius, even though they have operations worldwide."

IMC associates choose which community organizations to support and how to support them. IMC encourages their participation, but does not dictate how they should be involved. Associates, including the owners and officers, meet every business day at 8:15 A.M. to discuss what's going on at the company and with the people. Community and volunteer activities and opportunities are a normal part of the discussion, as are situations that call for ethical responses. "Doing what's right is instilled here," says Bloomstine. "That happens when you have a morning meeting every day to talk about what you did. Associates can see how situations are handled."

They can also see how community service is valued. The list of community activities by Bill Bloomstine is too long to list here but includes leadership in Boy Scouts and Cub Scouts, church and college organizations, Erie Rotary Club, Children's Welfare Association, Erie Building Code Commission, and United Way. The Bloomstine Family Foundation, through the Erie Community Foundation, contributes to the needs of the community throughout the year.

Through their actions, the leaders at IMC demonstrate the value of community service. Associates respond with widespread involvement of their own, including contributions that earned IMC the Gold Award of the United Way of Erie County.

"We want to treat people the way we want to be treated," says John Bloomstine. "The culture here is one of caring, of concern for others." And that culture extends to, and benefits, their community.

THE SHIFT IN THINKING

In the new business management model, corporate responsibility and citizenship—like quality—are integrated into the way people do their jobs. The parallels between changing a corporate culture to make public responsibility and citizenship part of everyone's job, and changing it to make quality part of everyone's job, are striking:

- *Both require leadership's commitment.* 3M, USAA, and IMC stand as models of citizenship because their leaders clearly communicate its importance by encouraging involvement and by getting involved themselves.

- *Both demand employee involvement.* The opportunities for protecting the environment and acting ethically present themselves to individuals and teams in the course of their work. The opportunities for serving their communities are less evident but equally compelling. Employees must be empowered to recognize and respond to these opportunities.

- *Both need clear direction.* The more explicit the expectations for conducting business ethically, protecting the public health and safety and the environment, and serving the community, the more focused the response will be. Leaders in this area establish values and policies for corporate responsibility and citizenship, develop objectives that act on their values, and measure their progress.

- *Both must be managed and measured.* To assume that, left alone, people will act responsibly and ethically and will serve unselfishly is tantamount to assuming that, left alone, people will improve quality. Measures need to be established and processes managed for corporate responsibility and citizenship to take root and grow.

The new management model looks outward as well as inward. It recognizes that customers are more than the people who buy products and services, and that all customers need to be satisfied if the company is to have long-term success. Companies that approach this responsibility with open minds often discover that active corporate responsibility and citizenship make good business strategy.

As we wrote in Chapter 1, the Baldrige criteria define the system for our new management model. This "company responsibility and corporate citizenship" part of the system accounts for just 30 of the criteria's possible 1,000 points, but it is the only part that can cause the Department of Commerce to pass on a company the panel of judges has recommended. The criteria state that *award recipients are to serve as appropriate models of total quality achievement for other U.S. companies.* In other words, if the rest of a company's system is world-class but its ethical or environmental record stinks, it is not fit to serve as a model. Or to win an award for quality excellence.

17 SYSTEM ASSESSMENTS

Eastman Kodak Company

AT&T

Graniterock

In the new business management model, the role of assessments has evolved from punitive to supportive, from a hunt for problems and mistakes to a search for ways to improve, from assigning blame to offering assistance. The change in attitude reflects the enlightened view that problems with operational performance or quality are almost always caused by problems with the system, not problems with people. To improve the system, you must first know what condition it is in and where the improvements need to be made. That is the purpose of a system assessment.

System assessments tend to be like annual physical examinations: You may check your blood pressure or cholesterol level regularly, and you may need a checkup when you are ill, but a thorough, general examination—a personal "system assessment"—comes but once a year. The same is true for an assessment of your organization's system. "We believe we should check our system annually," says Dale Myers, district manager of quality planning for AT&T. "Everyone reviews budgets and tracks financials monthly, but they are the result of all the processes that make up your quality system. It seems reasonable to check the health of that system once a year."

The subjects of the exam may disagree. Unlike an individual's physical examination, a system checkup relies on a self-assessment for accuracy and completeness—and the self-assessment is not a painless process. A business system is a complex set of elements. The interaction of those elements is what makes the system function, but it is also what makes an assessment so difficult. You cannot study the system by isolating and assessing one element in it, such as one functional area or one process, and ignoring how it affects and is affected by other elements in the system. For that reason, an effective system assessment has two components: (1) a team willing to do the hard work of performing the assessment and (2) a tool it can use to conduct a valid assessment.

The tool must be capable of assessing the entire system as well as the key elements that make up that system. High-performance companies, including the three companies we will study in this chapter, have embraced the only assessment tool with these capabilities: the criteria for the Malcolm Baldrige National Quality Award.

As we stated in Chapter 1, the Baldrige criteria represent a business management model that addresses every element in an organization. They have been scrutinized, debated, interpreted, and improved, but the criteria have not been replaced as the preeminent system assessment tool. As Kay Whitmore, former chairman, president, and CEO of Eastman Kodak Company, wrote in his company's self-assessment workbook: "I believe that performance against the national quality award criteria is a leading indicator of a unit's future success."

Other leaders concur. Kodak, Intel, Corning, Honeywell, and others have created internal system assessments using the Baldrige criteria as their tool. In Chapter 1, we quoted Robert Shafto, president of The New England, who said, "I've become more and more convinced that the Baldrige is a management guide for business success, and if you meet all the requirements, you'll end up satisfying the customer—hence, grow the business."

To meet all the requirements, a company must understand what they are, assess itself (or its candidate unit) based on the requirements, then use the findings of the assessment as a guide for improving. Each of these three steps requires a serious commitment if it is to be accomplished. In this chapter, we will look at how Kodak, AT&T, and Graniterock are using the Baldrige criteria to assess their business systems. We will use their experiences to explore these questions:

- Who does the assessment?
- How do we conduct a system assessment?
- How is the assessment evaluated?

- How are the results of the assessment used to improve?
- How is the assessment process improved?

We will devote this chapter to system assessments because such assessments, based on the Baldrige criteria, are critical to a company's ability to understand and improve its management model. We acknowledge that other quality assessments must also be done. Kodak, AT&T, and Graniterock perform frequent and diverse quality assessments that include such tools as employee satisfaction surveys, evaluations by customers, product quality testing, process analysis, and ISO certification. The key assessments are discussed in the relevant chapters of this book; for example, employee satisfaction surveys as an assessment tool are described in Chapter 9. In this chapter, we will focus on how our role models assess their systems by means of the Baldrige criteria.

MODELS OF EXCELLENCE

Eastman Kodak Company serves two primary business segments: imaging (photography, office imaging applications such as copiers and printers, printing and publishing, and motion pictures and television) and health (diagnostic imaging and information systems). Kodak has more than 132,000 employees at marketing and manufacturing operations in more than 50 countries. Its headquarters is in Rochester, New York.

AT&T is a global company that provides communications and information to more than 90 million customers, including consumers, businesses, and government. The company has annual revenues of more than $52 billion and 130,000 employees. AT&T operates in more than 200 countries and territories around the world. It has produced three Baldrige Award winners: Network Systems Group, Transmission Systems Business Unit (1992; now part of Lucent Technologies); Universal Card Services (1992); and Consumer Communications (1994).

Graniterock produces high-quality construction materials—rock, sand, and gravel aggregates; readymix concrete; and asphalt—for road and highway construction and maintenance and for residential and commercial building construction, and is a heavy engineering contractor under the name Pavex Construction Company. Founded in 1900, the company markets its products in the central coast region of California, where it operates the largest crushed-rock quarry west of the Mississippi River. It has nearly 500 employees. Graniterock won the Baldrige Award in 1992.

USING THE BALDRIGE AWARD CRITERIA
TO ASSESS YOUR SYSTEM

All three of our role models use the Baldrige criteria to assess their businesses. AT&T's assessment process, which is currently being revised to reflect changes in organizational structure, paralleled the Baldrige program's process. A board of examiners presided; the requirement that those business units were required to submit full-blown applications; the evaluation and judging process was at least as stringent as the Baldrige judging process; and there were several ways of sharing best practices.

Kodak offers two types of assessment to its business units:

1. A self-assessment using the Kodak Quality System Review.
2. An assessment by an examination team.

Graniterock has applied for the Baldrige Award every year since 1989 and will continue to write an application every year, solely for assessment purposes.

Kodak requires business units to perform assessments using the Baldrige criteria. The focus is on the voice of the customer and the soundness of key processes. In *The Baldrige Quality System: The Do-It-Yourself Way to Transform Your Business*, Stephen George identified the benefits of the application (assessment) process that will be visible in the activities of the role models described in this chapter. The application process:

1. *Involves and motivates people.* To accurately assess the quality of your system, you need to explore every nook and cranny of every process, work unit, team, department, and so on. You need people to do the research and people to provide the answers.
2. *Provides a proven quality system.* A system assessment is only as good as the assessment tool, which is why so many companies are using the Baldrige criteria.
3. *Focuses on the customer.* The goal of each company—of every company's business system—is to satisfy its customers. An assessment using the Baldrige criteria shows how satisfying customers must be the focus of the entire system.
4. *Assesses quality.* Not only do the criteria identify the elements in a business system, but they also provide a means of assessing the quality of effort for each element and for the system as a whole. As Joe Rocca, one of the writers of IBM Rochester's Baldrige Award-winning

application, said, "We thought we had a good quality program, and now we've got one that's ten times better for having gone through the application process."

5. *Demands data.* Without a formal system assessment, few people are able to describe with any accuracy the quality of their system or the elements in it. Instead, they offer a nice story or a good hunch or a best guess. A system assessment using the Baldrige criteria quickly dismisses such soft estimations by providing hard data.

6. *Provides feedback.* Any company that has performed a system assessment using the Baldrige criteria will tell you that the real value of the process is the feedback it provides. Graniterock's feedback reports, on its first two Baldrige applications, listed 110 areas for improvement. The company used the list to drive its quality improvement efforts (as we will describe later in this chapter).

7. *Encourages sharing.* The Baldrige criteria's common system, language, and metric promote sharing. AT&T has created a Pockets of Excellence report and sponsors sharing rallies to encourage internal sharing of best practices. (We will discuss the report and conference later in this chapter.)

8. *Stimulates change.* Kodak, AT&T, Graniterock, and hundreds of other companies that are using the Baldrige criteria to assess their systems understand that the goal of the assessment process is improvement. AT&T started its Baldrige assessment process to accelerate progress toward its goals. At the 1993 Quest for Excellence conference, in Washington, DC, all five 1992 Baldrige Award winners stated that applying for the Baldrige Award speeded up their pace of improvement.

9. *Builds financial success.* Continuous assessment and improvement in quality must lead to the improvement of the system's products and services. As we illustrated in Chapter 1, quality improvements are directly linked to increases in customer satisfaction and shareholder value. When you improve the system, the products of that system must also improve, and this improvement results in a growing market share and improved profitability.

Companies embrace Baldrige-like assessment processes because they understand the benefits. At larger companies, that understanding does not often extend to the people who must perform the assessments, who may then see the assessment process as a chore they must fit in around their regular jobs. Whether companies dictate that assessments will be done or inspire business units to participate, the assessment process is always more effective if business unit leadership supports and is involved in the process.

GETTING COMMITMENT TO THE ASSESSMENT PROCESS

One of the first problems a company faces as it is establishing an assessment process is how to get buy-in from the business units, divisions, or departments it wants assessed. "In the old days, a company's corporate headquarters dictated to a business unit that it must conduct an assessment," says AT&T's Myers. "That usually produced a half-hearted application, and feedback that was useless." AT&T wanted its people to give the application their best effort, so they made applying for the AT&T Chairman's Quality Award a voluntary process.

With the trend toward decentralization and increased autonomy for business units, companies are increasingly sensitive about telling those units what to do. Like AT&T, many are choosing to inspire rather than demand participation. The benefit of relying on motivation to get an assessment done is that the participants recognize its value and conduct a useful assessment. The disadvantage is that units can choose not to participate, thus denying themselves and the company the benefits of the assessment.

Kodak both inspires and demands participation. "We have eight business units that must assess themselves annually, using one of our assessment forms," says George Vorhauer, director of corporate quality initiatives. "We've said all along that this isn't something different from your business; this is to make you more competitive, to add value, and to better serve the customer." Vorhauer admits that not all business units appreciate these benefits. "Early on, there was a tendency to see this as a lay-on—something you do in addition to the important job you have—rather than a way to measure and improve. We've addressed that by focusing more on the units' plans to improve rather than their score on the assessment."

WHO SHOULD DO THE ASSESSMENT?

Graniterock's executive committee reviews and approves the company's annual Baldrige application and uses it to gauge companywide improvement. Kodak created a matrix and abbreviated report processes so that the executives could assess their unit in less time than a full application requires. AT&T, which encouraged its business units and divisions to participate, used to require full Baldrige applications. In 1992, 32 of slightly more than 50 eligible units applied for the AT&T Chairman's Quality Award.

What these and other companies have learned is that senior management involvement in the assessment process results in three major benefits:

1. It establishes the system assessment process as the unit for or the company's primary tool for continuous improvement.
2. It creates an annual learning and improvement cycle, beginning with feedback to the assessment, that includes planning, execution, and evaluation.
3. It improves senior executives' ability to understand and improve the system they oversee.

The degree to which these benefits are realized relates directly to the degree to which senior executives are involved in the assessment process. Those who take the time to learn what the criteria are asking and what their company or unit is doing become "systems thinkers," able to identify the elements in their system and to see how those elements work together to achieve the company's goals. This holistic perspective is available to all who work on the assessment process, whether they are executives or employees to whom the assessment has been delegated, but the organization gains most by executive involvement because executives have the greatest control over the system. Leaders who resist getting actively involved seem to believe that participating in the assessment process is not a good use of their time. The experience of our quality role models suggests they are wrong.

CONDUCTING A SYSTEM ASSESSMENT

An organization can conduct a system assessment for an internal or an external deadline. Any company or unit of any size can set its own deadline at any time of the year. AT&T states the annual deadline for its Chairman's Quality Award in the application guidelines it distributes with copies of the Baldrige criteria. For small companies intent on performing a system assessment, senior management must drive the process if it is to be completed by the deadline.

External deadlines offer the advantage of providing an immovable deadline. A system assessment packaged as a Baldrige application must be completed by the Baldrige deadline, which is typically in early April. Organizations can also submit their system assessments for state quality awards. More than half the states in the country now have or will soon have quality awards based on the Baldrige criteria.

The point is: Identify a firm deadline, or the assessment will never get done.

To assess your system using the Baldrige criteria, plan on a three-month process from start to finish. Kodak estimates that writing a full application takes around 2,500 labor-hours, which seems like a good average. Companies such as Xerox have reported spending much more time, because of the size of the organization represented in their application and because they were simultaneously working on improvement. At the other extreme, consider how the Globe Metallurgical executive wrote his company's award-winning application in one long weekend. How long it will take you depends on the size of your company or unit, the availability of system data and information, and the maturity of your quality improvement process. Size determines complexity; data availability determines research time; and maturity determines how easily you can match what you do with what the criteria measure.

The process of creating the assessment document, as described in *The Baldrige Quality System,* follows fourteen major steps:

1. *Involve senior management.*
2. *Establish application team(s).* Teams share the work, bring different perspectives to the task, and spread the learning experience to more people.
3. *Train team members.* The first exposure to the Baldrige criteria can be more confusing than enlightening, unless people receive some training in how to understand the criteria and apply them to their organization.
4. *Assign responsibilities.* The assessment process is most effective when there is clear accountability for gathering data and information, writing responses, and producing the report.
5. *Collect data and information.* The quality of the assessment depends on the quality of the data and information it presents. A system assessment that is vague or anecdotal or that reports glowingly on what the organization hopes to achieve is worthless.
6. *Identify areas for improvement.* Areas for improvement materialize in the course of conducting the assessment. Wise companies understand

that these areas are the primary goal of the process, the gold nuggets that make the assessment worthwhile.

7. *Communicate needs, ideas, and information.* As the assessment process proceeds, individuals and teams tend to focus on a particular category, work process, or functional area, thus losing sight of the system in which they exist. Constant communication helps to maintain a systems perspective.

8. *Edit the first draft.* Editing the responses to the criteria is an exercise in interpretation and communication that requires diligence and clarity. It is also very hard work, but the payoff—learning to think about what your organization does as a system—is worth it.

9. *Begin the layout, including graphics.* An essential part of clear communication is the presentation of information. Charts and graphs can help explain processes, information, and results.

10. *Evaluate the first draft.* Reviewers usually include the authors of the assessment document and the organization's senior people (if they did not write it). Internal and external quality experts and consultants may also be included.

11. *Write subsequent drafts.* The first draft evaluation always identifies sections that are inappropriate, weak, inaccurate, and wrongly placed. Subsequent drafts can only make the assessment stronger.

12. *Coordinate writing and graphics.* As the deadline approaches, an individual or team must coordinate all the pieces that will make up the document.

13. *Produce the final draft.*

14. *Print and deliver the assessment.*

Almost every organization that creates a system assessment document follows a similar process. Major variations occur when companies assign responsibility for the document to an individual or a very small team, but even then, data must be gathered, areas for improvement identified, drafts written, and the document assembled. Set a deadline, or the assessment will not get done. Expect resistance, no matter what deadline you establish; the people who will be involved in the assessment process are already busy. This is when senior executive leadership becomes critical.

Leadership is also needed when the assessment is used to drive improvement. People involved in the assessment are usually worn out from the process, but they are also aware of the weaknesses it has revealed. Because the assessment has little value unless it is used to improve, leadership must make it possible for employees to integrate the findings with their ongoing improvement efforts. As AT&T's Myers says, "From my observations, improvement only happens at a significant rate when leaders make it clear that the health of the goose that lays the golden egg matters as much as the golden egg."

ALTERNATIVES TO USING THE BALDRIGE AWARD APPLICATION

Kodak created two alternatives to help reduce the amount of time it would take to complete its assessments.

In 1997, the self-assessment using the Kodak Quality System Review and the Baldrige team assessment focused on anything related to customers. Each senior leader at Kodak has identified actions and goals that are important to his or her business unit. These goals and actions are captured in the Management Performance Commitment Plan (MPCP), which ties significant portions of leaders' take-home pay to customer satisfaction (30%), employee satisfaction (30%), and shareholder results (40%). Results are reviewed quarterly.

Some units choose to conduct the self-assessment using Kodak's own matrix, shown in Table 17.1 on pages 220–223. "The matrix allows you to arrive at a Baldrige-like score in eight hours," says Vorhauer. "If you multiply that by the number of executives who perform the assessment, you've got 80 to 100 hours for an assessment—significantly less than a full application—and you also get a way to improve." As it developed the matrix, Kodak had units write applications and complete the self-assessment, then compared the scores. It found a strong correlation between the matrix and application scores, suggesting that the scoring aspect of the self-assessment matrix would give units an accurate picture of their systems and of the areas that needed to be improved.

The matrix describes ten "ranks" for each of the seven Baldrige categories (based on the 1991 criteria). Each member of the assessment team, which is usually a unit's management team, scores every cell in the matrix, using the following codes:

Deployed (D)	The unit has fully applied the characteristics described in the cell.
Partially deployed (P)	The characteristics have been applied only to major areas within the unit.

Not deployed (N)   Application of the characteristics is minimal or anecdotal.

The ratings should be verifiable through available data. After each assessment team member has scored all 70 cells, the team meets to arrive at a consensus score for each cell and for the unit as a whole.

EVALUATING THE ASSESSMENT AT KODAK

At the Kodak consensus meeting, team members agree on what each cell is requesting, then on what score is appropriate for their unit. They work on one category at a time, proceeding from Cell 1 to Cell 10. When they have scored all cells, they figure the total score for the assessment. The team begins by identifying the lowest cell in a category that received a score of N (not deployed). Below that cell, each cell with a rank of D (deployed) is worth 1, and each cell with a rank of P (partially deployed) is worth ½. The total of Ds plus Ps is the rank for that category.

For example, assume your team agreed that your unit's scores for the leadership category were as follows:

Cell 10 = N
Cell 9 = N
Cell 8 = P
Cell 7 = N
Cell 6 = N
Cell 5 = D
Cell 4 = P
Cell 3 = P
Cell 2 = D
Cell 1 = D

The lowest cell with a score of N is Cell 6. The three Ds and 2 Ps below that cell add up to 4.0, which is the score for the leadership category. The P for Cell 8 does not count because it is in a higher cell than the first N.

To arrive at the total rank for the category, the number rank for each category is multiplied by the weight given to the category. The weights are shown in the matrix directly under each category heading. Using our example, the rank for the leadership category (4) times the weight for the category (10) equals a score of 40 points. The total of the scores for all

TABLE 17.1. Kodak self-assessment matrix

Rank	Leadership 10	Information and Analysis 6	Strategic Planning 9	Human Resources 15	QA of Products/ Services 15	Quality Results 15	Customer Satisfaction 30
10 Maturing	Quality is placed equal to profits, market share, and stock price.	Measures reviewed regularly to identify improvement opportunities; data and information directly affect behaviors and impact overall results.	Quality improvement plans are totally integrated into long-term and short-term plans.	Measures and trends of employee well-being and morale show "Best-in-Class" when benchmarked against peer companies and units.	Process in place for continually reducing cycle time (the amount of time required to develop and introduce new or improved products).	Sustained (> 3 years) results, clearly caused by approach (use of QLP), indicate "World Class" in major areas (supplier, product, service, and support).	"Best-in-Class" in customer satisfaction for products and services (include surveys, competitive awards, ratings by independent organization, trends in market share, trends in gaining customers).
9	Unit managers demonstrate Kodak's five Quality Principles outside the company and encourage/positively reinforce employees for doing the same.	All teams derive data/informational needs to support KRAs that have been developed using QLP.	KRA improvement plans in place at all organizational levels.	QLP usage is an essential element of reward and promotion systems.	Human factors and mistake proofing used to design and continually improve job functions.	Quality levels of products, services, and processes considered "Best-in-Class."	Evidence that improvement results are caused by Quality Leadership Process approach.
8	Reward and consequence processes reinforce QLP involvement.	Process in place and used to track data and identify areas for immediate corrective action.	Rewards/consequences are based on both behaviors and results.	Training is evaluated for improvement at four levels: (1) attitude about course (content, instructor), (2) immediate knowledge gained from course, (3) application to job and performance, and (4) impact on business results.	A formalized process, such as Quality Function Deployment, is used to translate customer needs during product/service development.	Significant improvement trends noted (3 years minimum) in major areas.	Customers actively involved in problem solving/improvement effort.

7	All teams have completed at least one full QLP cycle; management performance measures based on progress in meeting KRAs; decisions based on vision.	75% of teams derive data/informational needs to support KRAs that have been developed using QLP.	Planning processes are reviewed and improved at least annually.	All employees are trained in QLP; additional education and career development opportunities to support continuous improvement efforts widely available.	Cross-functional teams are used throughout product development cycle for major products and services.	Benchmark results show "World Class" in some areas.	Positive trends evident in all customer satisfaction indicators.
6 *Growing*	At least 75% of teams have completed at least one full QLP cycle.	Processes in place to improve reliability, insure consistency and validity of data, and reduce cycle time of data gathering, analysis, and dissemination.	A documented process for employee, supplier, and customer contribution to the planning process is used.	At least 75% of all employees have some QLP training and are involved in continuous improvement.	Evidence exists that quantitative measures of performance extend fully into both manufacturing and nonmanufacturing areas of the unit.	All improvement efforts and results are linked to KRAs.	Process for communicating customer information to appropriate units exists and is used.
5	At least top half of interlocking teams use QLP to guide all meetings.	50% of teams derive data/informational needs to support KRAs that have been developed using QLP.	Resource allocation is consistent with corporate/unit KRAs.	Resources are allocated for development and implementation of educational plans to support growth in core competencies.	Evidence exists that strong emphasis is placed on prevention rather than *fire-fighting* and inspection; root cause analysis is used where problems exist.	Positive quality result trends exist in most major areas.	Process exists and is in use for integrating customer satisfaction data into the continuous improvement cycle of the company.

Key: QLP = Quality Leadership Process, Kodak's process for improving quality; AOP = Annual Operating Plan; KRA = Key Result Area, a broad area of performance.

(continued)

TABLE 17.1. *(Continued)*

Rank	Leadership 10	Information and Analysis 6	Strategic Planning 9	Human Resources 15	QA of Products/Services 15	Quality Results 15	Customer Satisfaction 30
4	Management teaches QLP to their direct reports and serves as role model.	Data appropriately analyzed, reviewed, and disseminated to the right people in a timely fashion (e.g., trend analysis > 2 years, projections, performance evaluations).	QLP used for short-term and long-term planning; every unit has a written plan.	Education and career development plans exist and are linked to business unit goals, tactics, and strategies.	Process in place for ensuring precision and accuracy of measurement systems, including traceability to controlled international standards.	Trends of quality measures exist for processes that produced the products or services (e.g., lead times, yields, waste, inventory levels, rework of products and repeat services, first-time success rates, environmental improvements).	Processes exist for identifying and using: (1) market segments and customers, (2) product/service features and their importance to customers.
3	Have unitwide plan for implementation of QLP, including necessary resources.	Leading indicators developed and used for decision making and for taking preventive measures toward recurrence of problems.	AOP addresses: technology, human resources, suppliers, environmental issues, and competitive actions/reactions.	QLP training scheduled for all employees.	Process in place to ensure quality of products and services; audit process used for ensuring the total quality system; continuous improvement methods are used.	Positive results exist as a consequence of working with suppliers to improve their quality (include awards and other feedback).	Proactive processes exist for determining and improving customer satisfaction (beyond measurement of complaints, returns, and warranty rate).

2	Mission and vision defined, published, and understood by all stakeholders.	External data gathered (i.e., customer, supplier, competition, benchmark, environmental).	Process in place for linking customer/market needs with the strategic planning process.	Recognition/rewards (beyond performance appraisal) occur in specific, sincere, immediate, and personal ways.	Development and production of new products and services documented and followed/document control process in place and used.	Trends of key quality indicators exist for suppliers and their services.	Processes exist to promptly resolve customer complaints.
1 *Beginning*	Direct interaction of management with employees, customers, suppliers, and other stakeholders regarding Kodak Quality Principles.	Internal data gathered (i.e., product, operations, processes, employees, safety, health, environmental, regulatory, quality results).	A documented long-term (2–5 years) and short-term (1–2 years) planning process is used.	Measures and trends of employee well-being and morale exist.	Customer input used to develop and produce products and/or services with required characteristics.	Trends exist in key measures of product and service quality, including incoming supplies (e.g., reliability, timeliness, accuracy, performance, behavior, delivery, documentation, and appearance).	Contract/guarantee/warranty policy adhered to for product/service performance.

Key: QLP = Quality Leadership Process, Kodak's process for improving quality; AOP = Annual Operating Plan; KRA = Key Result Area, a broad area of performance.

seven categories is the unit's assessment score. (Later in this chapter, we will describe how to use the score and the rest of the self-assessment to improve.)

EVALUATING ASSESSMENTS THAT USE BALDRIGE AWARD CRITERIA

Evaluating a Baldrige application, whether internally or externally, also involves arriving at consensus scores; the difference is that someone outside the unit does the assessing and scoring. Many large companies have patterned their assessment process after the Baldrige process (also described in *The Baldrige Quality System*). Kodak trains about 50 people a year for its internal Board of Examiners. AT&T annually creates its own board of examiners; it trained 300 internal examiners in 1993. "The training for our examiners is based on materials from the National Quality Award process," says Myers, "but we strengthened the training on site visits and giving feedback. We also work hard to make sure each five- or six-person examiner team reflects a diversity of job levels and functional areas, such as manufacturing, finance, research and development, and so on."

Like the Baldrige application process, AT&T's process began with examiner teams scoring the applications. Only those that met certain thresholds proceeded to the site-visit phase, where the assessment was clarified and verified. Unlike the Baldrige Award, AT&T rewarded both

TABLE 17.2.   AT&T achievement awards (level of excellence)

Award	Point Score	Description
Gold	876–1,000	Outstanding effort and results in all categories. Effective integration and sustained results. National and world leaders.
Silver	751–875	Effective efforts in all categories, and outstanding in many. Good integration and good to excellent results in all areas. Full deployment. Many industry leaders.
Bronze	601–750	Evidence of effective efforts in most categories, and outstanding in several. Deployment and results show strength, but some efforts may lack maturity. Clear areas for further attention.
Crystal	500–600	Evidence of effective efforts in many categories and outstanding in some. A good prevention-based process. Many areas lack maturity. Further deployment and results needed to demonstrate continuity.

TABLE 17.3.   AT&T improvement awards (rate of progress)

Award	Point Score	Description
Gold	200 points per year	Improvement at a world-class rate
Silver	150 points per year	Improvement at an excellent rate
Bronze	100 points per year	Improvement at a very good rate

achievement and improvement. "If we hadn't done this, units in the 200-to 300-point range would have sat out the process," says Myers. "What we wanted most was to get everyone involved."

The descriptions of what it took to earn each level of the Achievement Award indicate what examiners looked for when they evaluated an application (see Tables 17.2 and 17.3).

The assessment process is a straightforward evaluation of how an application responds to the criteria. When the criteria request a process—how you do something—the examiners assess the approach you are taking—how sound, systematic, and prevention-based it is—and then determine how fully the approach has been implemented. When the criteria request results—the measures of what you are doing—the examiners study the direction and levels of trends in all key areas, and compare them to the trends of competitors and world-class benchmarks. For each item, the examiners identify what you are doing very well (strengths) and what you need to do better (areas for improvement), and then figure your score.

USING ASSESSMENT RESULTS TO IMPROVE

The results of a Baldrige assessment lend themselves to action. Such phrases as "process is not evident," "limited deployment," and "trends not given" are common in a Baldrige feedback report, and they always direct the organization's attention to specific areas for improvement. The problem many organizations face is how to tackle so many areas at once.

Graniterock organized the 110 areas for improvement listed in its first two Baldrige feedback reports into ten categories. It formed a corporate quality team to work on each category. Each team had a senior executive facilitator and five or six employees, usually including one middle manager and people from all levels of the company. "The executives' evaluations depend on the success of their teams," says Val Verutti, director of quality support, "while the vertical membership unified our purpose and our people to accomplish something. Each team has a definite mission, and they've all been reasonably successful at accomplishing what they set out to do."

Over time, baseline goals have replaced the work of most Corporate Quality Teams. Baseline goals are annual improvement goals that include before-and-after measurements of process or system improvement. Entire branches or departments are involved in accomplishing the goals.

This system assessment and improvement process is so important to Graniterock that it has continued to write Baldrige examinations annually, even though it could not actually apply again until 1998. It hires former Baldrige examiners to score its applications and conduct site visits.

Many companies lose the value of their Baldrige assessments by not having a plan for acting on the feedback. Part of the problem is that the feedback is nonprescriptive; it tells you when something is missing or weak, but it does not tell you how to fix it. AT&T addressed this issue in several ways. Its initial feedback, like its assessment process, paralleled the Baldrige feedback: clear, concise, and nonprescriptive. Copies of the feedback report were given to the head of the organization and the unit's application coordinator to use as they wished. A unit's score and the data in its application were not shared with any other unit or with corporate staff. "We were overly strict about enforcing confidentiality because we wanted to develop trust. We needed honest sharing through the application to make the feedback helpful," says Myers.

If the applicant requested it, AT&T required the examination team leader, the senior examiner, to give an oral presentation on the feedback to the applicant's senior management team. "Nearly every unit took advantage of that," says Myers. "It gave them a chance to ask questions and clarify the written report. But we still asked the team leaders to be nonprescriptive, primarily because we didn't want to undermine the quality manager in that unit." A quality manager who wanted a prescription could request an advisory session with the senior examiner and other team members. The session focused on what the team would do if it were responsible for acting on its report. However, the responsibility for actually doing something still belonged to the unit.

AT&T also used the assessment process to spread knowledge about best practices. At one-day "sharing rallies," representatives of the most successful units described to AT&T quality professionals and operational managers what the units were doing. In addition, a Pockets of Excellence report identified, for each Baldrige item, those units that scored 60 percent or higher. The report encouraged internal sharing and recognized those units that were excelling in specific areas.

The most coveted form of recognition comes with winning one of the Chairman's Quality Awards. To win, a unit had to meet the point ranges listed in Tables 17.2 and 17.3, have the score and assessment findings substantiated by a site visit, be recommended for an award by AT&T's internal panel of judges (17 senior managers and quality experts in 1992), and be considered a role model. Judges recommended winners to the Management Executive Committee, which reviewed the list to make sure everyone on it had earned the honor. As Myers notes, "All of these buy-ins and checks add credibility."

At the end of each October, AT&T brought in more than 1,000 people from all business units and divisions to its annual two-day AT&T Quality Conference. On the first night of the conference, the Management Executive Committee hosted a private dinner for the award winners, each of which was represented by the head of the organization and the quality manager. "This accomplished two things," says Myers. "The winners got to interact with the senior executives, and the senior executives got to learn what works."

The chairman presented the Achievement and Improvement Awards during the conference's plenary sessions. He described each unit's major accomplishments, invited the head of the unit and the quality manager to come onto the stage, and handed them their award, after which the unit head spoke briefly. The ceremony was broadcast live to over 100 AT&T locations. Such recognition further displayed AT&T's commitment to the quality improvement process—and it created more than a little desire among unit leaders to stand on that stage.

AT&T also studied the feedback reports for all units, to identify common threads that the company as a whole needed to work on. "We analyzed the results to find common strengths and areas for improvement, then fed these findings to the Management Executive Committee," says Myers. AT&T is currently creating a quality Website to help share information and provide wide access to quality resources.

At Kodak, each business unit is required to report its assessment data, obtained from an independent source or by self-assessment. Progress on actions initiated in response to the assessment is reported quarterly. "The idea that you've signed up for a goal and you're making or not making it— and management cares—is important," Vorhauer says.

Assessments using the Baldrige criteria yield a detailed snapshot of your system. You cannot realize the snapshot's value by passing it around for people to admire; it must be studied for clues about key areas that need to be improved, translated into a written improvement plan, and acted upon. Only then does the system assessment make the system better.

THE SHIFT IN THINKING

Until the Baldrige criteria came along, few organizations had ever assessed their entire business system. For one thing, no effective assessment tool existed. In addition, the search for ways to improve rarely revealed the need for a system assessment. Problems belonged to departments, work groups, and individuals, not to the system as a whole. Only when the quality movement began harping about the system being the problem did people wonder what condition their system was in.

Companies that are using the Baldrige criteria to transform their business start with an assessment. They need a new understanding of the nature of their system, a baseline for gauging their improvement, and a sense for what must be worked on first. All these are available through a Baldrige assessment, whether that assessment takes the form of a 50-page application or an improvement plan based on a matrix score.

However, our experience has shown that the more time people invest in the assessment process, the more value that process has for them and for their company. An organization's score for a full application may correlate with its score for another type of assessment, such as the Kodak self-assessment matrix, but the benefits will not be the same. People who must wrestle with the criteria to understand what they are asking, then assemble a response that meets the criteria, become "systems thinkers" during that process. They begin to assimilate the Baldrige values—customer-driven quality, management by fact, continuous improvement, and so on—and apply them to their daily tasks. They think more critically, ask better questions, look for root causes of problems, and strive to improve.

Ironically, a broad system assessment inspires personal quality. (We will discuss this more in Chapter 18.) The system assessment also produces a road map for continuous improvement. Graniterock builds its improvement efforts around the areas for improvement identified in its feedback reports. Kodak uses its measurement process to drive improvement plans in each of the units assessed. AT&T improved by sharing how its internal role models excelled in different areas of the Baldrige criteria.

A system assessment using the Baldrige criteria will identify strengths and weaknesses for every area we discuss in this book. By using the criteria to assess your system, you set in motion a process of discovery and improvement that can jump-start a failing system and energize a lumbering one. Just ask the Baldrige Award winners. (Or check their results at the Baldrige program's Website: http://www.quality.nist.gov/)

18 CROSSING THE RIVER: THE TRANSITION TO THE NEW MANAGEMENT MODEL

Three years, minimum! That's the time frame most companies of any size are looking at before the transition from a traditional management model to the new systems model begins to become institutionalized. Small companies can make the change more quickly; larger companies tend to take longer.

But you don't have to wait three years to realize the *benefits* of the new management model. Each of the action plans provided in this chapter offers immediate advantages. It may take three years before you have *all* the listening posts in place to tell you what customers are thinking, but your company will find itself getting closer to customers as each of those avenues of communication is established. It may be three years before employees feel empowered to shut down a manufacturing line or act on their own to solve a customer's problem, but the process of learning team and problem-solving skills and taking responsibility will bring steady improvement. The transition to systems management is an *ongoing process of continuous improvement* that begins when your company commits itself to managing by quality.

The transition is rarely smooth. Roles are being redefined. Responsibilities change. Routines are scrutinized. Like each person in the company, the company itself is changing jobs, *learning to take a systematic approach to satisfying customers.*

Nearly two decades ago, Marilyn Ferguson wrote about change in the workplace in her book, *The Aquarian Conspiracy* (J. P. Tarcher, Inc., 1980). She quoted Dick Raymond, the founder of a Bay Area network of

229

entrepreneurs called Briarpatch, on the transition from working for some-one to working for yourself. His insights are equally appropriate for peo-ple involved in the transition to the new management model:

> Crossing this river is difficult: it means leaving behind some of your old ideas about work and jobs. Most of us try to tiptoe around the pain, but it's important to talk about some of the agonies one is apt to confront. . . . When you start abandoning your old beliefs or values, some very primal circuits get ignited. . . . You may be stuck on the threshold for two or three years. Before moving on, you have to clear away all your cherished beliefs.

The process of clearing away cherished beliefs is one reason the tran-sition to the new model takes at least three years. This river is wide, the current is fast, and the riverbed is strewn with rocks. Even when they can see the need to cross, people will wish they could remain on safe ground—which is why an unshakable commitment to change is essential.

Gaining this commitment is the first step in your transition. You need to marshal your forces before crossing the river. In this chapter, we have organized the transition process into a logical sequence that any company can follow. The sequence *you* follow depends on your com-pany's unique situation. If you are in a hurry, you may need to jump to phase 4 and start grappling with your processes, then backfill with plan-ning, training, and determining customer requirements. If you have more time, you may want to begin with a system assessment to deter-mine what you have to work with and where you need to go first. *There is no single course we can prescribe for your company.* Use your under-standing of your company's needs to construct a transition plan that will guide you toward your goals.

As you consider the transition and then move through it, remember to focus on the *system.* It is easy to get caught up in the steps, to fall in love with employee involvement or process management or any of the other all-consuming phases you will pass through. *The goal is to align and im-prove your system for satisfying customers.*

In Chapter 1, we introduced the diagram of the new business man-agement model, repeated here as Exhibit 18.1. Each element in this model has been explained through the experiences of the 51 models of excellence featured in Chapters 2 through 17. Taken together, our role models suggest a systematic approach to focusing all your resources on meeting your customers' expectations. They demonstrate how any com-pany that has a clear and accurate understanding of its customers' expec-tations, and of their system for meeting those expectations, can achieve customer satisfaction.

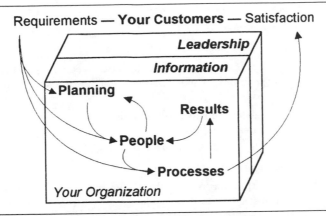

EXHIBIT 18.1.   The new management model.

This chapter sets the following course for gaining understanding:

- Phase 1 outlines the steps you can take to get senior management to commit to change.
- Phase 2 describes what you can do to determine your customers' perceptions of your company and the condition of your system.
- Phase 3 focuses on how you can institutionalize a customer focus.
- Phase 4 zeros in on strategic planning, employee involvement, and process management, and on your measurement system.
- Phase 5 addresses the alignment of every activity to meeting and exceeding customer expectations.
- Phase 6 looks at using the Baldrige criteria to assess your system and initiate the next round of improvements.

Each of the goals identified in Tables 18.1 through 18.5 lists the chapters where information about the subject may be found. For example, if you wonder what gaining senior management's commitment might look like (Table 18.1), you can refer to Chapter 2 for a description of how the senior executives at Corning, FedEx, and Marlow Industries lead their companies' quality improvement processes. Their stories, like the steps listed in the tables, suggest directions your company can take as it moves toward the new management model.

PHASE 1: COMMIT TO CHANGE

Senior managers are the system's gatekeepers. If, and only if, they open the gates to cultural change, will the transition begin. The leaders of

TABLE 18.1.   Action plan for committing to change

Goal	Gain commitment (see Chapter 2)
Participants	Senior managers and their staffs.
Steps	• Assess your company's performance and compare it to your perception of how much better it could be to industry and world-class leaders.
	• Learn about the new model through reading, attending conferences and seminars, and training.
	• Study the management styles of the Baldrige Award winners.
	• Look at your company from your customers' perspective.
	• As a staff, brainstorm what the company would look like with the new management model in place.
	• Identify the benefits, drawbacks, and obstacles of such a change.
	• Develop a new vision, mission, policies, and values that capture the company you wish to be.
	• Commit, as the company's leaders, to the long-term, permanent transition to management by quality.
	• Communicate this commitment throughout the company.
	• Begin work on a system of measures of senior executive and company performance based on the new management model.

world-class companies not only open the gates, they lead the transformation, putting their minds, hearts, and souls into this new management model. Table 18.1 provides an action plan for phase 1.

PHASE 2: ASSESS YOUR SYSTEM

By the time companies turn to a new approach to management, most do not have much time for assessments. Companies, like people, resist dramatic change until they run out of options. However, even a quick assessment is better than going with the first improvement program that catches your eye.

The assessment should be both external and internal, ascertaining what your customers think of your company and what your own measures tell you. The more thorough the assessments, the easier it will be to establish baselines by which you can gauge progress, and to identify and prioritize areas for improvement. Table 18.2 provides an action plan for phase 2.

TABLE 18.2.   Action plan for assessing your system

Goal	Determine customers' perceptions of your company (see Chapter 3).
Participants	Executives, managers, supervisors, and other employees who have direct contact with customers, particularly members of marketing, sales, and customer service.
Steps	• Identify the primary markets and customers your new system will target.
	• Gather information from every possible source about these customers' requirements, expectations, and needs, and how your company is doing at fulfilling them.
	• Aggregate and analyze this information to determine the customers' requirements and their view of your company.
	• Run your findings past key customers to verify their accuracy.
	• Document and present findings to senior management.
Goal	Perform system assessment (see Chapter 17).
Participants	Employees needed to conduct the assessment.
Steps	• Establish the assessment team, train, and assign responsibilities.
	• Collect data and information.
	• Document and present findings to senior management.
Goal	Develop action plan (see Chapters 2–5).
Participants	Senior managers and their staffs, other employees.
Steps	• Compare findings with vision of where company needs to be, to identify strengths and areas for improvement.
	• Prioritize areas for improvement and assign to executive owners.
	• Determine how progress will be measured.
	• Formalize a process for periodic system assessments.

PHASE 3: INSTITUTIONALIZE A CUSTOMER FOCUS

Because the new management model is customer driven, there's no time like the present to put the customer behind the wheel. Unfortunately, it is not as easy as slipping the customer into the driver's seat and handing over the keys. Institutionalizing a customer focus requires getting close to customers, then acting on what they tell you. Many of the steps that make this possible will be taken again and again throughout all phases of the transition. Table 18.3 provides an action plan for phase 3.

TABLE 18.3.   Action plan for institutionalizing a customer focus

Goal	Establish listening posts (see Chapter 3).
Participants	All employees, primarily those in marketing, sales, and customer service.
Steps	• Identify all possible sources of information about present and potential customers.
	• Formalize processes for gathering information from these sources.
	• Assess the tools used to determine customer satisfaction and to improve the quality of information gathered, timeliness, usefulness, and so on.
Goal	Aggregate and analyze customer information (see Chapters 3 and 10).
Participants	Senior managers, planning process participants, members of marketing, sales, and customer service.
Steps	• Formalize a process for aggregating customer information from various listening posts.
	• Formalize processes for communicating to appropriate units/individuals information that needs immediate attention.
	• Formalize processes for analyzing the aggregated information.
	• Formalize processes for communicating this information to appropriate units/individuals.
Goal	Use customer requirements to drive internal processes (see Chapters 3–6, 10–15).
Participants	All employees.
Steps	• Determine links between customer satisfiers and internal processes and measures.
	• Focus on these key processes and measures in Phase 4.

PHASE 4: INSTITUTIONALIZE THE NEW MANAGEMENT MODEL

The transition to the new model will remain a transition until the model is institutionalized. Companies that flit from quality program to quality program with no process for reweaving the fabric of their organizations never stray far from their old management model.

Companies convert to the new model in one or more of four ways: strategic planning, employee involvement, process management, and their measurement system. Examples of each have been described in this book. The avenues you choose depend on which are more appropriate for your company, because one does not seem to be better or more effective than another. Keep in mind that you can work toward all four of the following

TABLE 18.4. Action plan for institutionalizing the new management model

Goal	Align all activities through the strategic planning process (see Chapter 4).
Participants	All levels of employees, customers, and suppliers.
Steps	• Define a single strategic planning process by adapting the "best practices" of world-class companies to your organization.
	• Identify who should be involved in the process, including all levels of employees, key customer representatives, and key suppliers.
	• Establish channels of communication that will feed key data and information into the planning process.
	• Determine the vital few long- and short-term goals necessary to improve customer satisfaction and operational performance.
	• Assign executive ownership for each goal.
	• Decide on measures for each goal.
	• Deploy the plan to all employees, verifying that the activities of divisions, departments, teams, and individuals are aligned with corporate objectives.
	• Formalize processes for assessing progress and helping groups not performing to plan.
Goal	Involve all employees in continuous improvement (see Chapters 2, 5–7).
Participants	All employees.
Steps	• Communicate vision, goals, requirements, and expectations to all employees (via executives, managers, and supervisors).
	• Formalize processes for ongoing communication of corporate values to all levels of employees.
	• Clarify management's role in the new system, and provide training and support to assist in the transition.
	• Train employees in the skills they need to assume responsibility for their processes and results.
	• Formalize processes for providing employees with the feedback they need to assess and improve performance.
	• Train employees in the skills they need to participate in teams.
	• Initiate the use of teams to manage and improve processes and solve problems.
Goal	Manage and improve all key processes (see Chapters 11 and 12).
Participants	All employees.
Steps	• Identify core processes that link directly to customer requirements.
	• Train employees in process management and improvement.
	• Assemble cross-functional teams to analyze key processes that cross departmental boundaries.
	• Formalize processes for using teams' findings to manage and improve processes.

(continued)

TABLE 18.4.   *(Continued)*

- Reorganize the company around its core processes.
- Formalize processes for managing and improving processes involving suppliers.
- Assign responsibility for addressing processes within departments.
- Formalize processes for managing and improving these processes, and for solving problems within these processes.
- Establish methods of communicating feedback to teams, and results to the whole organization.

Goal	Establish a system of measurement (see Chapter 14).
Participants	All employees.
Steps	• Use information about customer and company requirements to identify key measures.
	• Measure only what you can control.
	• Make sure all measures are easy to collect, report, and understand.
	• Train employees in taking, analyzing, and using measures to improve.
	• Formalize processes for collecting and reporting data.
	• Formalize processes for reviewing, analyzing, and using the data to improve.

goals at once, and that the steps toward each are often overlapping and complementary. And remember that many successful companies test everything before implementing it across the company. Use pilot projects liberally, to test and fine-tune your approaches. Table 18.4 on pages 235–236 provides an action plan for phase 4.

PHASE 5: ALIGN AND EXTEND YOUR MANAGEMENT GOALS

One of the primary goals of the new model is to align every division, department, team, individual, function, process, plan, product, and service to meeting and exceeding your customers' requirements and your company's performance goals. Once the fundamentals needed to do this are in place, you can turn your attention to less urgent, though equally important, areas of your system. The transition to the new model begins with the areas that have the greatest impact on customers and the company, then spreads out to encompass all that the company does. Now is a good

TABLE 18.5. Action plan for aligning the system

Goal	Align compensation and recognition programs with new management model (see Chapter 8).
Participants	All employees, particularly human resources professionals.
Steps	• Survey employees to understand their expectations and requirements for compensation and recognition programs.
	• Form cross-functional teams that represent your employee base, to assess and improve existing programs and develop and implement new ones.
	• Work with the teams to clarify the purpose of such programs; focus first on doing no harm and then on promoting the company's vision, mission, and goals.
	• Establish measures of each program's performance and contribution to the company's mission and goals.
	• Study the issues affecting compensation, to determine the best course of action for your company.
	• Involve employees in running the company's recognition programs.
	• Make at-risk pay and formal recognition dependent on measurable performance, preferably team performance.
	• Formalize processes for regular review and improvement of all compensation and recognition programs.
Goal	Treat employees as the company's most important asset (see Chapter 9).
Participants	All employees, particularly senior executives and human resources staff.
Steps	• Determine from employees what they require and expect in their work environment, to be healthy and satisfied.
	• Align the goals for employee health, well-being, and satisfaction with the company's mission and goals.
	• Develop ongoing measures of employee health, well-being, and satisfaction.
	• Formalize processes for reviewing and improving employee health, well-being, and satisfaction.
Goal	Establish a benchmarking program (see Chapter 15).
Participants	All employees.
Steps	• Involve senior executives and other decision makers in learning about what benchmarking is and what benefits it offers.
	• Formalize your company's benchmarking process; define who is involved, the steps in the process, and the expected results.
	• Train employees in the benchmarking process.
	• Use input from customers, suppliers, and employees to identify benchmarking opportunities, then prioritize those opportunities and assign responsibility.

(continued)

TABLE 18.5.   *(Continued)*

	• Empower benchmarking teams to organize and conduct the studies and present their recommendations.
	• Formalize processes for translating recommendations into action plans, and for evaluating and improving the benchmarking process.
Goal	Provide leadership and support for publicly important purposes (see Chapter 16).
Participants	All employees, particularly senior executives.
Steps	• Establish your company's mission, goals, and values in the areas of public responsibility and corporate citizenship.
	• Communicate these values throughout the organization, orally, through involvement in relevant activities, and by supporting employee participation in community affairs.
	• Develop measures for employee and company involvement in such areas as waste minimization, environmental responsibility, volunteerism, charitable contributions, and community service.
	• Formalize processes for reviewing and improving performance in these areas.

time to remind yourself of the implications of managing the system. Place everything that is going on in your company in a holistic context.

Think of it as staging a play. You have chosen the play, assigned parts, begun practice, and booked theaters. Your attention now expands to include creating a set, designing costumes, and publicizing the event. You still work hard to fine-tune the performances, but you understand that the performances are only the most visible part of the production, and that each area you neglect has the potential to detract from or undermine your efforts.

Phase 5 focuses attention on four areas that have had to wait their turn: rewards and recognition, employee health and well-being, benchmarking, and corporate citizenship. Table 18.5 on pages 237–238 provides an action plan for this phase.

PHASE 6: REFINE YOUR SYSTEM

The new management model focuses on continuous improvement. The only way to continuously improve is to periodically look at where you are, compare it to where you want to be, and change course, speed up, or leap ahead. System assessments give you the information you need when you must decide what to do next.

They also help you develop the discipline of "refinement." Most companies, including many of the role models in this book, fail to close the loop on their processes by leaving out the refinement cycle. They develop a terrific approach, deploy it throughout the company, then move on without leaving behind a process for regularly evaluating and improving the approach. The same concept applies to the entire system; the approaches you are taking need to be evaluated and improved on a regular basis.

We recommend an annual assessment based on the Baldrige criteria (see Chapter 17). No other tool on the market is better at helping you explore, understand, and improve your entire system.

CONCLUSION

We understand that this is an imposing list of steps. The transition to the new management model cannot be done in haste or without thought. We hope, however, that the list will not deter you from stepping into the river of change.

At the beginning of this chapter, we quoted Dick Raymond's thoughts about crossing this river. He concludes with an observation that captures the promise for each individual who sets foot on the new land:

> The people I know who have successfully made this transition are the most joyful, the most outgoing, the most well-rewarded people I know.

This is the ultimate benefit of total quality management for the people involved, from senior executives to frontline workers. In our experience, the companies that involve everyone in continuous improvement, that make customer satisfaction their top priority, that value people for who they are, and that see their systems as treasure chests filled with endless opportunities—these companies have the most joyful, outgoing, and well-rewarded people we know. Their enthusiasm is infectious, their commitment is inspiring. They invariably seem more alive and fulfilled and challenged than the millions who just go through the motions day after day. They stand on the riverbank called total quality management and shout out the wonders of working together for the good of all.

We encourage you to join them.

Appendix A

RESOURCES

To get a copy of the Baldrige criteria and/or the requirements for applying for the Baldrige Award, contact:

Malcolm Baldrige National Quality Award
National Institute of Standards and Technology
Route 270 and Quince Orchard Road
Administration Building, Room A537
Gaithersburg, MD 20899-0001
301-975-2036

To contact the authors:

Stephen George
3381 Gorham Avenue, Suite 203
Minneapolis, MN 55426
612-927-7437
e-mail: *SteveGeorge@baldrige.com*
Website: http://www.baldrige.com

Arnold Weimerskirch
Honeywell
Vice President, Corporate Quality
PO Box 524
Minneapolis, MN 55440
612-951-0225

Appendix B

COMPANIES PROFILED IN THE BOOK

To find out more information about the companies featured in this book, write or call the contact people listed in this section. If you wish to explore specific topics, please review the benchmarking process described in Chapter 15 before contacting these companies.

3M Corporate Quality Services
Ron Kubinski
Quality Manager
Building 525-5E-02, 800 East Minnehaha
St. Paul, MN 55144-1000
612-737-8406

ADAC Laboratories
Doug Keare
Vice President of Quality
540 Alder Drive
Milpitas, CA 95035
408-321-9100

Alcoa
Ron Hoisington
Manager, Corporate Quality Group
1501 Alcoa Building
Pittsburgh, PA 15219
412-553-3925

American Express Financial Advisors
Kristin Kooda-Chizek
IDS Tower 10
Minneapolis, MN 55440
612-671-3016

Ameritech Services
Vicki Karfias
2000 West Ameritech Center Drive
Hoffman Estates, IL 60196-1025
847-248-4892

Ames Rubber Corporation
Chuck Roberts
Vice President, Total Quality
23-47 Ames Boulevard
Hamburg, NJ 07419
201-209-3200

AMP Inc.
Dean Hooper
Vice President, Customer Satisfaction/Business Effectiveness
470 Friendship Road
Harrisburg, PA 17111
717-564-0100

Armstrong Building Products
Operations
Melvin Pugh
Human Resources Manager
2500 Columbia Avenue
Lancaster, PA 17604
412-553-3925

AT&T
Dale Myers
District Manager, Quality Planning
AT&T Corporate Quality Office
One Oak Way
Berkeley Heights, NJ 07922
908-234-6684

AT&T Consumer Markets Division
Susan Grove
Quality Director
Room 4A100Y
900 Route 202/206
Bedminster, NJ 07921
908-221-5831

Ben & Jerry's
Ann Viets
Senior Manager, OD/HR
30 Community Drive
South Burlington, VT 05403-6828
802-651-9600, ext. 7568

BI Performance Services
Betsy Schneider
Director, Marketing Services
7630 Bush Lake Road
Minneapolis, MN 55439
612-844-4655

Bose Corporation
Lance Dixon, Executive Director
JIT II Education & Research Center
The Mountain
Framingham, MA 10701-9168
508-766-7515

Cadillac/General Motors
Corporation
Joseph Bransky
Director, Quality and Reliability
30007 Van Dyke Avenue, Room 142-
37
Warren, MI 48090
810-492-7704

Carrier Corporation
Dr. Larry Sweet
Vice President, Operations
1 Carrier Place
Farmington, CT 06032
860-674-3425

CIT Commercial Services
CIT Group Holdings Inc.
Larry Marsiello
President and CEO
1211 Avenue of the Americas
New York, NY 10036
212-382-6829

Corning
Martin Mariner
Director, Quality Management
HP CB 067
Corning, NY 14831
607-974-7970

Custom Research Inc.
Jeffrey Pope and Judith Corson,
Partners
10301 Wayzata Boulevard
PO Box 26695
Minneapolis, MN 55426
612-542-0800

Dana Commercial Credit
Corporation
Jim Beckham
Director of Quality
PO Box 906
Toledo, OH 43697-0906
419-322-7460

Eastman Chemical Company
Katherine Watkins
Communications Technologist
PO Box 511
Kingsport, TN 37662
800-695-4322, ext. 1150

Eastman Kodak Company
George Vorhauer
Director, Corporate Quality
Initiatives
343 State Street
Rochester, NY 14650-0543
716-724-9819

Engelhard
Ken Rogers
General Manager
9800 Kellner Road
Huntsville, AL 35824
205-464-6371

FedEx
Darlene Faquin
2005 Corporate Avenue
Memphis, TN 38132
901-395-5406

Globe Metallurgical
Norm Jennings
Quality Director of Foundry
Products
PO Box 157
Beverly, OH 45715
614-984-2361

Graniterock
Val Verutti
Director of Quality Support
PO Box 50001
Watsonville, CA 95077-5001
408-761-2300

GTE Directories
Michael English
Director, Quality and Customer
Services
PO Box 619810
Dallas/Fort Worth Airport, TX
75261-9810
972-453-7988

IBM Rochester
Steve Hoisington
Director, Market-Driven Quality
3605 Highway 52 North
Rochester, MN 55901-7829
507-286-4434

Insurance Management Company
John Bloomstine, President
123 West Ninth Street
Erie, PA 16501-1302
814-452-3200

Intel Corporation
Pamela Olivier
Strategic Planning Manager
Microprocessor Products Group
220 Mission College Boulevard
Santa Clara, CA 95052
408-765-4285

Kennametal
Chris Lowe
Director of Operations
6865 Cochran Road
Solon, OH 44139
216-349-5737

L.L. Bean
Catherine Hartnett
Media Specialist
Freeport, ME 04033
207-865-4761, ext. 4507

Louisville Redbirds
Dale Owens
Vice President and General Manager
PO Box 36407
Louisville, KY 40233
502-367-9121

Lyondell Petrochemical
Jackie Wilson
Director, Public Affairs
1221 McKinney, Suite 1600
PO Box 3646
Houston, TX 77253-3646
713-652-4596

Marlow Industries
Ray Marlow, President
10451 Vista Park Road
Dallas, TX 75238-1645
214-340-4900

Motorola Inc.
Richard Buetow
Corporate Quality
1303 E. Algonquin Road
Schaumburg, IL 60196-1065
847-576-5516

The New England Mutual Life
Insurance Company
Scott Andrews
Consultant, Quality Commitment
501 Boylston Street
Boston, MA 02117
617-578-3049

The Northern Trust Company
Debra Danziger-Barron
Senior Vice President
50 South LaSalle Street
Chicago, IL 60675
312-444-7701

Randall's Food Markets
Randall Omstead, President
3663 Briapark, PO Box 4506
Houston, TX 77210
713-268-3462

Raytheon TI Systems
Karen Hollingsworth
Director, Center for Business
Excellence
PO Box 405, Mail Station 3461
Lewisville, TX 75067
972-462-3222

The Ritz-Carlton Hotel Company
Patrick Mene
Vice President of Quality
3414 Peachtree Road, NE
Atlanta, GA 30326
404-237-5500

Seitz Corporation
Verna Moran
Human Resources Manager
PO Box 1398
Torrington, CT 06790
203-489-0476, ext. 2120

Solectron
Sae Jae Cho
Director of Customer Satisfaction
777 Gibraltar Drive, Building 5
Milpitas, CA 95035
408-956-6669

Sprint
Margie Linck
Director, Business Resources
7171 West 95th Street
Overland Park, KS 66212
913-534-3801

Staples Inc.
Kim Shea
100 Pennsylvania Avenue
Framingham, MA 01701
508-370-8345

Tennant Company
Rita Ferguson Maehling
Employee Programs Manager—
Involvement and Recognition
PO Box 1452, Mail Drop 31
Minneapolis, MN 55440
612-540-1402

Thomas Interior Systems
Thomas Klobucher, President
192 Spangler Avenue
Elmhurst, IL 60126
708-832-4200

Trident Precision Manufacturing
Joe Conchelos
Vice President of Quality
734 Salt Road
Webster, NY 14580-9796
716-265-2010

USAA
Paul Ringenbach
Senior Vice President
USAA Building
San Antonio, TX 78288

210-498-0949

Wainwright Industries
Mike Simms
Plant Manager
PO Box 640
St. Peters, MO 63376
314-278-5850

Xerox
Sam Malone
Director, Quality Services
Xerox Square—018-A
100 Clinton Avenue S.
Rochester, NY 14644
716-423-9190

Zytec
Ron Schmidt, President and Chief
Executive Officer
7575 Market Place Drive
Eden Prairie, MN 55344
612-941-1100

Index